Immigration

A Wadsworth Casebook in Argument

Sharon K. Walsh
Loyola University Chicago

Evelyn D. Asch
Northwestern University

Australia • Canada • Mexico • Singapore • Spain
United Kingdom • United States

Immigration
A Wadsworth Casebook in Argument
Sharon Walsh/Evelyn Asch

Publisher: Michael Rosenberg
Senior Acquisitions Editor: Dickson Musslewhite
Associate Project Manager, Editorial Production: Karen Stocz
Senior Print Buyer: Mary Beth Hennebury
Permissions Manager: Bob Kauser
Marketing Manager: Carrie Brandon
Compositor/Project Manager: Argosy Publishing
Photo Manager: Sheri Blaney
Cover Designer: Joseph Sherman
Printer: Malloy Lithographing, Inc.

Cover Art: © Smithsonian American Art Museum, Washington, DC/Art Resource, NY

Printed in the United States of America
1 2 3 4 5 6 7 09 08 07 06 05

For more information about our products, contact us at:
Thomson Learning Academic Resource Center
1-800-423-0563

For permission to use material from this text or product, submit a request online at **http://www.thomsonrights.com.**

Any additional questions about permissions can be submitted by email to **thomsonrights@thomson.com**.

Library of Congress Control Number: 2004112974

ISBN 1-4130-0664-7

Credits appear on pages 305–306, which constitute a continuation of the copyright page.

Thomson Higher Education
25 Thomson Place
Boston, MA 02210-1202
USA

Asia (including India)
Thomson Learning
5 Shenton Way
#01-01 UIC Building
Singapore 068808

Australia/New Zealand
Thomson Learning Australia
102 Dodds Street
Southbank, Victoria 3006
Australia

Canada
Thomson Nelson
1120 Birchmount Road
Toronto, Ontario M1K 5G4
Canada

UK/Europe/Middle East/Africa
Thomson Learning
High Holborn House
50–51 Bedford Road
London WC1R 4LR
United Kingdom

Latin America
Thomson Learning
Seneca, 53
Colonia Polanco
11560 Mexico
D.F. Mexico

Spain (including Portugal)
Thomson Paraninfo
Calle Magallanes, 25
28015 Madrid, Spain

Contents

Preface

We have focused this book, both the section on argument and the Casebook on Immigration, on the relationship between reading and writing and readers and writers. Our philosophy of teaching and our classroom practice have convinced us that good writing is stimulated by the challenges that meaty texts present. The readings you will find here come from the fields of political science, history, sociology, and anthropology and from the genres of the essay, personal narrative, letters, memoirs, autobiography, interviews, and oral history. They center on an issue central to the history of the United States, immigration, and they record the experiences of immigrants as well as several of the debates about immigration that our country has had during its history. The writers of these texts are immigrants themselves, theorists who attempt to make sense of immigrant experience, and writers who propose immigrant policy. We envision them all entering into conversations, civil discourse, and, perhaps, heated debates that we too can join. We will find that many of the stories engage us. Some of us will be convinced by arguments in support of or in opposition to restricting immigration; others will want to debate the claims and conclusions. But since immigration is all around us, we can hardly avoid the topic.

The two parts of the book move from reading to writing. In Part One, Chapters 1 and 2 focus on understanding argument and its failures, with emphasis on analyzing exemplary texts. Chapter 3 presents a method for writing argumentative essays that are based on reading and research. Part Two, the Casebook on Immigration, also moves from reading to writing. Each chapter supplies background for each author included, provides questions about the texts and their argument, raises issues worth exploring, and suggests ideas for writing as both conversation and argument. We have designed these features of the text to make challenging readings accessible to students. Chapter 4 explores examples of the immigration debate over time and presents narratives of nineteenth- and early twentieth-century immigrants. Chapter 5 presents some of the contemporary theories about the impact of immigration as well as the stories of later twentieth-century immigrants. Chapter 6 focuses on the recent debate about Hispanic immigration.

There is also another relationship between readers and writers that we would like to explore: between you the readers of this book and us the authors. We imagine that you instructors are like us, enjoying the give and take of the classroom, sometimes snowed under by the papers we assign, but convinced that our students can learn to write well. We want our students to learn to write well by observing good writers in action, engaging in worthwhile discussion, and experiencing the urge to have their say. We imagine that your students are like ours: lively; bright; often engaged with the class, but sometimes not; sometimes unsure of what you think; sometimes unwilling to say what you think; often lacking confidence in your writing skills.

We write this book for you, hoping that you will discover, as we did, that it is satisfying to chew on the ideas, engaging to enter a conversation with the writers and each other, and—even—fun to make one's own voice heard through argument.

Acknowledgments

This Casebook on Immigration, like our previous Casebooks on Just War and Civil Disobedience, owes much to the Loyola University Chicago English Department Shared-Text Project. Many colleagues shared their ideas with us and provided feedback on *Just War*, and we have enjoyed the give-and-take of collegial discussion with them. Research colleagues at Northwestern University have encouraged the asking of hard questions and have been understanding and supportive of the joys and pains of writing.

Loyola writing students continue to make teaching challenging and rewarding. English 106 students in particular have contributed to this casebook by their stimulating discussions of the casebook readings and by their unexpected and insightful responses. Special thanks go to Caitlin Cunningham, whose work appears in Appendix B.

Once again, we are grateful to Jain Simmons, of Thomson Higher Education, for her ongoing support. We thank our editor, Dickson Musslewhite, and Karen Judd and Karen Stocz at Wadsworth, who have shepherded this text through the perils of publication.

And, finally, our families continue to encourage our project, despite the hours we spend away from them. We truly could not have written this book without them. We thank Richard Hartenstein and John, Rachel, and Nathaniel Tingley for their unfailing love, support, and encouragement.

Is Immigration Good for Us?

Mary Antin's question, "Is immigration good for us?" has been asked throughout American history. In her book, *Those Who Knock at Our Gates: A Complete Gospel of Immigration* (1914), she asks as well, "Have we any right to regulate immigration?" and "What is the nature of our present immigration?" Writing seven years after the largest influx of immigrants in U.S. history and ten years before the landmark Immigration Act of 1924, Antin provides a cogent approach to understanding immigration.

Her first question begs for a definition. The *Oxford English Dictionary* defines the term "immigration" as "entrance into a country for the purpose of settling there" and distinguishes it from "migration," which implies the action of movement without the necessary purposeful quality. Those who immigrate—"immigrants"—seem to differ from the original English colonists, who initially considered the American colonies an extension of the mother country and then later separated from it. Thus, colonists became American citizens after the Revolution, and "immigrants" seem to have come afterwards. As Benjamin Franklin complained in 1757, however, non-Englishmen came to the colonies in significant numbers well before the Revolution. Immigration seems also to imply a voluntary, rational choice, so that would preclude calling African slaves immigrants because they were brought to America by force and against their will.

Other distinctions between the terms "migrants" and "transnationals" are important for contemporary immigration theorists. Migrants move from country to country to work without putting down (or being allowed to put down) roots. Transnationals have their feet in at least two countries, participating in both societies but not relinquishing their cultural identity or assimilating fully into the country where they have come to settle.

Antin's second question, "Have we any right to regulate immigration?" has been answered by the series of laws that have done so. The Constitution limits the presidency to a native-born American; a 1790 law required two years of residency before naturalization; an 1864 law allowed the importation of contract laborers; and the Chinese Exclusion Act of 1882 forbade new immigration of Chinese laborers. Other important legislation includes the Immigration Act of 1924, which provided quotas for European immigrants and halted Far Eastern immigration. The Immigration Act of 1965 reformed the 1952 Immigration and Nationality Act, which still limited immigration from the eastern hemisphere by setting limits of 20,000 immigrants per country, encouraging family reunification, and giving preferences to skilled workers.

Immigration legislation, of course, had a great impact on who was allowed to settle in the United States and who was refused admission, but to answer the question "What is the nature of our present immigration?" we must look at other causes as well. The immigration panorama that Mary Antin would have seen in 1914 included numerous Irish, Poles, Italians, and Russians. Fewer Chinese and Japanese would have been represented. Economic conditions like the Potato Famine of 1845 drove more than 500,000 Irish to come to America in five years. Religious persecution and adverse economic conditions after 1860 account for the two million Poles settled in the United States by 1914. Italians immigrated in large numbers after 1880 due to crop failures and economic instability. Over three million Russians, primarily Jews, fled oppression after the May Laws of 1882.

The immigration tapestry looks quite different today. Communism, poverty, unemployment, and persecution account for much of the movement. About 700,000 Cubans settled in Miami in the '60s, '70s, and '80s to escape Castro, and 500,000 Vietnamese fled the Communist takeover of Vietnam. Mexican immigrants first came after the Mexican Revolution of 1910, but they have arrived in much larger numbers (approximately 5 million) between 1950 and 1990 to escape poverty and unemployment. Dominicans, Haitians, and Jamaicans have come for the same reasons. East Asian, Southeast Asian, and Middle Eastern immigrants populate our colleges in notable numbers.

Our casebook provides several kinds of answers to the question, "Is immigration good for us?" Some sociologists raise concerns about immigrants remaining in the lowest socio-economic class—a trend known as "segmented assimilation." Immigration restrictionists such as Samuel Huntington caution us to enter a serious discussion of what our values are and what we want our society to be. Others remind us that immigrants have enriched our country for more than two centuries and agree with the noted historian Oscar Handlin that "the history of the United States is the history of immigration." A study by the National Foundation for American Policy (released July 19, 2004) found that the children of immigrants accounted for 60% of the finalists in the 2004 Intel Science Talent search, 65% of the U.S. Math Olympiad's top scorers, and 46% of the U.S. Physics Team. We leave it to you to decide.

PART ONE

Analyzing and Writing Arguments

CHAPTER

1

Analyzing Arguments

Recognizing Arguments

Imagine this scene: Two adults are screaming at each other, hurling insults and accusations back and forth. Or this: Children trying to decide on which game to play engage in a shouting match. Because we describe these activities by the term "argument," we often think of argument as a negative activity. We might ask our children or our friends not to argue, as if arguing were only the equivalent of fighting or disagreeing. For our purpose though, argument refers to a very common and widespread process by which we draw conclusions from evidence that has been laid out or make decisions based on reasons provided. Argument is not so much about winning or losing, though we do talk about debate in those terms; it is more about concluding, deciding, solving or resolving, persuading—all very positive and practical human activities.

Where Is Argument Found?

Argument pervades our private and public discourse. We make arguments, whether in speech or in writing, when we raise questions and answer them; demonstrate problems and solve them; or outline issues or alternatives and delineate the ways to address or decide them. Through argument we weigh evidence, alternatives, and competing claims. Through argument we may come to theoretical answers and solutions, but we also make decisions or choices that will lead to action in the real world.

The Private Sphere

Argument is a large component of our private thoughts, our stream-of-consciousness. A writer debates internally how she should organize her text; she sketches out possibilities, evaluates them, and then chooses. A student lays out problem-solving strategies and selects the one most likely to succeed. We argue with ourselves: I should major in business because I'll be able to get a job. We engage imaginary opponents: Dad, you should help me with grad school because I received a scholarship for college tuition.

Important also to family life, argument ranges from the trivial to the serious as a way to negotiate differences: Who will sit in the front seat? What movie shall we see? Where shall we go on our vacation? How shall we budget our money? What values shall we teach our children?

The Professional and Business Domain

Argument is central to contemporary medical practice as doctors can no longer rely on their patients' unquestioning acceptance of the doctors' dictates. Rather, canny doctors list the pro and con reasons for a medical procedure or treatment, weigh them, and offer a medical opinion.

Underpinning business and commercial life, argument appears in business plans, proposals, loan applications, marketing strategies, ad campaigns, and stock recommendations. From team decision making to the deliberations of the board, both employees and managers use argumentative strategies to arrive at decisions.

The Public Forum

Intrinsic to making a case in our law courts, argument structures a trial as the prosecutor opens with what is to be proved, provides the requisite evidence to support this claim, and makes a closing statement demonstrating what has been proved. The defense's role is to undermine or rebut the prosecutor's argument. Demonstrating that the prosecutor's evidence is flawed, countering it with other evidence, or constructing an alternative theory of the case are all ways defense attorneys strive to attack the prosecutor's case.

Argument is crucial to our democratic deliberations, particularly in the debate format where the reasons for or against an issue or proposition are weighed. We see it in speeches given in Congress to argue for the passage of a bill or by the president to the American people to lay out the reasons for going to war.

The Academic Classroom and Symposium

Finally, argument is fundamental to our academic discourse. Every time we formulate a thesis and prove it, or establish criteria and weigh the value of a work of art against them, or provide statistics or other evidence to support an assertion, we engage in argument. Students write essays, professors write articles, and scholars give papers. Faculties debate curricula and policy, departments argue for appointments and tenure, and students debate issues. These argumentative strategies have a long history, begun by Aristotle in his *Rhetoric.* More recent discussions of argument include the Toulmin and Rogerian methods. **Toulmin** argument is rooted in Aristotelian logic but replaces the syllogism with a **claim** and **warrants** for that claim. The **Rogerian** method (explained fully in Robert Miller and Robert Yagelski's *The Informed Argument* [Wadsworth]) focuses on locating a common ground between arguers or arriving at consensus.

What Are the Components of Aristotelian or Classical Argumentative Strategy?

Argument is closely allied to **rhetoric**, the study of how language may be used to achieve a desired effect. Those who follow Aristotle's guidance utilize or respond to three elements of argument: **ethos**, the persona that speakers or writers project to their audience; **logos**, the type of reasoning on which the argument is based as well as the content of the argument; and **pathos**, the emotional appeals that speakers and writers make to their audience. Each of these strategies may be used legitimately or validly, or they may be used fallaciously.

Notice that both speakers and **audience**, the listeners to or readers of the argument, have reciprocal roles in each element of this triad. Speakers and writers must always keep the audience in mind when trying out an argumentative strategy. Unless the audience responds as expected to this strategy, the argument cannot be called truly successful

Ethos: Evaluating the Writer's Assumptions, Credentials, Reputation, and Use of Authority

Discussions of argument based on the Aristotelian model generally begin with ethos because we intuitively give much weight to the trustworthiness of the speaker or writer. If we do not trust the speaker or believe the writer to be qualified, we are likely to dismiss the argument no matter how good the logic. We can determine the persona that writers project to their audience by asking questions like the following: What kind of person is the speaker or writer? What does he or she believe? How do those beliefs underlie the argument? Is this someone with appropriate credentials? How do we know from evidence within the text? Are there sources outside the text that will help us find out? How do other experts and the writer's peers esteem this writer? What sources or authorities does the writer rely on? Given the answers to the preceding questions, how can we judge the writer's credibility?

Assumptions

What are the speaker's assumptions, premises, beliefs, and values that underlie or stand behind the argument? Does the speaker or writer make them explicit, presume the readers share them, or hide them?

Thomas Jefferson's *Declaration of Independence* (see p. 58) makes explicit a set of beliefs or convictions from which his premises follow. His thinking is grounded in eighteenth-century political philosophy. He spells out his assumptions, so all his readers can make the connections between his assumptions and premises. Probably few of Jefferson's readers could have enunciated the basis for the claim that "whenever any Form of Government becomes destructive of these ends, it is the right of the People to alter and abolish it," so Jefferson does it for them, making an interlocking chain of assumptions: Men are created equal and are also given inalienable rights by their creator to "Life, Liberty, and the pursuit of Happiness"—the divine rights of humans rather than the Divine Right of Kings! And wonder of wonders: "to secure these rights, Governments are instituted among Men"! Governments are not put in place merely to perpetuate power or to ensure the prosperity of the rulers, nor should they be imposed upon the governed through might; rather, they derive their power from the consent of the governed. When all these preconditions are in place, then and only then can Jefferson state his first premise with some possibility that it will be accepted.

In "The Hispanic Challenge" (p. 211), Samuel P. Huntington's argument rests upon a set of assumptions that he calls a "creed." This creed, drawn from the Anglo-Protestant culture of the founding American settlers, includes such features as basic values (the work ethic, for example), language, religion, and concepts of law. As put forth in *The Declaration of Independence*, this creed that stresses basic human rights is what, Huntington assumes, has drawn most immigrants to this country. Immigrants embrace the creed and bring elements of their own culture to enrich American culture. Apparently, Huntington does not think these assumptions need explanation, for he does not provide any, presuming his readers' acquiescence to them. Huntington is certainly aware that the greater the acceptance of the assumptions, the greater the likelihood that readers will be convinced by the argument. For even if an argument follows the rule of logic, if one does not accept the assumptions, one will not be persuaded by the logic. However, Huntington cannot presume that all his readers will accept his assumptions because any critical reader of an argument will question assumptions. Thus, in order to accept that contemporary Hispanic immigrants may be threatening the cultural base of our country, one must first agree on what the cultural base is.

Credentials

What education, training, experience, knowledge, and expertise does the speaker or writer have? What evidence of the speaker's credentials is there within the text? What outside sources can help us determine these credentials? We suggest consulting such biographical and bibliographical sources as the *Encyclopedia Britannica, Who's Who, Contemporary Authors,* university or department websites, and library listings.

Even if we did not know that Jefferson had a wide-ranging intelligence and would serve his country as ambassador to France and as president, we can discern from *The Declaration of Independence* his skills as a logician and rhetorician.

Samuel P. Huntington's credentials are likewise beyond reproach. By modern standards, his Harvard Ph.D., his position as University Professor at Harvard, holding an endowed chair, his "real-world" experience on the National Security Council at the White House (1977), as well as his editorship of *Foreign Policy* give him exemplary status in his field. His books have broken new ground and raised healthy controversy and discussion. For example, *The Clash of Civilizations* brought new awareness of the divide between Western culture and Islamic fundamentalism. Though colleagues at Harvard and elsewhere have criticized his arguments, they have also taken him seriously.

Reputation

How do peers and colleagues review the work? Do they value its contributions to the field? What is the quality of the forum in which the writer is published? Is it a major newspaper or a respected press? How has the response to a writer or speaker changed over time? Has the reputation increased or diminished? To find book reviews, good sources are the London *Times Literary Supplement* (TLS), *New York Times, New York Review of Books, Book Review Digest, Chicago Tribune,* journals of opinion, and professional and scholarly journals. *Contemporary Authors* and the *Dictionary of Literary Biography* provide assessments of authors' reputations.

To illustrate the importance of evaluating both the credentials and reputation of a writer, let us take as an example Charles Colson, a member of the Nixon White House staff and participant in the Watergate scandal. His credentials include undergraduate education at Brown and a J.D. at George Washington University, work experience in the offices of the Secretary of the Navy and Senator Leverett Saltonstall, and a position as special counsel to President Nixon from 1969 to 1973. He founded Prison Fellowship Ministries and has written prolifically, including theology, autobiography, and Christian fiction. He is also a contributing editor to *Christianity Today*. Despite these accomplishments, he is usually remembered for the part he played in Watergate, for which he was convicted and served prison time. While awaiting trial, he underwent conversion, becoming a born-again Christian, and has served in prison ministry for over thirty years. Nonetheless, some question the sincerity of his conversion and his motives. What he writes is therefore read against the backdrop of his reputation as Watergate criminal and convict.

Use of Authority

We use the word *authority* in various ways. For example, a CEO has the authority (from the board or the stockholders) to make a decision; here, the CEO derives his power from those who employ him. As another example, I have the authority to sign checks for my aunt who signed a legal power of attorney permitting me to act in her name. The writer, however, speaks with the authority earned by credentials and position. The words writers choose and the rhetorical and argumentative strategies they employ most certainly help create ethos. But authors can also add weight to their words by appealing to the authority of someone higher, more expert, more experienced, or more credible. Important questions to ask about credentials include the following: How does the writer use other authorities? Whom does the writer enlist or cite as an authority? Are they people with better credentials than the writer's, ones pertinent to the topic, ones that readers will understand and appreciate?

Thomas Jefferson has authority to speak for the colonists, having been designated by the Continental Congress to draft *The Declaration.* He also uses God as his ultimate authority. In the introduction, he claims that "Nature's God" entitles a people, having found it necessary to dissolve its "political bands," to have a "separate and equal station." He assumes that "all men are created equal" and that "they are endowed by their Creator with certain unalienable rights." In his conclusion he also calls upon God as "Supreme Judge of the world" to witness their right intentions and expresses their "firm reliance on the protection of divine Providence." Calling on God as Creator, Providence, and Judge reminds his readers of their commonly held beliefs that God is all-encompassing and all-powerful, and reassures them that the colonists' cause is just, binding them together in a series of morally necessary actions. For those among the British or the colonists who are frightened by the revolutionary nature of *The Declaration,* calling upon God strengthens the case for revolution.

Many writers find their authority in books, using the information and analysis of other authors to buttress their own ideas. Students writing literary essays, for example, often use literary critics as well as the primary text to support their positions. The sociologists included in the casebook rely heavily on statistical sources for their authority. For example, many of the tables that Richard D. Alba (p. 161) and Alejandro Portes and Rubén G. Rumbaut (p. 178) use come from U.S. Census data. This material is considered authoritative, based on the commonly accepted ways that the data have been collected. Alma M. Garcia (p. 203) and Nina Glick Schiller, Linda Basch, and Cristina Blanc-Szanton (p. 193) use interviews and observations (vignettes) on which to base their conclusions. To demonstrate their authority, they provide information about interview questions and procedures and review the literature in the field to show how their work fits into or takes issue with other work being done in the field.

Audience: Considering the Reader's Needs

The writer usually has a specific initial audience in mind, and the greater the writer's knowledge of those who comprise this audience, their values and assumptions, their desires, their knowledge, and their mental capacity, the more likely the argument is to succeed. Crucial questions for the writer are: Who is the intended audience? Does this differ from the actual audience? Is the audience likely to be receptive to or agree with the writer's assumptions? Is the audience either uninformed or neutral about the writer's argument? Is the audience likely to be hostile to the argument? Given that a writer may be addressing all these audiences at once, what strategies might be used to find some common ground to get the audience on the writer's side? Is the audience likely to agree with the writer's assumptions? What are the tone and language appropriate for the intended audience? In addition to the intended audience, we can think of the actual audience as a series of concentric circles radiating from the original audience. For a speech, the actual audience is people in the room, people who see it on television or the Web, people who hear it on the radio, people who read it the next day, and so on. Writers like Jefferson who see their works as possibly extending to a wide-ranging audience must hope to keep in mind the needs of all their readers.

The audience must also assess the choices the writer has made. Has the writer kept the needs and desires of the various audiences in mind? Has the writer given them the information they need to understand the argument and done so without talking down to them or talking over their heads?

Jefferson, for example, must have had the colonists first and foremost in mind because he wishes to convince them that action to overturn the government is justified. The lengthy list of grievances must be intended to persuade them as well to pay "decent respect" to the views of the world. King George III and Parliament are unlikely to be convinced by this argument, so Jefferson can expect only to declare that the American colonies are independent, not that Britain will accept this action. As for their British brethren, Jefferson hopes for some sympathy; from other countries like France that are sympathetic to the desire to overturn a tyrannous king, he hopes for more concrete forms of support like money and troops. Of course, Jefferson, well aware of the momentous nature of *The Declaration,* must also have been writing for the ages.

We can get an idea of the audience for Samuel P. Huntington's article, "The Hispanic Challenge," by looking at the journal in which it appears, *Foreign Policy*, noting that it was co-founded by Huntington, a Harvard political scientist, and observing that it includes lengthy, serious articles on a range of foreign policy issues. The immediate reader response to Huntington's article provides a snapshot view of the readership in the letters to the editor published in the following edition (May/June 2004). Only two letters come from readers whose affiliation is not given; five are from professors at Harvard, Johns Hopkins, University of Cincinnati, California State, and University of California, San Diego; one from the pastor of a Methodist church; several from various institutes and councils: the Pew Institute, the Cato Institute, the National Council of La Raza, and the Carnegie Endowment for International Peace. What can we infer from this information? We can see that well-educated readers take careful note of the argument and respond in most cases cogently and promptly to significant disputed points. We cannot, however, conclude that the letters represent a statistical sample of the readership. We also know that Huntington takes his readers seriously because he takes the time to address their concerns.

Rogerian Argument: Finding Common Ground with Readers

Anyone who has worked on committees, boards, or councils understands the importance of finding common ground on which to base a decision; otherwise, decisions may be delayed or, if reached, so displease some members of the group that the group cannot function effectively. Here is where listening techniques derived from the field of psychology, especially from the work of Carl Rogers, are very valuable. If listeners can restate the positions of the other group members clearly and fairly, acknowledge the strengths of a position they disagree with, recognize the weaknesses of their own position, and remind themselves of their common goals, the group will have a much better chance of reaching the consensus needed to make a decision. The outcome is less likely to be a narrowly won victory and more likely to be a satisfactory determination.

While it is certainly possible to construct a written Rogerian argument using the process indicated above, argumentative essays are less likely to follow the Rogerian pathway, especially with hotly debated issues. Effective arguers do, however, borrow elements from this approach, particularly in introductions intended to draw readers into a discussion.

Mary Antin, in "Have We Any Right to Regulate Immigration?" (p. 103), effectively wins readers to her side by introducing her argument for open-door immigration by finding common ground with her readers, many of whom might not concur with the policy. The common ground is *The Declaration of Independence*, which she calls "the fundamental American law," granting life, liberty, and the pursuit of happiness to all. Few readers then or today would fail to accept *The Declaration* as foundational to our system of government. When she goes on to compare *The*

Declaration to the Mosaic Law and then to the Gospel, she assumes her readers will see the relevance of these religious codes and writings to our secular document. Given the familiarity with scripture that most people in 1914 would have had, she can count on their understanding of and agreement with the comparison. When she then moves to arguing that this American law, like the religious codes, has general applicability to immigrants as well as citizens, she has a much greater chance of winning a hearing for her argument than if she had begun with a more threatening claim like open-door immigration policy is the only just policy.

Raising objections to their own arguments is another way writers acknowledge the importance of their readers' positions. The latter strategy fails, however, if writers see readers' objections only as impediments to be removed from the argumentative ground. Rather, writers must sincerely explore the strengths of a position contradictory to their own. In "Too Many Immigrants?" (p. 114), Tamar Jacoby exhibits this kind of fair-mindedness in granting a point of one of the arguments against immigration and refuting that same argument. For example, in discussing the post-September 11 calls for keeping track not only of students but also of foreigners already in the United States, she admits, "This is not an unreasonable idea." She goes on to say, though, "it would be almost impossible to implement," demonstrating the latter point by estimating the numbers of entries and exits of our ports in a year as half a billion. She also grants the bad news about immigration, stating that "restrictionists" are correct in some respects because "Immigrant America is not monolithic, and some groups do worse than others, both economically and culturally." Such concessions are important strategies for keeping skeptical readers reading what may be an unpalatable argument.

Logos: Understanding the Writer's Reasoning

Although logos suggests the English word "logic," it goes beyond logic to consider the ways we think or proceed rationally. We think of logos as the heart of argument, for here we provide both the necessary information and the logical structure to convince our readers.

Induction

Inductive reasoning is the process by which we draw conclusions or generalizations based on a series of experiences or examples. It is the way much of our learning takes place. For example, if a child gets sick every time she drinks milk, we conclude that the milk has caused the illness. If a toddler burns himself by touching the lit burner of a stove and a lighted candle, he very quickly concludes that flames burn.

How Does Inductive Reasoning Translate to Argumentative Writing?

Induction can lead to very sophisticated and successful arguments. *The Declaration of Independence* relies heavily on a series of examples to prove its case. The body of the document is a lengthy list of the outrages perpetrated by the government of Great Britain against the American colonists. Jefferson lists eighteen categories of outrages that King George III has perpetrated against the colonies, what Jefferson calls "a history of repeated injuries and usurpations, all having in direct object the establishment of absolute Tyranny over these States." A short list of grievances would not have the same impact. He also builds his case by saving the most heinous offenses, assaults on life, for the last five positions in his list. At the end of these "Facts . . . submitted to a candid world," few could argue that his generalization is unfounded.

Induction also plays a significant role in some of the writing assignments in the casebook as well as sociological studies we have included. When you are asked to draw conclusions about differences in immigrant experiences based on several readings, for example, you are being asked to use an inductive process. You might look at the way men and women view relationships with relatives at home or at the ways they assimilate to American society. After collecting your data from the stories, you can make a generalization or claim warranted by the data. Richard D. Alba uses the inductive method in "Assimilation's Quiet Tide" (p. 161) when he draws conclusions from statistical data drawn from a sample of the 1990 U.S. Census. In Table 5-1 (Educational attainment by ethnic ancestry—men), there are significantly fewer men of all ethnic groups attending college and receiving college degrees in the group born between 1916 and 1925 than in the group born between 1956 and 1965. Even groups like the Italians and Polish that trailed the higher-performing British group in the 1916–1925 cohort had almost caught up with them in 1956–1965. Alba concludes that, based on educational attainment, "there has been a growing and impressive convergence in the average socioeconomic opportunities of members of white ethnic groups."

Argument by Analogy

Argument by analogy is a legitimate form of inductive reasoning that uses similarities between examples to draw conclusions. When we draw on our experiences, we may reason by analogy. For example, a teacher might reason that students in class A are like those in class B and that the same lesson would therefore work as well in class B as it did in class A.

Many writers also seek out historical analogies to bolster a point. Mary Antin draws an analogy between *The Declaration of Independence* and the Mosaic Law: "What the Mosaic Law is to the Jews, The Declaration is to the American people. It affords us a starting-point in history and defines our mission among the nations." She finds that both "must be taken literally and applied universally." Tamar Jacoby claims that there is an analogy to be made between Puerto Ricans and Mexicans: The former stopped flowing into the United States when economic conditions improved enough so that people did not feel the need to immigrate. Mexicans too will stop coming in such numbers because as its population growth slows with the concomitant economic improvement, fewer will immigrate. Samuel P. Huntington uses an extended analogy between Miami and Los Angeles and the southwest to make this point: Mexicans in the southwest will, like Cubans in Miami, choose not to assimilate, forming a large ethnic enclave that speaks a different language than English and embraces different values. As you read each piece, decide how useful such analogies are in making a case.

The analogies in the preceding paragraph raise the question of how many points of similarity are necessary to make the analogy valid. In the following example, there appear to be important points of comparison:

Jewish immigrants to the United States have thrived economically due to their strong belief in education and solid family structure. Korean immigrants also value education highly and have tight family networks. Therefore, Korean immigrants will succeed the way the Jews did.

These apparent similarities may not hold up under scrutiny, however. Perhaps the two groups may have different views of the role of education. Other differences may also be significant: Jews came earlier to the United States in large numbers, they have a different religion from the American majority, and they are not racially identifiable. Koreans, on the other hand, have arrived more recently, almost all are Protestants, and are racially distinct in appearance. Such differences outweigh the similarities given above.

Deduction

Deductive reasoning starts with a generalization (either drawn from induction or stated as an unproven assumption), applies it to a particular case, and draws a conclusion.

Syllogisms

These are the classic format for deductive reasoning. A syllogism has two premises, or propositions, from which a conclusion may be drawn. The following is Aristotle's famous syllogism, illustrating the deductive process:

All men are mortal. (Major premise)

Socrates is a man. (Minor premise)

Socrates is mortal. (Conclusion)

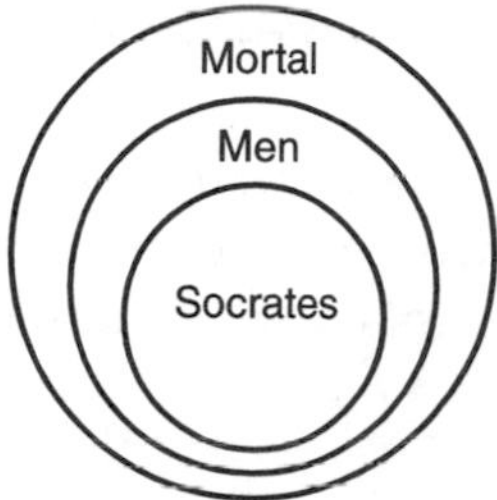

Figure 1-1

Note that here the **major premise** results from an inductive premise (though this is not always the case): All the people who lived in the past eventually died; we know people who have died; we do not know of any exceptions. It thus makes sense to state as a proposition that all men are mortal. The **minor premise** places Socrates in the category of men, that is, he shares the characteristics of men. Given that the entire category of men belongs within the category of mortal beings, it makes sense that Socrates, who belongs to the category of men, must also be included within the category of mortal beings. Thus, we can conclude that Socrates is mortal.

To test whether a syllogism is valid, we can both apply rules and diagram the syllogism. Note that validity is not the same as truth. A syllogism may follow all the rules and still not be true because one or both of the premises are not true.

Rule 1. There must be three and only three terms (men, mortal, Socrates), each of which must refer to a discrete entity.

We can draw no secure conclusion from the following premises because the meaning of the middle term shifts. Being a Marxist and teaching Marxism are not the same. Belonging to one group does not mean automatically belonging to the other group:

All Marxists are communists.

Professor Jones teaches Marxism.

Professor Jones is a communist.

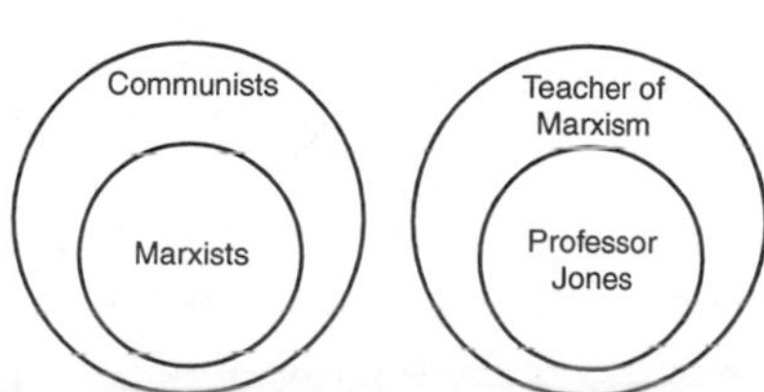

Figure 1-2

Rule 2. The middle term must be distributed at least once.

The **middle term** appears in both premises (in our first example, the middle term is "men") but not in the conclusion. To understand **distribution**, think of the meaning of the statement "All men are mortal." In a positive proposition or statement, the subject term "men" is distributed because "all" refers to every member of the group. Had "men" been modified by "some" or "most," it would not be distributed. The predicate term "mortal" is undistributed. We are essentially saying that men are only some of the mortal beings—others would be dogs, cats, carrots, roses, and so on. Note the illustration of this statement:

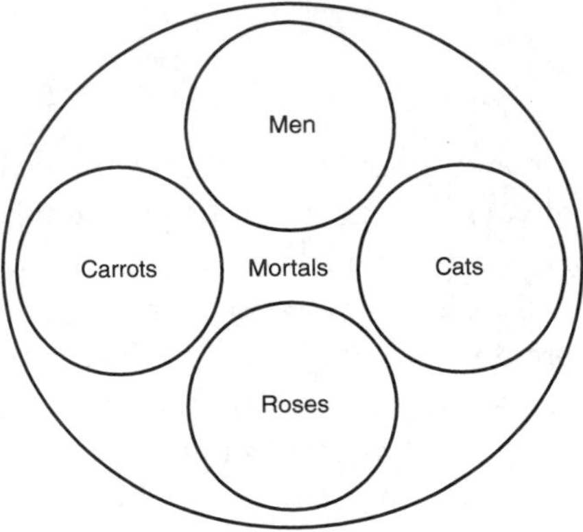

Figure 1-3

In a negative proposition or statement, the subject term is distributed if it is modified by "no." The predicate term is also distributed. In the statement "No cat is a human," we are saying that no member of the class of cats is any part of the class of humans. A diagram illustrates this proposition with two nonintersecting circles:

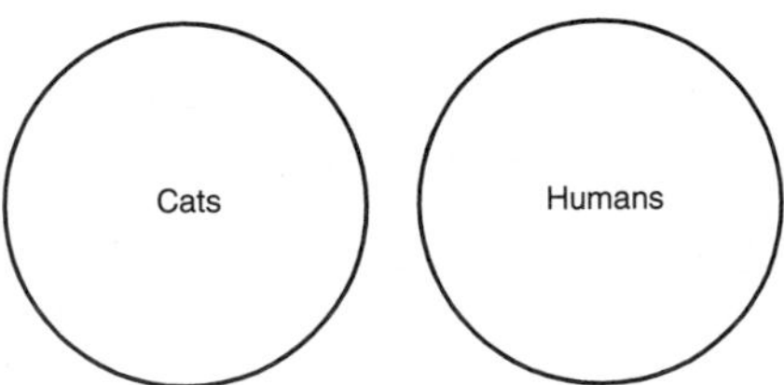

Figure 1-4

Rule 3. If a term is distributed in the conclusion, it must be distributed in the premise.

No local students are dormitory residents.

Some seniors are local students.

Some seniors are not dormitory residents.

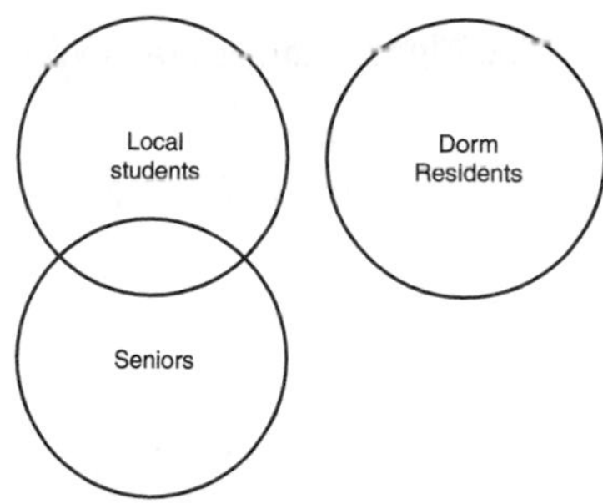

Figure 1-5

The conclusion is valid. Here the term "dormitory residents" is distributed both in the conclusion and in the premise. Look at what happens, though, in the following syllogism:

All local students are dormitory residents.

Some seniors are local students.

All seniors are dormitory residents.

The above conclusion is not valid. We cannot conclude "All seniors are dormitory residents" because the term "seniors" is now distributed in the conclusion although it is undistributed in the premise. We cannot make the extension from "some seniors" to "all." Try to draw your own diagram to illustrate this syllogism.

Rule 4. If a premise is negative, the conclusion must also be negative.

No British are Germans.

Carla is British.

Carla is not German.

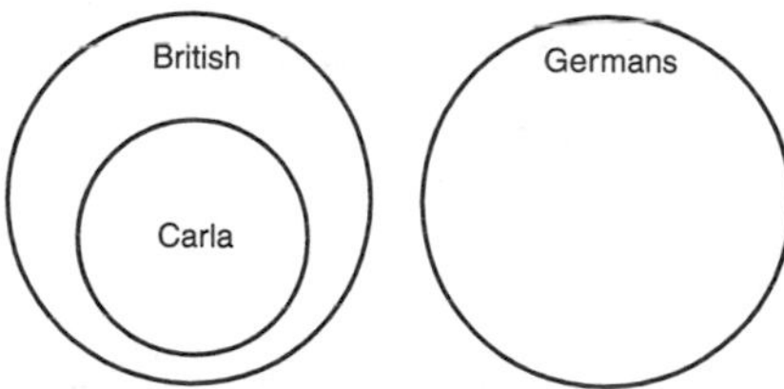

Figure 1-6

In this example, if Carla belongs to one group, she cannot belong to the other. Thus, we cannot logically conclude that "Carla is German."

Rule 5. No conclusion may be drawn from two particular premises.

Some cats are mean animals.

Some mean animals are rabid.

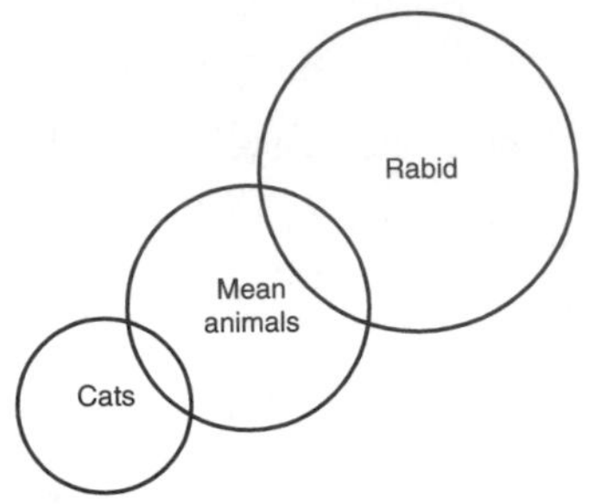

Figure 1-7

Here we cannot conclude "some cats are rabid." Because there are, in addition to cats, other types of mean animals, and because some of these other mean animals are rabid, we cannot know for certain whether cats are rabid. We could draw a valid conclusion that "some cats are rabid," if we were to say that "all mean animals are rabid" and "some cats are mean animals" because then the middle term would be distributed.

Rule 6. No conclusion can be drawn from two negative premises.

All bimsy are not fimsy.

All fimsy are not mimsy.

We cannot conclude either that "all bimsy *are* mimsy" or "all bimsy *are not* mimsy." They may or may not be:

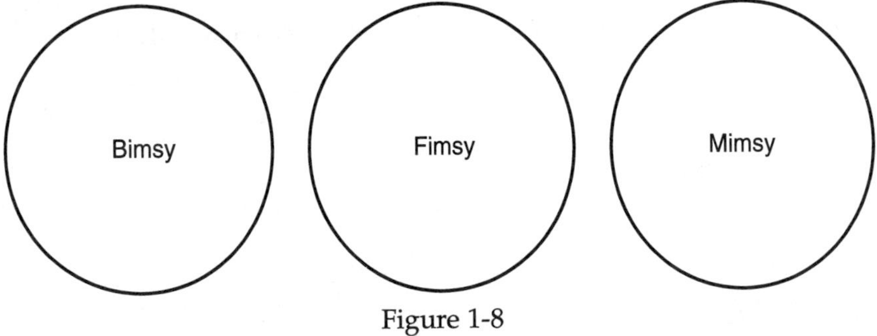

Figure 1-8

Exercises

Test the validity of the following syllogisms both by diagramming them and applying the rules. If no conclusion is supplied, supply the conclusion that will follow logically from the premises.

All humans are rational animals.
Mary is a human.

All humans are rational animals.
Mary is not a rational animal.
Mary is a human.

All good students study for finals.
Marge did not study for finals.

Some people are robots.
All robots are intelligent.
Some people are intelligent.

Some A are B.
All B are C.
Some A are C.

Some robots are intelligent machines.
Some intelligent machines are expensive.
Some robots are expensive.

No A are B.
No B are C.
No A are C.

All A are B.
All B are C.

Hypothetical Syllogisms

These syllogisms start with a first premise consisting of an **antecedent** from which a **consequent** follows: If students get 70 percent or above (antecedent), they will pass the course (consequent). The second premise may either **affirm** or **deny** the antecedent or affirm or deny the consequent. The syllogism is **valid** if the second premise affirms the antecedent or denies the consequent.

If students receive 70% or above, they will pass the course.

This student received 70% or above. She will pass the course.
(Affirms the antecedent, so it is VALID.)

This student did not receive 70% or above.
He will not pass the course.
(Denies the antecedent, so it is INVALID. There are other possibilities. Perhaps the teacher decided to curve the grade, so the student passed.)

This student will not pass the course.
She did not receive 70% or above.
(Denies the consequent, so it is VALID.)

This student will pass the course.
Therefore, she received 70% or above.
(Affirms the consequent, so it is INVALID.)
(That same kind teacher!)

Enthymemes

Enthymemes are shortened syllogisms that we use frequently in speech and sometimes in writing. We might say, "John is mortal because he's human." Or "John is human, so he's mortal." In such structures, it is usually the major premise we omit, perhaps because it is obvious. Sometimes, though, we may not want to call attention to the major premise because it does not fully meet the test of distribution. For example, in the enthymeme "Professor White is a good writer because she teaches English," we may not be able to preface the major term with *all* but only *nearly all* or *most*. We certainly cannot say that *all* professors of English are good writers, but we probably can say that *many* or *most* are. The following examples show strategies for expanding the enthymeme. Note that such linguistic clues as "because" and "so" may signal a premise or conclusion:

Because Mary was elected class president, we know she is popular. Because the word "because" points to a premise—usually the minor premise—the main clause must be the conclusion. So far, the syllogism is taking shape like this:

Major premise: [What belongs here?]
Minor premise: Mary was elected class president.
Conclusion: Mary is popular.

"Elected class president" must be the middle term because it appears in a premise, but not in the conclusion, and it also must be distributed at least once. So the major premise must be "All those elected class president are popular." The syllogism is valid, but is it true? Must a student be popular to be class president? Certainly this is often the case, but is it always the case? Might someone be elected because she is competent or a good leader though not popular? Probably the best we can do is say that *most* or *almost all* of those elected class presidents are popular.

When linguistic clues are missing, it can be harder to expand the enthymeme. If we are told, "John must be frugal. He was elected class treasurer," we assume there must be some connection between the two statements, but we cannot assume that the first statement is the premise and the second the conclusion. We can try each statement as the conclusion and work back from there to see if we can derive a major premise that will make a valid syllogism.

If "John is elected class treasurer" is placed as the conclusion, the syllogism would look like one of the following:

Major premise: Those elected class treasurer are frugal.
Minor premise: John is frugal.
Conclusion: John is elected class treasurer.

Or

Major premise: Frugal people are elected class treasurer.
Minor premise: John is frugal.
Conclusion: John is elected class treasurer.

But in the first case the middle term, "frugal," is not distributed at least once. In the second case, there is also a problem because we certainly cannot claim that all frugal people are elected class treasurer. If we make "John is frugal" the conclusion, we can get closer to validity, especially if we qualify the statement: Those elected class treasurers are likely to be frugal; John is elected class treasurer; therefore, John is likely to be frugal.

Exercises

Try your hand at analyzing the following hypothetical syllogisms, rephrasing the statements as necessary to determine their validity. Do not merely apply the rules, but try to think through why the conclusion does not follow from the premises:

1. If you file your taxes late, you will receive a penalty. You received a penalty. Therefore, you must have filed your taxes late.
2. I know you cannot graduate if you don't complete 168 units. Because you will graduate, you must have completed all 168 units.
3. If you don't have your passport, you won't be allowed on the plane for France. You have your passport. So you must have been allowed on the plane.

Expand the following enthymemes to make a valid syllogism. Is the syllogism also true?

4. Martha wears glasses, so she must be studious.
5. George is sick because he ate green apples.
6. Heather is gorgeous. She gets lots of dates.

How Do Deductive Reasoning and Syllogisms Transfer to Longer Arguments?

Essentially, deduction not only logically structures the reasoning process but also provides a framework for the argumentative essay or speech.

In *The Declaration of Independence,* for example, Thomas Jefferson sets up his first or major premise that a "government which becomes destructive of these ends" (ensuring the right to life, liberty, and pursuit of happiness of its citizens) may rightfully be altered or abolished. The body of the argument provides plentiful support for the second or minor premise: The government of Great Britain is destructive of these ends ("The history of the present King of Great Britain is a history of repeated injuries and usurpations, all having in direct object the establishment of an absolute Tyranny over these States").

The conclusion of the argument also provides the ineluctable conclusion of the syllogism: The government of Great Britain may rightfully be and is abolished ("We, therefore, the Representatives of the united States of America . . . are, and of Right ought to be Free and Independent States; that they are Absolved from all Allegiance to the British Crown, and that all political connection between them and the State of Great Britain, is and ought to be totally dissolved").

Though "Letter from Birmingham Jail" may at first sight appear primarily as a refutation, Martin Luther King, Jr., derives his own argument that it is justified to break an unjust law from two categorical syllogisms:

Major Premise:	A just law is a manmade code that squares with the law of God.
Minor Premise:	Segregation laws are not manmade codes that square with the law of God.
Conclusion:	Therefore, segregation laws are not just laws.

And

Major premise:	Unjust laws may be broken.
Minor premise:	Segregation laws are unjust laws.
Conclusion:	Therefore, segregation laws may be broken.

Another example of deductive reasoning used to structure an argument is Mary Antin's "Have We Any Right to Control Immigration?" Taking the same principles that underlie *The Declaration of Independence*, that all men are created equal and endowed by the Creator with unalienable rights to life, liberty, and the pursuit of happiness, she adopts these principles as her first premise: All humans have these rights. Her second premise is that immigrants are humans. And thus it follows that immigrants too have these rights. Probably, her readers will grant the logic of her syllogism. It is the extension she makes in the rest of the argument that immigrants have the right to claim these rights in the United States that some—perhaps many—readers may have difficulty admitting.

Toulmin Argument: Moving from Certainty to Probability

The contemporary philosopher Stephen Toulmin has contributed another way of understanding deductive reasoning in his book, *The Uses of Argument* (Cambridge UP), by allowing for a lesser degree of certitude. The Aristotelian syllogism sets up a system that leads ineluctably from a universal statement or major premise to a conclusion. As our discussion of the enthymeme has suggested, though, there are many cases where we cannot argue with complete certainty. How often can we say something that applies to every member of a group? Instead of saying *all*, we may hedge our bets and say *almost all, most,* or *many.* We often use adverbs to qualify our statements: *usually, frequently, often.* The terms Toulmin uses for the elements of argument reflect this lesser degree of certainty: The **claim** is what is to be proved; **qualifiers** indicate exceptions to or limitations of the claim; the **data** are the evidence or support for the claim; and the **warrants** are the assumptions, principles, and beliefs—stated or, often, unstated—that both underpin the claims we make and allow us to link the data with the claim. Toulmin includes two other terms: the **backing**, additional support for the warrant, and the **rebuttal**, either critiques of an argument or counterarguments.

The Toulmin method, though quite complex, can be simplified and adapted for the composition classroom; we call this a claim/reasons/specific evidence method, which many students agree is a useful process for analyzing and constructing arguments.

Claim: What is the proposition to be argued or defended? What, if any, qualifications or exceptions does it have?

> Motorcyclists and bikers who do not wear helmets should not be covered by insurance because this risky behavior often contributes to the severity of accidents and to raising their cost.

The qualifier here is the word *often.* Is the fact that risky behavior does not always lead to severe accidents or high cost enough to undermine the claim?

Reason I (or subclaim) for supporting the claim: *Not wearing helmets contributes to the severity of accidents.*

Specific evidence (data) supporting this reason or subclaim: *Frequency and types of severe motorcycle and bike accidents.* **Warrants:** *These injuries must clearly relate to having the head unprotected.*

Reason II: *Not wearing helmets helps to raise the cost of accidents.*

Specific evidence: *Head injuries can lead to various types of mental and physical impairment, necessitating costly treatments.* **Warrants:** *Must show both how the injuries lead to impairments and provide data on the cost of such treatments.*

Reason III: Does not apply here, though many arguments have multiple reasons and specific evidence to support them.

Reason IV and so on: Does not apply here.

Warrants: How can one justify connecting each reason with the claim as well as each piece of evidence with the reason it supports? The main warrant for the argument is *"Risky behavior that often contributes to the cost and severity of accidents should not be covered by insurance."* Whether one accepts this reasoning or not probably depends on how much store one places on taking responsibility for one's own acts.

Refutation

Dealing with objections raised about an argument or countering evidence supplied to support an alternative position is an essential strategy to win a hearing from readers who may be leaning to the other side or have already made up their minds. Many readers will raise objections that you fail to raise and may then decide your argument is not worth following because you have not shown yourself to be fair-minded.

Tamar Jacoby devotes a significant portion of "Too Many Immigrants?" to refutation, realizing that when there are pronounced views vociferously articulated, one cannot ignore them. The first section of her article presents the arguments restrictionists use against immigration: security, scarcity, economics, and lack of assimilation. Though she is conscientious about stating what she considers to be their valid arguments, in the second part of the article she is also careful to point out where she finds the arguments inadequate: tracking all who come or go in the United States is almost impossible; it is impossible to predict which immigrant groups will want to come to America and how their populations will increase; immigrants do not take jobs from Americans; "the immigrant drive to succeed is as strong as ever," and if they fail to assimilate we need to provide services to help them do so. Nor does she merely make these counterclaims; she provides multiple reasons to support her refutation.

Pathos: Weighing Appeals to Emotion

Appeals to emotion can be a very powerful part of argument. Such legitimate appeals often speak to the best parts of our humanity, our sympathy for the sufferings of others, our altruistic desires to improve our world, and our outrage against those twisted individuals who inflict harm on the innocent, the unprotected, and those who cannot protect themselves.

Through pathos, we also recognize that we are subject to multiple fears that may paralyze us or move us to action. Even when used judiciously, such appeals to emotion may, however, raise the hackles of some readers, so they must be used carefully.

Some useful questions to ask of appeals to emotion are: Does the argument lend itself to emotional support? Most likely, a medical discussion of the advisability of taking one drug therapy or another does not lend itself to the use of emotion. Is the audience one that will respond positively or negatively to emotion? An academic audience may be turned off by emotional appeals, for example. Does the use of emotion strengthen or weaken the argument? Does the emotional appeal substitute for a strong logical structure?

Appeals to emotion can function legitimately in arguments as an adjunct to the logic they employ. *The Declaration,* for example, appeals for solidarity with the colonists' British brethren: "We have appealed to their native justice and magnanimity, and we have conjured them by the ties of our common kindred to disavow these usurpations." The list of causes, though generally couched in measured terms, does in fact name heinous deeds: "He has plundered our seas, ravaged our Coasts, burnt our towns, and destroyed the lives of our people." The powerful verbs Jefferson uses must heighten the sense of outrage the colonists feel.

Jefferson makes emotional appeals that, while effective, are subordinate to the logical structure. Martin Luther King's use of pathos in the famous paragraph 14 of "Letter from Birmingham Jail" is much briefer than his use of logos, but it is truly a stunning example of the appeal to emotion. Most of the paragraph consists of a periodic sentence: a long sentence that withholds its main point until the end or period. This sentence is constructed of a series of subordinate clauses beginning with "when." Each depicting a moving situation, the clauses are designed to enable readers to participate imaginatively in the black experience: lynch mobs attacking one's parents; policemen beating black brothers and sisters; 20 million Negro brothers "smothering in an airtight cage"; a six-year-old daughter who cannot go to a public amusement park; a son who asks, "Why do white people treat colored people so mean?"; a family on a cross-country trip who cannot find a motel that will accept them. These experiences, even stripped of King's moving descriptors, evoke powerful images of discrimination by the surrounding society. The next set of "when" clauses turn inward to trace the psychological alienation inflicted by signs addressed "white" and "colored"; the depersonalization caused by the loss of one's name and title; the constant discomfort of "living constantly at tiptoe stance"; and the ultimate sense of the loss of self or "nobodiness" that results. Of course, many of King's readers would not have experienced these things firsthand, but the cumulative impact of piling up example after example is great. King intensifies this impact by repeating "when" again and again, like nails pounded into a wall. He also uses the repetition of alliteration to underscore his point: "lynch . . . at will" and "drown . . . at whim"; policemen who "curse, kick, and even kill"; "harried by day and haunted by night." Only after one has experienced all of the above, King says, "only then you will understand why we find it difficult to wait." It is difficult to imagine that any reader could fail to grasp the power of this writing. To be sure, such high-voltage writing should be used sparingly if it is to be effective. King knows this.

Samuel P. Huntington provides a recent example of the use of pathos to galvanize his readers into action. In the penultimate paragraph of "The Hispanic Challenge," he writes:

> Continuation of this large immigration (without assimilation) could divide the United States into a country of two languages and two cultures. . . . The transformation of the United States into a country like these [Canada and Belgium] would not necessarily be the end of the world; it would, however, be the end of the America we have known for more than three centuries. Americans should not let that change happen unless they are convinced that this new nation would be a better one.

He has also used this formulation of two cultures and two languages in paragraph 5, but only after a fairly lengthy historical introduction. Here the idea seems merely a part of an academic debate. The idea gathers momentum as he discusses what he considers the disturbing realities of Hispanic immigration so that by the end he has primed his readers, both Hispanics and non-Hispanics, to engage in a real-world debate, probably under the impetus of fear.

This discussion of pathos should make us remember our obligations to our readers if we have forgotten them as we become preoccupied with the mechanics of arguments. Readers are flesh-and-blood people who occupy a moral universe and care what ethos we present. They want to see our character as well as our credentials, reputation, and skill in finding authorities to support us. Readers are intelligent people who dislike being talked down to and recognize when we play fast and loose with logic or evidence. They respect order and clarity and truthfulness. Readers have hearts that make them respond to the predicaments of others, to the poor, the victims, the unfortunate. At the same time, readers resent being manipulated by writers who overdo appeals to emotions by relying on sentimentality or exaggeration. In the next two chapters, we will explore both how we can lose the trust of our readers by fallacious reasoning and how we can gain it by careful, respectful reading, research, and writing.

CHAPTER

2

Avoiding Fallacies

Fallacies, whether deliberate or inadvertent, are failures in logical reasoning and argument. They can be categorized as failures in ethos, in logos, and in pathos. These fallacies may be found at every level of argumentative discourse. The child arguing that she should be allowed to go to bed late because her mother does and the teenager claiming that he should be able to have a beer because his father does are both making fallacious claims. Newspaper letters to the editor are gold mines of fallacies with some writers oversimplifying issues, creating false dilemmas, and attacking leaders and candidates based on spurious reasons. Political ads may attack the character of a candidate rather than her positions or may misstate the position of a candidate. To sell a product, television commercials, whether selling beer, lingerie, or cars, often appeal to multiple human desires, relying little on the intrinsic worth of the product and more on the product's purported ability to make the buyer happy or desirable.

Recognizing fallacies is important to you as a reader or viewer so that you can evaluate the claims that others make. It is crucial to you as a writer so that you can avoid distorting facts, overstating a claim, or drawing invalid conclusions.

Attacks on Ethos

Usually, attacks on ethos are unjustified or irrelevant assaults on the character or credentials of the speaker. Not every attack on credentials or character is unjustified, however, so it is necessary to make clear distinctions. Making a claim without the credentials to back it up can make the speaker a legitimate target. For example, Linus Pauling, who advocated large doses of vitamin C without the nutritional background or studies to support his claim, was excoriated by the scientific community despite being a Nobel laureate. A failure in ethics can also undercut a speaker's credibility. People charged with enforcing laws cannot break them without losing credibility. Both Presidents Nixon and Clinton discovered that the American people take covering up wrongdoing and lying under oath very seriously.

Ad Hominem or Attack on the Person

An ad hominem attack is on the speaker rather than the argument, focusing on something that has nothing to do with the argument:

- He's divorced. How can he have anything to say about funding for childcare?

Tu Quoque or You Too

A favorite of children addressing their parents, this fallacy suggests that people cannot advise against or prohibit a behavior that they themselves practice.

- You smoke. How can you tell me not to do it?
- You're telling me to save my money? Look how much money you spent last year!

False Authority

We know that legitimate authority is vital to the writer's ethos. In the false authority fallacy, the argument relies on someone without the knowledge, position, or credentials to be an authority on the issue discussed. This fallacy is often seen in ads.

Michael Jordan may be granted authority to promote a brand of athletic shoes. However, this authority most likely does not extend to promoting a particular restaurant or car. There is no reason to think he has those credentials.

Failures in Logos

Errors in Reasoning

Many logical fallacies are related directly to failing to derive valid conclusions or construct valid syllogisms. The following might be called errors in reasoning.

Hasty or Illicit Generalization

Induction requires sufficient relevant examples on which to base a conclusion. A hasty generalization occurs when too small a sample leads to a suspect conclusion:

- I know two redheads who have bad tempers. It's clear that redheads have bad tempers.
- Terrorists who were Muslim were responsible for the attacks on September 11. Muslims are a threat to the United States.

Stereotyping

Related to hasty generalization, a stereotype begins with a conclusion drawn about a group of people from a too-limited sample and then applies that conclusion to a member of the group, implying that every member of the group shares that characteristic:

- Joan must be a gossip. You know what women are like.
- Men are sports freaks. Mark must spend his weekend glued to the TV watching football games.
- The Irish (or the Polish, French, Russians, Jews, Catholics, or Protestants . . .) are all __________ (fill in the blank). What can I say? She's Irish.
- I saw a picture of an Arab terrorist the other day. I'll avoid anyone who looks like him.

Stacked Evidence

Here the evidence supporting an assertion may be valid, but the writer or arguer omits other evidence that may weigh against it. In a criminal trial, for example, if the prosecutor were to omit a relevant fact that might lead to exoneration—perhaps an alibi—that would be stacked evidence.

Invalid Syllogisms

In deductive reasoning, failure to follow the rules of the syllogism, whether categorical or hypothetical, leads to an invalid conclusion, often called a non sequitur. You will recall that hypothetical, categorical, and invalid syllogisms are discussed in Chapter 1.

Faulty Analogy

Analogies can become faulty when similarities are stretched too far or are outweighed by the differences between the examples being compared:

- A teacher reasons that two students, both named Meghan and both having blond hair, should receive the same grade.

Obviously, the unimportant similarities between the two students are inadequate for reasoning by analogy.

Fuzzy Thinking

These next fallacies may be attempts to sound as if one is arguing logically. Instead, they are fuzzy thinking or replacements for logic.

Begging the Question

Begging the question means restating a claim, in one form or another, without supplying any proof:

- The theory of evolution is just that, a theory. Charles Darwin has not made his case for evolution. Evolution has not been proven.

Circular Reasoning

This is an attempt at argument that goes nowhere, landing us back at the beginning:

- I have to have a car in order to get to work. And I need to work in order to buy the car.

False Cause

Assigning the wrong cause for an outcome or an incident is a kind of oversimplification, assuming that there is only one cause for an effect:

- Our sales shot up by 25 percent after we started using an Internet pop-up.

This alone *might* have produced the result, but other factors might apply: The product might have been improved or the proximity of Christmas might have stimulated sales.

Post Hoc Ergo Propter Hoc or "After This, Because of This"

Another type of false cause involves saying that because something happened first in time, it caused what followed. Eating spicy food may indeed produce heartburn, but many superstitions ascribe causality to an incident merely because it preceded the effect in time:

- You walked under a ladder today. That's why you had bad luck.
- Your horoscope warned you not to engage in financial transactions today. No wonder you lost money on the stock market.

"What's One More or Less?"

The question implies that numbers do not really matter, but they do. Too many people in a boat **will** make it capsize. Other examples include:

- I know the registration system says the class is full. Please let me in anyway. One person won't make a difference. (Not true: The teacher will have more work to do and the students will have fewer chances to participate.)
- Why should it matter if we have less than the required number for the tour group? What difference can one person make? (The missing person's fare would have helped cover the expenses of the chaperone.)

Attempts to Deceive

The following fallacies are usually deliberate attempts to deceive, sometimes by oversimplifying, sometimes by misdirection, sometimes by narrowing options.

Straw Man

This fallacy consists of constructing a weak or exaggerated argument in order to tear it down, claiming that it is the argument your opponent is making. However, your opponent has not made this argument. For example:

- Consider this argument against pacifism: Pacifists always oppose violence. They think that the world can be changed by not responding to violence. They clearly do not understand the real world because they are blinded by their idealism. If pacifists were elected, we would be invaded the next day.

Here the arguer, by distorting the pacifist position, makes the argument seem poorly reasoned, even dangerous.

Red Herring

The red herring is named after a strategy used to train hunting dogs to follow the original scent. Dogs learn to ignore a strongly scented object like a herring that has been drawn across a trail. Thus, irrelevant or misleading statements that pull the audience away from the real argument are called red herrings. For example:

- You've argued that our candidate has not been fiscally responsible. She has, however, beautified the city, constructing planters along every major street.

False Dilemma

Sometimes called **black or white reasoning** or the **either/or fallacy,** this fallacy is usually improperly couched as an either/or proposition. As long as there might be another possibility, the statement is fallacious:

- To have peace in the Middle East, either Ariel Sharon or Yasser Arafat must resign. (Note that another possibility is that both must resign.)
- Either we go to war with Iraq, or Iraq will sell nuclear weapons to terrorists who want to attack us. (Certainly there are other possibilities, including pursuing arms inspection and elimination through the United Nations.)

Inappropriate Appeals to Pathos

Though appeals to emotion may be a legitimate adjunct to logic (see pp. 27–28 for Martin Luther King Jr.'s powerful use of the harm that discrimination does to children in "Letter from Birmingham Jail"), they can also be used to *replace* logic.

Ad Populum or Pandering

These are appeals to emotions or desires that many people feel. Commercials and ads might appeal to sexual instincts, selling cars by implying that the gorgeous model will come with them.

At Christmas, children's toys are much more than toys, and Christmas cards more than a seasonal greeting: Ads for these products are targeted to adults as well as children and bring with them happy memories of home and a promise of warmth and good times.

The ad populum fallacy may also involve an appeal to fear. It was used during World War II to justify interning Americans of Japanese descent with the claim that they might aid the Japanese in attacking the U.S. mainland. In the current war on terror, it might take this form:

- Look at Ground Zero and the grieving survivors. Terrorists are plotting another massive attack on the United States. We must suspend civil liberties in order to prevent this attack.

Bandwagon

This fallacy invites us to join the parade or jump on the bandwagon. Because everyone is doing something, we should too. A favorite ploy of political consultants, the bandwagon appeal often involves showing a large group of people rallying around a candidate. A commercial example is the well-known Coke ad showing a huge group of diverse people while the jingle "I'd like to teach the world to sing" is playing.

Slippery Slope

This is a kind of fearmongering that argues that any step down a path will lead to the worst possible outcome:

- Any restriction of abortion means that *Roe vs. Wade* will be overturned.
- Experiments with gene therapy for diseases will lead to designer or made-to-order babies.

Exercises

1. Work in groups to review the letters to the editor of several newspapers. Read a week's worth of these letters, selecting those letters with weak arguments. In your group, decide which fallacies are represented.
2. Also in groups, review the ads in several magazines that you read regularly. What needs, instincts, or feelings do these ads appeal to? Which do you think are legitimate appeals; which are not?
3. Identify the fallacious thinking in the following examples:

   - Susan Sarandon, a famous actress, and other entertainment figures used the Academy Awards ceremony to protest the war in Iraq. You should listen to what they have to say.
   - I don't get good grades because my teachers don't like me.
   - 98 percent of my high school class are attending college, many because "it's what everyone does."
   - Adopting the Equal Rights Amendment will mean that women will be drafted.
   - In his zeal to make his argument a strong one, Joshua presented all the evidence that supported his position, omitting any data that seemed to weaken it.

- After the plane crash, investigators discovered that the airline's ticket agents had allowed several passengers to bring on excess baggage even though they knew the plane was carrying a full cargo load.
- My dad told me that if I do not finish college, I will end up as a waitress or a sales clerk.
- When a ship disappeared after entering the Bermuda Triangle, investigators of paranormal phenomena reasoned that the Bermuda Triangle had triggered the disappearance.

CHAPTER

3

Writing the Source-Based Argumentative Paper

Becoming the Arguer: Creating a Conversation among Writer, Readers, and Authorities

The first two chapters of Part One have focused on understanding how argument works and reading arguments written by others to determine how they make their argument and whether they avoid fallacious reasoning. The kind of repeated careful analysis that we undertake together in class has undoubtedly honed our analytic skills. As we study how masters of the form make their case, we no longer read passively. We question; we disagree; we put forward our own arguments; we demand additional evidence; we contradict the support that is provided. No longer do we think of reading argument as a private activity, but we enter a conversation with the writer, other readers, and the authorities cited in the text. We say to the writer, "Who are you to tell me what I should think? Prove to me that you are competent to make this case." "My, you really did make a powerful *Declaration,* Mr. Jefferson." Or, "Mr. Huntington, I've been amazed at how differently you and Mary Antin have used *The Declaration of Independence* as part of your argument." With other readers, we dispute their interpretations and evaluations and sometimes reach an agreement: "You are just plain wrong that Samuel Huntington is a racist, but you have convinced me that there is another side to his argument that Hispanics will not fully integrate into American society." The sources and authorities cited within the text are thus no longer merely providers of dry data but people whose ideas and arguments are so familiar that we feel as if we actually know Jefferson, Polacheck, Antin, or Jacoby.

No matter how actively we have engaged in the conversation described above, at some point we decide to initiate our own conversation. Sometimes it is our own need to clarify or defend our ideas that urges us to write; often it is an assignment that requires us to do so. Whatever the motive, we need to take charge of the conversation, acquiring and demonstrating expertise, respecting our readers, and taking heed of their needs. Most of all, we need to lay claim to our position with conviction, passion, and authority, to be as willing to engage with our readers as we were to be critical readers.

The following steps work for any source-based argumentative writing, though some may be eliminated for a shorter essay based on a few primary sources. For the longer argumentative research paper, following the process in detail will assure a carefully researched, thoughtful, well-written paper that creates the kind of conversation we have been discussing.

Choosing a Topic

Select a topic that interests you and lends itself to research. For a successful paper, you will need to find multiple relevant and academic sources (that is, from significant journals and magazines, respected national newspapers, and books by scholars and experts). Your topic should raise important questions about serious issues.

You will be spending a great deal of time doing research and writing your essay, so you need a project that you will find worthwhile. Even if your topic has been somewhat limited by the topic of this casebook or by your assignment, you can find a way to tailor it to your interests. You might connect your topic with what you have been learning in another class or with a subject in which you are already interested. For example, one student decided to examine the argument in *Antigone* and used what she had been learning in a communications class to find a framework for analyzing the speeches. Another connected his peace studies class with his topic from the casebook, finding good sources for his support of the pacifist position. Others took historical periods that fascinated them and focused on the nineteenth century or the Vietnam War.

A quick survey of the topic will help you decide whether your topic is doable within the time frame and manageable within the parameters of the assignment. Read about the subject in a good encyclopedia like *Britannica.* Look at the bibliography provided after the article, as well as the bibliography provided in the casebook. Does your library have a good selection of these sources, or are public and other university libraries easily accessible? Do a quick subject search of your library's catalog and databases and of InfoTrac® College Edition to determine whether there is ample and varied material available on your topic.

Narrowing a Topic and Developing a Working Thesis or Claim

Try to narrow your topic as soon as possible. Do not research poverty in general, but research and explore the causes of poverty, the governmental or private remedies for poverty, or the impact of poverty on children. Narrow down the topic of capital punishment to the morality of the death penalty, or its deterrent effect, or the question of retribution, or the question of whether capital punishment is fairly administered. Focus on one war, not several; on a few speeches, not ten. Narrowing allows you to focus on more specific sources and to avoid getting lost in reading sources that will not be relevant to your project. Narrowing will also ensure that you can develop adequate support in the time and space you have. Always keep in mind that you need to be able to make a claim and that you will be writing an argument, not merely a report.

As soon as you can, write a working thesis (or claim). It is often helpful to start with a question. Given the information you have already, which questions are most appropriate; for which do you have the most supportive information? For example: Is capital punishment moral? Does it deter murderers? Does it provide retribution? Is it unfair in its application? In a short paper you might want to try to answer only one of these questions; in a longer paper you might want to tackle them all. Next, provide a tentative answer to your question. This answer is your thesis or claim. Be sure that it is arguable, that not everyone is in agreement: "Capital punishment is moral because _________." Or, "Capital punishment is unfair in its application because __________."

Your subsequent research will help you determine whether your claim is defensible, whether it will hold up to scrutiny. It is helpful to think of your claim as a hypothesis, one that you will test. Should the evidence not support the claim, you as a responsible and honest arguer will need to reformulate your thesis. One student, for example, began with a claim in which she argued that Richard Alba's article "Assimilation's Quiet Tide" (p. 161) explained well the assimilation process of the immigrants whose stories she had read. However, after she read Melvin G. Holli's "E Pluribus Unum," which argues in addition that when immigrants moved to progressive, tolerant societies they assimilated more fully, she concluded that Holli had the better argument.

Selecting and Evaluating Sources

Make effective use of library resources to find good sources. Check your library's online catalog of books and articles, and locate articles through databases such as InfoTrac College Edition. Books provide a more comprehensive look at a topic and often include extensive data or thorough development of important ideas; articles are, of course, shorter and more focused on a portion of the topic. Your bibliography should usually include both types of material.

Depending on your topic, your most up-to-date sources will be from journals, magazines, newspapers, and websites. Be wary of websites because they differ widely in source, reliability, and usable content. Look for those set up by universities, reputable institutions, and authorities. The following are useful questions to ask in order to evaluate sources:

1. Examine the cover of a magazine or journal, the front page of a newspaper, or the opening pages of websites. Determine how the publication's opening images and words affect you. What feelings do they stimulate? What would motivate someone to buy the magazine or newspaper or to continue reading the website or other electronic publication?
2. What is the publication's social and political viewpoint? Who owns or publishes it?
3. Study the table of contents, look at the range of subjects offered, and skim some articles. What can you infer about the political orientation, purpose, and assumptions of this publication?
4. Look at ads and generalize about which sponsors sell their products in this publication. What social class would they appeal to? What kinds of advertisements are missing? How might the advertisers influence the publication's policies and attitudes?
5. Analyze the language in the articles. How does the language indicate the targeted readers and their level of education?

Taking Notes

As you read, you will need to keep track of material helpful to your argument. It is a good idea to print out or copy any sources not in your text because transcribing material directly into your text can lead to many types of errors and, in some cases, to charges of plagiarism. In addition, your instructor may wish that you submit this material with your completed essay in order to check that you have cited material correctly, either by direct and accurate quotation, paraphrase, or summary. Many researchers start by highlighting relevant material in a source. Some researchers are then reluctant to allocate the time to take notes, but omitting this step can make it difficult to locate a quotation or piece of information and arrange material in the best order. When downloading sources, try to find sources that indicate original page numbers, such as PDFs.

We recommend using note cards or fairly small slips of paper for your notes. This way, you avoid having too much information on one card and do not lose the flexibility of shuffling cards to determine the correct ordering of the information you have amassed. Usually it is a good idea to have three types of note cards: a card with complete bibliographic information for each source; cards containing the background information, quotations, or evidence you think will be helpful for your argument; and cards on which you jot down ideas, questions, examples, and so on as they occur to you. Bibliography cards can then be alphabetized to serve as the source for your Works Cited or References page. The notes you take on each source should have at least the author and an abbreviated title at the top left and a topic on the right (these topics will help you sort your cards). Be sure to indicate page number (or paragraph number for an Internet source). Use quotation marks to indicate quoted material. For summarized or paraphrased material, be sure to rewrite the material in your own words. Do not merely change a word or two. These three types of cards are invaluable when you write your draft. Many students have told us that after they have arranged their notes in a logical order, the paper almost writes itself. The note cards on pages 41–42 will give you an idea of how to proceed. Some students find it convenient to take notes on the computer and then print them out for easy reference.

Construct your Works Cited or References page (for example, a minimum of 8–10 sources for an 8–10-page essay) from your bibliography cards. As you add sources, add them to a computer file you have created to list your sources. You can directly copy or download the bibliographic information from your library catalog. Include a wide range of sources: books, articles, and websites covering a time frame appropriate for your topic. For each source, do you have complete bibliographic information, including pages or paragraph numbers? Have you used correct MLA or APA bibliographic format?

Alba, Richard D. "Assimilation's Quiet Tide." Public Interest 19 (1995): 3–18.

Alba provides the classic explanation of the three-generation immigration model.

Holli, E Pluribus Unum — Progressive tolerant society

Holli adds to the traditional model (which looks at end results) an explanation of those results (he calls them "measures and predictors of results" p. 19): Progressive, tolerant societies provide better motivation and opportunities for assimilation. pp. 19–25

My Ideas

—Won't Asian Indian immigrants—even though in some ways they are transnationals moving back and forth between U.S.—more likely assimilate here since U.S. can offer them greater opportunities than a third world country?

—The immigrant experiences of Polacheck, Acuna, and Kim should fit into Holli's categories or measures of assimilation, even though they are all second generation (Polachak wasn't born here, but she came as a child).

Annotating a Bibliography

Many instructors require more than an initial list of your sources as a way to help decide whether you have the sources you need. The annotated bibliography includes the following steps: Skim each source you have selected. Write your own brief, but specific, summary of the source. Using the abstract in the database is not acceptable because it may often not include the specific information that makes the source valuable to you. Include a paragraph indicating your evaluation of the source: What is its relevance to your project? How pertinent and accurate is the information it contains? Does it make an argument that supports yours, or does it provide important counterarguments to your position? Keep looking for additional sources as you find holes in your research.

The following examples should provide you with a guide for preparing your annotated bibliography. Note that the first paragraph states the main points of each source. Try to be as succinct as possible. The second paragraph provides a reflection on the source's utility for the paper. Try to represent diverse viewpoints in these annotations, including good recent thinking, as well as more classic views, about the topic. Using correct MLA citation form here will ensure that you will use it in your finished essay.

Annotated Bibliography

Alba, Richard D. "Assimilation's Quiet Tide." Public Interest 19 (1995): 3-18.

Alba argues that assimilation "need not imply obliteration of all traces of ethnic origins" (3), but that it is characterized by increasing socioeconomic parity (due largely to improved education); decline of the mother tongue; moving from the ethnic neighborhood to the suburbs; and by intermarriage across racial and ethnic lines. As second and third generations succeed the first generations of immigrants, they are less ethnic and thus the ethnic group as a whole becomes less ethnic.

This seems to be a good statement of the classic assimilation model with Alba standing by his belief that assimilation is still continuing. It gives me a base for understanding immigration. The material on educational patterns (pp. 6–8) is very helpful in explaining why there is socioeconomic progress.

Holli, Melvin G. "E Pluribus Unum: The Assimilation Paradigm Revisited." Midwest Quarterly 44.1 (2002): 10-26.

Holli also examines the assimilation model because he wants to find out whether the new way of looking at recent immigrants as "transnationals" is truly useful. Will Asians and Latin Americans fail to assimilate? Will they bring their ethnic hatred and quarrels to America? He uses the same categories or factors as Alba does, but Holli calls them "measures" and "predictors." Holli is more interested than Alba in figuring out why these measures occur. His hypothesis is that in countries that are forward-looking and tolerant, immigrants assimilate well because they see the benefits. For example, Germans kept to themselves in Russia and Poland, but followed the typical immigrant pattern in the U.S. The same is quite true for Jews who stayed entirely apart in Eastern European countries and Russia, but have integrated well in England and the U.S.: They have been "eroding and assimilating not from hate [which kept them apart] but from love" (24).

Alba and Holli both agree on the four indicators of assimilation. Alba does a fine job of exploring the importance of education in social mobility. Holli looks in detail at immigration dispersion in

Chicago and adds an important perspective by trying to show how these indicators can work. He shows how important the openness and progressiveness of the welcoming country is. He makes the assimilation model useful today by showing how it, rather than transnationalism, will predict better how today's immigrants will assimilate. Both should be useful in my essay.

Focusing the Thesis

Once you have completed your research, you should be able to write a very focused thesis that not only indicates the conclusion you have reached but also provides the reasons or main points of support for your assertions. Such a focused thesis also serves as a kind of road map to the organization of your essay, allowing readers to keep track of where they are in the argument.

1. Capital punishment is moral because it is imposed by the rightful authority of the state, it allows for retribution, it safeguards the community, and it provides avenues of appeal.
2. Capital punishment is unfair in its application because members of minorities and the poor who must use public defenders are more likely to receive the death penalty.
3. Capital punishment is moral except in the case of young offenders, those with low IQs, and those found to be legally insane.

Note how the first two claims include the reasons that support them. The third indicates the exceptions. In both cases, readers will expect you to develop each point in the order given.

Planning an Argument: The Outline or Argument in Brief

Write a plan that will help you discover what you think, that will help you focus on the elements of argument you need to include, and that will help you determine whether you need additional material. You should include answers to the following questions:

- In light of your topic, what are your values and what assumptions do you make as the **writer?**
- Consider the **audience.** Who are your readers? What views may they already have about your issue? What kinds of values does the audience have? How can you make common ground with them? What will your audience need to know?
- What is your **claim** or thesis?
- Consider **reasons** or **subclaims** that will provide the main framework of your argument. These can provide the main points of an outline or an argument in brief.
- What kinds of **evidence** or **support** will best substantiate your thesis or claim?
- Think about what kinds of **objections** your readers are likely to raise. Forestall them by raising them first. This tactic helps to keep your readers with you. How will you **refute** these objections?

As you focus your thesis and plan your essay, think about the type of argumentative structure best suited for your topic. For example, if you are setting up general principles of a theory of civil disobedience against which you will test a particular action, a deductive framework may work for you. In this case, you might find *The Declaration* a useful model. In your essay, you might examine whether one or more models of immigration truly explain the data you gleaned from the immigration stories. For example, you would first clearly set up an extended definition of segmented assimilation and use it as your major premise; then you would use the body of your essay to examine how particular immigrant stories conform—or fail to conform—to the definition. You would then draw your conclusion from this evidence: Polacheck, Kim, and Mukherjee do (or do not) demonstrate the positive model of segmented assimilation.

If you wish to focus your essay on what conclusions may be drawn from specific evidence, an inductive approach, you may decide to use sociologists such as Richard Alba as models. Using this approach leads you to collect and present sufficient material about a topic from which you can generalize. After studying a series of personal narratives concerning immigration, for example, you might determine what common elements these narratives have, and then decide which elements are essential to persuade readers that the basic process of acculturation remains the same for these immigrants. The strategies of Rogerian argument may work well if, for example, you want to make an argument that is particularly difficult for an audience to swallow. Here you would look for the common concerns and values that the members of your audience share, and you would take care to illustrate that you understand and accept at least some of the arguments your readers would make.

Another way to proceed is to use the modifications of the syllogism that Toulmin proposes, which we might call the claim/reasons/specific evidence method.

Brief for Argument Paper

My Audience: The class and the teacher have all read the same material that I have. I need to be fair and also find a way to engage them. I think admitting where both writers agree and then focusing on what Holli adds to the discussion will do both things.

Claim: Alba and Holli both agree on four factors indicating that immigrants generally assimilate over three generations. Their claims are borne out by the immigrants whose stories I studied. However, because Holli explains why these measures of immigration occur, arguing that progressive and tolerant countries provide an environment that encourages assimilation and implying that recent immigrants (whom "transnationalists" say will probably not assimilate) will also follow the pattern of assimilation, his theory is more satisfying.

Warrant for the Claim: A claim is more "satisfying" when it more fully accounts for the data or facts.

Reason I: Alba and Holli both use the same criteria for assimilation—social mobility, increasing adoption of English, decline of ethnic neighborhoods, and intermarriage across ethnic and racial lines—and explain them convincingly. These criteria can be confirmed by the immigration stories.

Specific Evidence: Show how they both provide excellent explanations by using examples (e.g., Alba's discussion of education's role in social mobility and Holli's study of ethnic dispersion in Chicago) and show how the immigrant stories back them up (Polacheck, Acuna, and Kim—coming from different immigrant periods—have all mastered English and become upwardly mobile, for example).

Reason II: Holli claims that a country like the United States—progressive and tolerant—provides an environment conducive to immigration.

Specific Evidence: Examine his German example. It is good support. Also use Polacheck's coming from a repressive country and finding a home here.

Reason III: It makes sense to conclude that, given the advantages of living in the United States, recent immigrants, even those who are more affluent and can travel back home easily, will make a home here.

Specific Evidence: Kim's story provides good support for this statement.

Warrant: Reason II allows me to make the leap to the conclusion in Reason III.

Conferring with Your Instructor

If possible, arrange a conference with your instructor to which you bring your bibliography, sources, notes, argument in brief, and so on. Be sure to bring your questions as well. Ask for help if you are having problems finding sufficient information, if your thesis is not as focused as it needs to be, or if any part of your paper is giving you particular trouble.

Drafting the Essay

As you write your **introduction,** think about how you are engaging with your sources and your readers in a kind of conversation. How can you interest your readers in your topic? Can you pose a question that demands an answer, write a scenario that engages them emotionally, jolt them with startling or horrifying statistics, or draw them in with a quotation that provides the pith of your argument? How can you let your readers know both what you are arguing and how you will proceed? A carefully crafted thesis can do both, combining your claim and your reasons and thus providing a road map of your argument.

If you find that you are stalled somewhere in your introduction, move on to the body of your paper. For some writers, laying out the evidence is a very helpful way to get started. Then you can return to the introduction, having discovered what you really want to say. Use your outline or plan to guide the writing of the **body** of your draft. For each point turn to your notes, arranging them in the best order to supply the evidence you need to support each reason or subclaim. Keep checking back with your thesis or claim to see whether what you are writing advances it. As you introduce each section of your essay, be sure to use **topic sentences** that relate that section very specifically to your thesis and that show readers where you are in your argument. For example, if your thesis is *Whereas Tolstoy argues that violence will disappear once Christians refuse to participate in a government that is based on violence, Gandhi and King* *understand that violence is a possible outcome of nonviolent resistance,* you might introduce the section on Gandhi as follows: *Like Tolstoy, Gandhi embraces nonviolence, but he recognizes that his followers will encounter violence and trains them accordingly.*

Be careful to introduce your source material accurately, providing parenthetical citations so that you can check later that you have cited material correctly (see Appendix B). Consider whether each quotation, paraphrase, or summary is necessary to make your point. Do not merely drop one into the text but introduce and explain it. Do not allow your text to become a pastiche of quotations. Be true to your sources by presenting them accurately and fairly. Be true to your readers by constantly asking yourself, "What do they need to know? How will they respond to what I have written? How can I show that I respect them even if I suspect they will not be sympathetic to my claim?"

Even if you are not required to submit a draft with your completed paper, do not give in to the temptation to make your first draft your last! You may encounter difficulties or problems that require time to correct. Write a complete draft, including all the support you have gathered from your sources. This is an invaluable step that allows you to see exactly what you have and where you are missing necessary material. When you see gaps or holes in your research, this is a point at which you must return to your sources for additional information or locate new sources. Sometimes you may discover that the organizational structure you proposed in your plan is not working. To clarify the logical progression of your ideas, you may need to try a different order for your reasons or subclaims or even to employ another argumentative strategy.

Many writers find **conclusions** difficult to write. The temptation is to restate the thesis and leave it at that. Certainly you do need to demonstrate that you have proven your thesis or supported your claim. At this point, look back at your introduction to see if you have changed your mind in the course of writing the paper or inadvertently proven a different thesis, and adjust your conclusion accordingly. But a mechanical ending does not do justice to the conversation you have been having with your readers and sources. You might inquire whether the conversation about your topic has really been exhausted. What other questions are left to resolve? What problems remain? Where are you least satisfied with what you have discovered? Where do you think additional research needs to be done?

Revising the Draft

Revision means to see again; it implies re-viewing, re-thinking, and re-writing where necessary. Most likely, you have been revising as you write your draft, catching errors as you see them, and rearranging the order of material in a kind of ongoing, recursive process. Until now, your writing process has probably been rather solitary. Now it is time to seek out what Donald Murray calls a "test reader" in *The Craft of Revision* (Wadsworth). This reader may be a peer-editing partner or group in class or someone you have identified outside of class who can provide responses to your work. Ask this reader to comment on your work as specifically as possible so you can see how a reader responds to what you have written. Of course, you must be willing to do the same for your reader. The following are questions to guide your reader's response. You might also ask your reader to focus on an area with which you have had particular difficulty.

1. Does the introduction grab readers and draw them into the discussion? What tactic is used? How can it be improved?
2. At the end of the introduction, is there a focused claim that predicts the organization of the essay? What is the claim? Underline it on the draft and write it here. How can it be improved?
3. Does the organization of the essay follow from the thesis? If it deviates from the claim, where does this happen?
4. Does each section of the essay have a topic sentence or subclaim, showing how the section relates to the thesis?
5. Are there transitions that connect sections? Where are transitions needed?
6. Are judiciously chosen quotations included? Are they introduced well and discussed sufficiently, or are they merely dropped into the text?
7. Does the essay include ample, pertinent, and specific support from the sources? Where is more information needed? Where is additional support needed?
8. Are in-text citations present and correct? Is the Works Cited or Reference page properly formatted?
9. What are the most successful parts of the essay? Where would you suggest more work is needed?

Proofreading

Proofread carefully. Remember that this is a different process than revision. An error-ridden paper is distracting or even insulting to the readers, so check for spelling, punctuation, and typographical errors. One helpful technique is to put the paper aside for a few hours or a day so that you can see it with fresh eyes. Then start at the bottom of the page, looking only for errors. Another technique is to keep a list of the errors you make frequently and focus on those. Still another is to read the paper aloud. Often the ear will catch what the eye does not. Many people, including the authors of this text, need to proofread more than once. Check also that you have followed MLA or APA format exactly for both in-text citations and the Works Cited or References page.

Along with your well-edited final essay, submit your annotated bibliography, your argument in brief, copies of your sources, your notes, and your draft. Submit these items in a pocket folder or a manila envelope.

As a guide for your final revision and proofreading, we have also included the kind of checklist many instructors use to evaluate your essay.

Checklist for Argumentative Research Essay

Quality of research
(20 points total) ______
- Authoritative sources (15) ______
  - Pertinent
  - Ample
  - Varied
- Notes (5) ______
  - Accuracy
  - Documented
  - Labeled clearly
  - Complete

Success of argument
(50 points total) ______
- Claim (15) ______
  - Arguable
  - Focused
  - Provides major points of support or subclaims
  - Provides map of argument
- Assumptions clearly enunciated (5) ______
- Objections/refutation (5) ______
- Subclaims (20) ______
  - Topic sentences
  - Complete development
  - Necessary definitions
  - Specific evidence
- Conclusion (5) ______
  - Valid
  - Convincing

Documentation
(10 points total) ______
- Acknowledgment of all borrowed material
- Accurate quotations
- Complete paraphrasing
- Smooth inclusion in sentence
- In-text citation
- Works Cited or References page format

Paragraphs
(10 points total) ______
- Effective transition sentences
- Logical order of ideas
- Full development
- Appropriate length

Sentences
(10 points total) ______
- Clear
- Grammatical
- Correct spelling and punctuation
- Exact word usage
- Elimination of unnecessary words
- Smooth transitions

Total: ______

PART TWO

Casebook on Immigration

CHAPTER

4

Open the Door, Close the Door

Fundamental as immigration is to our identity as Americans, our attitudes and laws governing immigration have always reflected a tension between seeing our country as a haven for immigrants and protecting our national identity and freedoms from being transformed by immigrants. As early as the mid-eighteenth century, Americans debated the effect of immigration on their society and the necessity for either open or limited immigration. In his 1757 essay, "Observations Concerning the Increase of Mankind, Peopling of Countries, &c.," Benjamin Franklin wonders why so many Germans were allowed into Pennsylvania when there were plenty of English people to emigrate: "[W]hy should the *Palatine Boors* be suffered to swarm into our Settlements, and by herding together establish their Language and Manners to the Exclusion of ours?" He worries that Pennsylvania, founded by the English, would "become a Colony of Aliens, who will shortly be so numerous as to Germanize us instead of our Anglifying them, and will never adopt our Language or Customs. . . ."

Twenty-five years later, Hector St. John Crèvecoeur published *Letters from an American Farmer*, in which he praises the influence of America on the immigrant and the great country that this "mixture of English, Scotch, Irish, French, Dutch, Germans, and Swedes" has produced. "From this promiscuous breed, that race now called Americans has risen," he declares with pride. And in a famous passage, he writes:

> I could point out to you a family whose grandfather was an Englishman, whose wife was Dutch, whose son married a French woman, and whose present four sons have now four wives of different nations. He is an American, who leaving behind him all his ancient prejudices and manners,

> receives new ones from the new mode of life he has embraced, the new government he obeys, and the new rank he holds. He becomes an American by being received in the broad lap of our great Alma Mater. Here individuals of all nations are melted into a new race of men, whose labors and posterity will one day cause great changes in the world.

Thomas Jefferson makes no mention of immigration in *The Declaration of Independence,* which is included in this chapter, but he did express some concerns about the European immigrants whom Crèvecoeur saw as good Americans in the making. In *Notes on the State of Virginia* (1781–82), Jefferson highlights the gulf between the unique American government, based on the principles of English freedom and the natural rights he so memorably enshrined in *The Declaration,* and the absolute monarchies European immigrants were fleeing. He fears that these immigrants "will bring with them the principles of the governments they leave, imbibed in their early youth; or, if able to throw them off, it will be in exchange for an unbounded licentiousness, passing, as is usual, from one extreme to another. It would be a miracle were they to stop precisely at the point of temperate liberty." Like Franklin, Jefferson also thought that the immigrants' children would speak the language of their parents, as well as follow their parents' principles and beliefs. Nevertheless, Jefferson always expected that immigrants would be naturalized and take their rightful part as citizens in governing and legislating.

Lyman Beecher, Protestant preacher, seminary president, and father of Harriet Beecher Stowe, the author of *Uncle Tom's Cabin,* shared Jefferson's worst fears and added more of his own. In his *Plea for the West* (1835), Beecher also points to the background of absolute monarchy that many European immigrants left. But he is also especially worried by the religious allegiance to their church and their pope of Central European Roman Catholic immigrants. To Beecher, the prospect of their participation in government and legislation raises the specter of an America controlled by a foreign church. He urges that Americans counter such frightening possibilities by strengthening Protestant education and by exposing Catholicism's potential power over the United States.

The immigrants themselves also had thoughts and beliefs about their adopted country, and we read several pieces here that allow us to hear immigrant voices directly. William and Sophie Seyffardt, Ann McNabb, Rosa Cassettari, and Hilda Satt Polacheck reflect on their experience as immigrants and on American society. We can evaluate their contributions—actual and potential—as we read their words.

Mary Antin had little doubt about the actual and potential value of all immigrants to the United States. A Russian Jewish immigrant herself, she wrote an impassioned defense of open immigration based on her reading of *The Declaration of Independence*. In her 1914 piece, she argues from first principles that America had to open her gates to all who needed her. She rejects closing America to any particular ethnic or racial group. Yet many Americans in both the nineteenth and twentieth centuries feared or disdained certain types of immigrants, as is clear from editorial cartoons. Included here are just a few examples of visual commentary on the ongoing American division between open and restricted immigration.

Finally, we end with a contemporary, post-9/11 discussion of restriction on immigration by Tamar Jacoby. She examines current restrictionist arguments yet reminds us of earlier objections to immigration. Even today's fears of terrorist infiltration by immigrants may seem to echo the motives of Congress when it passed the Alien and Sedition Acts of 1798 that required aliens to wait fourteen years instead of five to become citizens and allowed the President to deport aliens "dangerous to the peace and safety of the United States" during peacetime.

Thomas Jefferson, *The Declaration of Independence*

The Declaration of Independence, approved July 4, 1776, as "The Unanimous Declaration of the Thirteen United States of America" by the Second Continental Congress, announced the formal separation of the colonies from Great Britain. Thomas Jefferson (1743–1826), John Adams, Benjamin Franklin, Roger Sherman, and Robert R. Livingston made up the drafting committee, but Jefferson wrote the initial draft, which was revised once by Franklin, Adams, and Jefferson before it went to Congress and then was revised a second time in Congress. The document established the new revolutionary government and allowed it to seek aid from foreign countries in its war with Great Britain. *The Declaration* draws on ideas of the Enlightenment, especially those of John Locke, and puts them into political practice as well as justifying, through a series of grievances, the break with British rule. Since its proclamation, *The Declaration* has influenced and inspired revolutionary movements throughout the world.

IN CONGRESS, July 4, 1776.

The unanimous Declaration of the thirteen united States of America,

When in the Course of human events, it becomes necessary for one people to dissolve the political bands which have connected them with another, and to assume among the powers of the earth, the separate and equal station to which the Laws of Nature and of Nature's God entitle them, a decent respect to the opinions of mankind requires that they should declare the causes which impel them to the separation.

We hold these truths to be self-evident, that all men are created equal, that they are endowed by their Creator with certain unalienable Rights, that among these are Life, Liberty and the pursuit of Happiness.—That to secure these rights, Governments are instituted among Men, deriving their just powers from the consent of the governed,—That whenever any Form of Government becomes destructive of these ends, it is the Right of the People to alter or to abolish it, and to institute new Government, laying its foundation on such principles and organizing its powers in such form, as to them shall seem most likely to effect their Safety and Happiness. Prudence, indeed, will dictate that Governments long established should not be changed for light and transient causes; and accordingly all experience hath shewn, that mankind are more disposed to suffer, while evils are sufferable, than to right themselves by abolishing the forms to which they are accustomed. But when a long train of abuses and usurpations, pursuing invariably the same Object evinces a design to reduce them under absolute Despotism, it is their right, it is their duty, to throw off such Government, and to provide new Guards for their future security.—Such has been the patient sufferance of these Colonies; and such is now the necessity which constrains them to alter their former Systems of Government. The history of the present King of Great Britain is a history of repeated injuries and usurpations, all having in direct object the establishment of an absolute Tyranny over these States. To prove this, let Facts be submitted to a candid world.

He has refused his Assent to Laws, the most wholesome and necessary for the public good.

He has forbidden his Governors to pass Laws of immediate and pressing importance, unless suspended in their operation till his Assent should be obtained; and when so suspended, he has utterly neglected to attend to them.

He has refused to pass other Laws for the accommodation of large districts of people, unless those people would relinquish the right of Representation in the Legislature, a right inestimable to them and formidable to tyrants only.

He has called together legislative bodies at places unusual, uncomfortable, and distant from the depository of their public Records, for the sole purpose of fatiguing them into compliance with his measures.

He has dissolved Representative Houses repeatedly, for opposing with manly firmness his invasions on the rights of the people.

He has refused for a long time, after such dissolutions, to cause others to be elected; whereby the Legislative powers, incapable of Annihilation, have returned to the People at large for their exercise; the State remaining in the mean time exposed to all the dangers of invasion from without, and convulsions within.

He has endeavoured to prevent the population of these States; for that purpose obstructing the Laws for Naturalization of Foreigners; refusing to pass others to encourage their migrations hither, and raising the conditions of new Appropriations of Lands.

He has obstructed the Administration of Justice, by refusing his Assent to Laws for establishing Judiciary powers.

He has made Judges dependent on his Will alone, for the tenure of their offices, and the amount and payment of their salaries.

He has erected a multitude of New Offices, and sent hither swarms of Officers to harrass our people, and eat out their substance.

He has kept among us, in times of peace, Standing Armies without the Consent of our legislatures.

He has affected to render the Military independent of and superior to the Civil power.

He has combined with others to subject us to a jurisdiction foreign to our constitution, and unacknowledged by our laws; giving his Assent to their Acts of pretended Legislation:

For Quartering large bodies of armed troops among us:

For protecting them, by a mock Trial, from punishment for any Murders which they should commit on the Inhabitants of these States:

For cutting off our Trade with all parts of the world:

For imposing Taxes on us without our Consent:

For depriving us in many cases, of the benefits of Trial by Jury:

For transporting us beyond Seas to be tried for pretended offences:

For abolishing the free System of English Laws in a neighbouring Province, establishing therein an Arbitrary government, and enlarging its Boundaries so as to render it at once an example and fit instrument for introducing the same absolute rule into these Colonies:

For taking away our Charters, abolishing our most valuable Laws, and altering fundamentally the Forms of our Governments:

For suspending our own Legislatures, and declaring themselves invested with power to legislate for us in all cases whatsoever.

He has abdicated Government here, by declaring us out of his Protection and waging War against us.

He has plundered our seas, ravaged our Coasts, burnt our towns, and destroyed the lives of our people.

He is at this time transporting large Armies of foreign Mercenaries to compleat the works of death, desolation and tyranny, already begun with circumstances of Cruelty & perfidy scarcely paralleled in the most barbarous ages, and totally unworthy the Head of a civilized nation.

He has constrained our fellow Citizens taken Captive on the high Seas to bear Arms against their Country, to become the executioners of their friends and Brethren, or to fall themselves by their Hands.

He has excited domestic insurrections amongst us, and has endeavoured to bring on the inhabitants of our frontiers, the

> merciless Indian Savages, whose known rule of warfare, is an undistinguished destruction of all ages, sexes and conditions.

In every stage of these Oppressions We have Petitioned for Redress in the most humble terms: Our repeated Petitions have been answered only by repeated injury. A Prince whose character is thus marked by every act which may define a Tyrant, is unfit to be the ruler of a free people.

Nor have We been wanting in attentions to our Brittish brethren. We have warned them from time to time of attempts by their legislature to extend an unwarrantable jurisdiction over us. We have reminded them of the circumstances of our emigration and settlement here. We have appealed to their native justice and magnanimity, and we have conjured them by the ties of our common kindred to disavow these usurpations, which, would inevitably interrupt our connections and correspondence. They too have been deaf to the voice of justice and of consanguinity. We must, therefore, acquiesce in the necessity, which denounces our Separation, and hold them, as we hold the rest of mankind, Enemies in War, in Peace Friends.

We, therefore, the Representatives of the united States of America, in General Congress, Assembled, appealing to the Supreme Judge of the world for the rectitude of our intentions, do, in the Name, and by Authority of the good People of these Colonies, solemnly publish and declare, That these United Colonies are, and of Right ought to be Free and Independent States; that they are Absolved from all Allegiance to the British Crown, and that all political connection between them and the State of Great Britain, is and ought to be totally dissolved; and that as Free and Independent States, they have full Power to levy War, conclude Peace, contract Alliances, establish Commerce, and to do all other Acts and Things which Independent States may of right do. And for the support of this Declaration, with a firm reliance on the protection of divine Providence, we mutually pledge to each other our Lives, our Fortunes and our sacred Honor.

Questions about the Passage

1. Outline the passage. What are the major sections into which you would divide it? What principles of classification have you used to make your divisions?

2. Jefferson includes a long, undivided list of grievances. Into what subcategories might they be divided? Look at the verbs he uses; consider the types of grievances he lists. Defend your decision.
3. Thinking of this document as a kind of template for other societies, what grievances against Milosevic might the Serbians make or the Afghanis against the Taliban or the Iraqis against Saddam Hussein and the Baath party? Following the logic of *The Declaration*, are the grievances sufficient to justify a change of government?

Questions about the Argument

1. Do you think the truths that Jefferson enunciates in his second paragraph are indeed "self-evident"? Might his immediate audience have seen them differently?
2. Throughout *The Declaration*, identify words that carry emotional weight. To which emotions do they appeal?
3. *The Declaration* is often used as an example of effective argument. Make a case for its efficacy. How does Jefferson use appeals to ethos, audience, logos, and pathos to defend his position?
4. Why do you think Jefferson does not mention immigration? Why does this document belong in a casebook on immigration?

Lyman Beecher, "The Threat of Catholic Immigration"

Lyman Beecher (1775–1863) was one of the best known Protestant clergymen of his day. Born in Connecticut, he attended Yale College and was ordained in the Presbyterian Church in 1799. His revivalist sermons won him fame, and he accepted pulpits with increasingly prestigious congregations in Connecticut and then Boston. In 1832, Beecher became the first president of the Lane Theological Seminary, a Presbyterian training school for ministers in Cincinnati. Raising funds two years later in Boston, Beecher gave a series of three highly charged anti-Catholic sermons. Following one of them, a mob burned the Ursuline Convent in Charlestown, two miles north of Boston; Beecher denied any responsibility for inciting the anti-Catholic destruction, but historians have connected his sermon to the mob's actions.

The passage below appears in *A Plea for the West* (1835). In this published series of speeches, Beecher describes the American West, which at that time included the Ohio Valley where his seminary was located, as a key battleground between the Catholic and Protestant faiths. His theory, soon associated with the political platform of the Native American Democratic Association (the "nativists"), casts the Catholic immigrant as a pawn of his church who will obey the pope in all political decisions. He fears that Catholic education would attract Protestants, and he thus urges the necessity of Protestant education such as his own seminary. He also hopes to limit immigration and the naturalization of immigrants in order to prevent his ultimate fear—that Catholic immigrants will take over the country and unite church and state under the pope's control.

> In the first place, while the language of indiscriminate discourtesy towards immigrants, calculated to wound their feelings, and cast odium on respectable and industrious foreigners, is carefully to be avoided; an immediate and energetic supervision of our government is demanded to check the influx of immigrant paupers, thrown upon our shores by the governments of Europe, corrupting our morals, quadrupling our taxation, and endangering the peace of our cities, and of our nation, it is equally plain, also, that while we admit the population of Europe to a participation in the blessings of our institutions and ample territory, it is both our right and duty so to regulate the influx and the conditions of naturalization, that the increase shall not outrun the possibility of intellectual and moral culture, and the unregulated action of the European population bring down destruction on ourselves and them. In what manner the means of self-preservation shall be applied, it does not belong to my province to say. Doubtless a perfect remedy may be difficult, perhaps impossible; but should we therefore look upon the appalling scene in pale amazement and trembling impotency? It would be the consummation of infatuation, and the precursor of ruin. *Nothing is impracticable for the preservation of our liberty and national prosperity which ought to be done, and nothing can ruin us but presumptuous negligence or faintness of heart.* But we must act, and act quickly, and with decision, or the stream will be too deep and mighty to be regulated, and will undermine foundations and sweep away landmarks, and roll the tide of desolation over us. Nor can the patriotic solicitude of the people, and the states, and the nation, be brought to bear on this subject, immediately, to the extent of our political wisdom and practical energy, and not

mitigate the evil, and avert the danger. But our past utter neglect on this subject, is as wonderful as the carefulness of the nations of the continent. Not an individual from this country can traverse Europe without the inspection of a host of spies and police agents, who make his person, character, and business, as well known to the government as they are known to himself, and no small portion of this vigilance is for the purpose of precluding the possibility of any political republican action, adverse to their institutions. While we, around the entire circumference of our nation, leave wide opened the door of entrance, and all the vital energies of our institutions, accessible to any influence which the anti-republican governments of Europe may choose to thrust in upon us. Do these governments indulge a vain fear in thus environing the political influence of Americans, though only temporary residents, and even wayfaring men? And have we nothing to apprehend while European paupers flood us, and Europeans occupy the soil, rear institutions, wield the press, control suffrage, and rush up rapidly to a competition of numbers? Is our government so compact and iron-sinewed as to bid defiance, safely, to every possible disturbing influence from abroad, which can be made to bear upon it? Ought there not to be a governmental supervision of the subject of immigration, which shall place before the nation, annually, the number and general character of immigrants, that the whole subject may experience the animadversion of an enlightened public sentiment, and the voice of the people aid in the application of the remedy?

We entered upon the experiment of self-government, when a homogenous people, with diffidence, and multiplied checks, and balances in our constitution, and have watched and encountered, with decision and care, the dangers developed in the progress of its administration; but why should there be such vigilance to guard our institutions from domestic perils, and such reckless improvidence in exposing them, unwatched, to the most powerful adverse influence which can be brought to bear upon them from abroad?

In respect to the Catholic religion, and its political bearings, there is an obvious and safe course. It is the medium between denunciation and implicit confidence, between persecution and indiscriminate charity. It includes a thorough knowledge of the principles, history, and present conduct of the papal church, where its power is unobstructed. To this end, a book is eminently needed, containing the authentic documents of the Catholic church, accessible to ministers and intelligent laymen of all denominations. These now are scattered through massy folios, or quoted in versatile discussions, and cannot be readily appealed to or consulted. A book of well authenticated documents, *without note or comment*, would nearly supersede the necessity of controversy, and afford ample material for public sentiment to act upon, which, while it would not encroach on the rights of Catholics, would, by no means, confide to their care the education of large and influential portions of our republic. A book of this description would not be invidious. If the Catholic system does not contain principles and usages adverse to free institutions, it would clear it of unmerited odium; and if it does contain such principles it is the right and duty of the nation to know it. There is nothing in Catholic more than in Protestant human nature, to demand implicit confidence, or preclude investigation and vigilance. No denomination of Christians, and no class of politicians, are so good as to justify implicit confidence, or supersede the necessity of being watched. *Responsibility to an enlightened public sentiment is the only effectual guarantee of unperverted liberty and political prosperity.*

But to a correct and universal observation must be added efficient universal action, to rear up, immediately, those institutions, literary and religious, which are indispensable to the intellectual and moral culture of the nation. Our own population is fast outrunning the influence of Christian and literary institutions; and if to us republicans it seems evil to supply them—if it grieves us to encounter the expense of maintaining the discipline which is necessary to the perpetuity of government in our way, we have no cause to complain that the powers of Europe should extend to us a gratuitous education, which shall enable them to avert the annoyance of our example, and govern us their way. If we do not provide the schools which are requisite for the cheap and effectual education of the children of the nation, it is perfectly certain that the Catholic powers of Europe intend to make up the deficiency, and there is no reason to doubt that they will do it, until by immigration and Catholic education we become to such an extent a Catholic nation, that, with their peculiar power of acting as one body, they will become the predominant power of the nation, or if not predominant, sufficient to embarrass our republican movements, by the easy access and powerful action of foreign influence and intrigue. We have no right to complain that the Catholics of this country, aided from Europe, should seek to accomplish a work which we neglect,—and we do not complain either of his holiness of Rome or of his majesty of Austria, or his wily minister Metternich. They pursue the policy in supplying our deficiency of education, which, with their views of right and self-preservation, they ought to pursue, and the Catholics in this country have a perfect right to gather funds from Europe to purchase lands—rear cathedrals—multiply churches—and sustain immigrant ministers, and to sustain the unendowed bishoprics for fifty years to come, and establish nunneries, and support the sisterhood, and establish cheap and even gratuitous education amid all the destitute portions of our land. They have a right to do it, and, according to their principles, they ought to do it, and they are doing it, and they will do it, unless as a nation of republicans, jealous of our liberties, and prompt to sustain them by a thorough intellectual and religious culture as well as by the sword, we arise, all denominations and all political parties, to the work of national education.

The sole object of this argument touching the Catholics is not 5
to repudidate them, but to present the facts in the case, and appeal to the nation, whether it will sustain its own institutions for the education of its own people, or depend on the charity of the Catholic despotic governments of Europe. I do it because when the facts are stated, and the eye of the nation is fixed on the subject, unless infatuation has fastened on us, there can be no doubt of the result. Education, intellectual and religious, is the point on which turns our destiny, of terrestrial glory and power, or of shame and everlasting contempt, and short is the period of our probation. Indolence and neglect will soon extend over the land the lamentation, "The harvest is past, the summer is ended, and we are not saved." The things which belong to our peace are now before our eyes, and our sufficiency to secure them is vast and manifold. As a nation we are disincumbered of debt, and from our perilous resources might at once make provisions to endow forever the colleges, academies, and schools of the land. Each state, alone, is able to endow its own institutions,

and were all legislative provision withheld, there are in the nation individuals of sufficient wealth and patriotism, and munificence, when they perceive the perils and the safe-guards of our liberty, to call into being all those orbs of light which are indispensable to the safety and perpetuity of our institutions. And were even those unmindful of their privilege and duty, a republican phalanx, such as once fought the battles and paid the taxes of the revolutionary war, would now command institutions for the defence of liberty to arise, as their fathers did the forts and munitions of their day. Every denomination would organize its willing multitude to give and toil till intelligence and holiness should cover the land as the waters cover the sea. But this various and superabundant ability and willingness of the nation must be called forth in plans of peaceable efficacy—the means must be multiplied of providing and sustaining the requisite host of qualified instructors. Institutions, male and female, must be endowed to secure cheaply, the requisite qualification. The national intellect and morals, will never rise to the exigencies of our preservation, accidentally, or spring up under the hand of ephemeral and inexperienced instructors. The early culture of the national intellect, and heart, is worthy of becoming a *profession*, and must become a profession, in the hands of duly qualified men and women—embracing the experience of the past, and the accumulating knowledge of coming generations. The education of the nation—the culture of its intellect—the formation of its conscience, and the regulation of its affection, heart, and action, is of all others the most important work, and demands the supervision of persons, of wise and understanding hearts—consecrated to the work, and supported and highly honored in accordance with their self-denying, disinterested, and indispensable labors. It is here that we faulter, and that the Catholic powers are determined to take advantage of our halting—by thrusting in professional instructors and under-bidding us in the cheapness of education—calculating that for a morsel of meat we shall sell our birth-right. Americans, republicans, Christians, can you, will you, for a moment, permit your free institutions, blood bought, to be placed in jeopardy, for want of the requisite intellectual and moral culture.

One thing more only demands attention, and that is the extension of such intellectual culture, and evangelical light to the

Catholic population, as will supercede implicit confidence, and enable and incline them to read, and think, and act for themselves. They are not to be regarded as conspirators against our liberties, their system commits its designs and higher movements, like the control of an army, to a few governing minds, while the body of the people may be occupied in their execution, unconscious of their tendency. I am aware of the difficulty of access, but kindness and perseverance can accomplish any thing, and wherever the urgency of the necessity shall put in requisition the benevolent energy of this Christian nation—the work under the auspices of heaven will be done.

It is a cheering fact, also, that the nation is waking up—a blind and indiscriminate charity is giving place to sober observation, and a Christian feeling and language towards Catholics is taking the place of that which was petulant, and exceptionable. There is rapidly extending a just estimate of danger. Multitudes who till recently regarded all notices of alarm as without foundation, are now beginning to view the subject correctly, both in respect to the reality of the danger, and the means which are necessary to avert it, and both the religious and the political papers are beginning to lay aside the language of asperity and to speak the words of truth and soberness. Under such auspices we commit the subject to the guardianship of heaven, and the intelligent instrumentality of our beloved country.

Questions about the Passage

1. In the first paragraph, what two kinds of immigrants does Beecher identify?
2. What does Beecher mean, in paragraph 1, when he urges that immigration and naturalization be limited so "that the increase shall not outrun the possibility of intellectual and moral culture"? In the same long paragraph, what contrast does he draw between American and European political society?
3. What specifically does Beecher recommend to combat the influence of Catholicism in paragraph 4? How does he think his solution will work?
4. What is the role of education in Beecher's defense against Catholic influence in the United States?
5. In what ways are American republicanism and the immigrants' Catholicism in opposition?

6. In the final paragraph, Beecher commends the nation's attitude toward Catholic immigrants as improved because it falls between two extremes. What are the two extremes?

Questions about the Argument

1. What assumptions does Beecher make about his audience's beliefs and attitudes?
2. Does Beecher use appeals to pathos? If so, are they legitimate?
3. Does Beecher support his points? If so, how?
4. What strategies does Beecher use to make his ethos a reasoned and calm one, despite his message of urgency?

William and Sophie Seyffardt, "Letters Home to Germany, 1851–1863"

Nearly 1.4 million German immigrants came to the United States between 1840 and 1860, about a third of all immigration during this period. In the fall of 1850, August Frank and his younger sisters, Sophie (1827–74) and Christiane, and Christiane's husband, Edward Barck, arrived in Saginaw County, Michigan, from the town of Dietlingen, in the southern German state of Baden. The Franks' father was a prosperous Evangelical Lutheran pastor, and he provided some of the funding for the farm property acquired by the family along the Titibawassee River. Sophie Frank married William Seyffardt (1829–71), another German immigrant, in 1852. William's parents were also well-off people. Sophie's and William's letters home to their parents reveal a network of German immigrant settlements in the midwest as well as the importance of continued financial assistance from Germany. The letters also allow us to glean details of ordinary immigrants' lives—their work, their homes, their families, and their aspirations.

1851
William Seyffardt to his parents.

Titibawassee, October 1.

I visited several German settlements on horseback. About 4 miles from Frankentrost[1] I became lost, and in the growing

1. Frankentrost, Saginaw County, Michigan, was one of several German settlements established in that area during the late 1840s. The persons mentioned further on by Seyffardt became a part of the circle of acquaintances of the Barck-Seyffardt-Frank families.

darkness, was thrown from the horse by a branch. I found lodging in Frankentrost where an inn-keeper let himself be paid well for weak coffee and yard-long prayers. The next morning I was received in a friendly way by Mr. Veenfliet in Sheboyonon. After two days, I rode home by way of the friendly settlement at Frankenmuth. There are social gatherings at Titibawassee on Sundays in which Count Salms and a Hungarian Baron von Espenberg, an excellent musician, participate in target shooting, etc. A daughter was born to the Roeser family, at which time I made a trip to the doctor, 25 miles away. At this time I killed a deer, using a piece of board to stun it. Two large bears were killed by Indians. My plan is to buy a 100–160 acre farm, and I therefore ask for a loan of $3,000.

1852
William Seyffardt to his father.

Titibawassee, January 10.

At this time I can give no report about buying, but am busy looking, for one must not make a lot of noise when one wishes to buy at a low price. Wellington Farm has been my residence since I came here. It is leased by G. Roeser for 5 years for $350. Our Sunday get-togethers with indispensible dancing and target shooting angered only a few Yankees and German old-Lutheran pietists, the participants, however, were well pleased. I was out of sorts for a week for my horse fell on me, but nevertheless I could carry an 80-pound deer home $1^1/_2$ miles. Christmas eve was at Roeser's with punch, cake and whist for the neighbors.

William Seyffardt.

1852
William Seyffardt to his father.

Saginaw, February 17.

On this date I have purchased Wellington's farm for $1160. I will build a suitable house next year. The farm consists of 67 acres, 45 clear, is the nicest location along the river, and recognized as such. From Roeser, who had rented the farm, I received a team of horses with harness for $105 and eight tons of hay for $80, also a lean-to shed for $30. Household goods, $20. Not to forget 3 cows ($36), 7 pigs, etc.

William Seyffardt.

As concerns thoughts of marriage, I merely mentioned them to Louis, because it is necessary for a farmer to have a wife, and to be frank, the choice here is small. But I would 10-times sooner not have a wife than an uncultured or frivolous one.

Your *William.*

1852
William Seyffardt to his parents.

Titibawassee, March 30.

I have important news to tell you, namely my engagement to Sophie Frank. The father of my bride-to-be is a minister at Dietlingen and may come over here this year. I became acquainted with my Sophie on the farm of Barck and Frank. To praise her good qualities is not the thing for a bridegroom to do, but I will get a dear good wife. I would prefer bringing her to you but the ocean prohibits that. I have learned the value of a home only since I own a farm. I cannot tell you how happy I am not to be so alone in America any more, and I am convinced that you will have no opposition to this marriage. The wedding date is set for the end of June. My farm is 67 acres, 40 cleared, 20 acres of meadow, which pays with the high prices of hay ($10 a ton). I have 2 horses, 2 cows, 7 pigs and 30 hens. I took over the equipment from Roeser.

1852
Sophie Seyffardt to the parents of William Seyffardt.

Titibawassee, July 5.

Now at last, after the wedding is past and I am united with my William forever, I get to greet you and to tell you how happy I feel being your daughter. Because of obstacles, the wedding had to be postponed until June 26, and since Roesers moved out before this day, William had to cook for himself for five weeks. I often felt sorry for him, when, tired from his work and bathed in sweat, he would stand at the stove and prepare his dinner. As a result of this he often caught a cold. The wedding was celebrated with only the family present. We were also sad that father and mother could not stand at our side. William did everything to make the most favorable impression. Everything was brightened, the windows cleaned, the room was white-washed, and even the garden was prepared. We are happy together and my housekeeping gives me great pleasure.

I am adding my thanks for the valuable gift. William bought me a ladies' saddle with it and now we ride together on the farm. At first I was afraid, but William gave me a very gentle horse—maybe a bit too calm, as William who rode at my side had to help with his foot at times. From our two cows I get 8 pounds of butter weekly, but from the 40 hens in the coop, I get only one egg every other day. That is unpleasant since, with a lack of fresh meat, one is limited to a flour diet. The mosquitoes this summer were very kind, but still bother us enough. Since yesterday we have 8 men cutting wood for the barn. William exerts himself so much at it that I am worried about him because of the great heat. It is questionable if my parents will ever come, for the trip is being postponed from year to year. The older they get, the harder the trip will be. Cheer us often with letters for it is one of the greatest pleasures to get mail from our dear ones.

1852
William Seyffardt to his Father.

Titibawassee, August 6.

There was quite a commotion in our household. We had 8 men at the table daily. My barn was erected July 30, and we had 24 men for this job and they had to be well fed. I was in bed for three days with a violent fever. My poor wife, who because of all the people could not get away from the stove, had also caught a cold and could hardly stand on her legs after the evening meal. We rested on the following day, Sunday, and played our woes by notes. The fever left us after three days, leaving a great feeling of lassitude, which was improved by a few hearty deer soups. A sore on my wife's neck opened on Tuesday and since then she has been as lively as ever.

My brother-in-law, August Frank of Milwaukee, was married to Miss Kerler several weeks ago. Her father is wealthy and he opened a credit account of $5,000 for him in New York.

August has associated himself with a substantial man. But since the credit would not be good until three months from now and August needs money immediately to enter into the partnership, I gave him $550, I have a legal note for it and will receive 7%, and can get my money back after four weeks' notice. If I would not be sure of it, I would not have done it. I still have $400 in Saginaw, $250 of which will be needed for my barn.

Aug. 9. A half day of mowing caused the fever to return and I am glad that brother-in-law Henry has come to help me. My Sophie is always being called to the neighbors to cut out clothes, or to help with other well-known women's jobs. We are very much dependent upon helping one another and it is unpleasant for me to have to be lazy. I subscribe to the New York "Staatszeitung" (Democratic, weekly $2.80) and the weekly "Tribune" (Whig) $2.30 with postage.

Aug. 21. I believe that I am rid of all the fever now, but if things remain this way I cannot do any work, as I feel too weak, I had a great desire for bouillon this afternoon, but could only satisfy this craving by shooting a chicken. A short time ago I shot three deer, one right after the other in the creek in front of my house. We use deer meat here the same as beef. Because of the heat we keep only a quarter at most in the summer (of course if one is a hunter, the hind quarter). What is not eaten at once is put into sour milk. In this way one dabbles in the kitchen and becomes half a "kitchen-Peter." The first melon was ripe today, for they ripen quickly when it is so dry. I will try to describe the farm to you. The drawing of the ground plan is nearly ready. It is hard for me since I am no artist, in spite of the certificate from Aachen. Sophie will include a short letter.

1852
Sophie Seyffardt to the Seyffardt parents.

Titibawassee, October 16.

When my last letter was sent I believed William to be free of all fever, but it returned after 14 days and weakened him very much. Added to that was a cholera attack, and you can imagine my fear and fright. The attack lasted from 2 a.m. until 12 noon. I am glad that Mr. Schlegel is a help to William. Our nearest German neighbors is a family named Vasold from Thueringen. They live diagonally across the creek, so near that we can talk to each other. The family consists of a daughter and five grown sons. One daughter is married to William Roeser. The nearest neighbors on our side are Yankees, quite friendly, obliging people. Unfortunately, I have so much trouble with English that I cannot say a decent sentence. Not only does it give me a headache, but William laughs at me on top of it. The farm of Gustav Roeser is a half mile from us, we often go there as they are the kind of neighbors that anyone could wish for. A young couple lives just below our farm; the husband is 18, the wife 15. The woman lived in a barrel in the open before they built a hut. Two families, the Bernhards from Frankfurt, and the Liskows from Pomerania, live some distance from us, six miles along the way to Saginaw. Count Solms of Austria lives three miles farther. When we visit them, we pick up Barcks with our horses for they have only oxen. Tomorrow I will ride with William to Saginaw, and will stay overnight there in order to go to church the next day. There are only 20 of our 70 chicks left as a result of the cold. The cabbage, which William planted when a bridegroom, bore such nice heads as I never saw in Germany. We are waiting for Indian summer, but it looks as though it will snow today. Winter is not unpleasant to me—it is so nice to sit in a warm room.

1852
William Seyffardt to his parents.

Titibawassee, October 17.

The three Roeser brothers are living in three houses upward along the river. Otto Roeser (law student), the hunter, runs a bachelor's hall and sometimes supplies us with deer meat. I have shot nothing recently and Schlegel (traveling salesman) with a residual south-German stoutness, tells us, mostly panting, that the deer ran through the river faster than it was possible for him to run. I consoled him and myself for better days. Barck has big trouble. A German, named Fischer, whom Barck had persuaded to come to the farm because he became melancholy in Saginaw, is completely insane now and must be watched all the time. I do not know what will come of that.

Tomorrow will be the first German meeting concerning County affairs, and I hope that the Germans will take a more active part than I have had the opportunity to observe up till now. The Presidential election is approaching and the Democratic and Whig newspapers are attacking each other like biting dogs. I have not been converted to either of these parties. The Whigs have spent a lot of money and are flooding the country with brochures, and with pictures of the invincible General Scott, who through the conquest of splintered Mexico is on a level with the first generals of Europe?!! There is no mention of administrative virtues. The Democrats have set up Pirie [Franklin Pierce], but their statement of principle is so undemocratic (for protection of slavery) that a free-minded person can not agree with them.[2]

As far as the land is concerned which I intend to buy, I have my eye on two pieces of 80 acres each. They are to cost $2½ and $5 per acre respectively, but I will inquire further.

I ask you to tell Moritz that the no. 5 key on my accordion is broken, and that the nickle silver given to me by Band is no good. Maybe he can find out what the trouble is.

I am concerned about the beetles, as there are few to be had. In any case, there are fewer here than in Pennsylvania.

1853
William Seyffardt to his Parents.

Titibawassee, August 15.

Many thanks for the congratulations on the birth of our little one. She is gaining well, is very dear, and sleeps from evening until morning. She smiles by day, and is friendly, so that she is the darling of the German as well as the Yankee neighbors. We had our pictures taken recently. I will send beetles and daguerrotypes soon. It was a busy summer for us as we were building a house. The house will cost $370, the stone cellar $130. We hope to move in by November. On August 10, I drew $210 on Curtis & Co. as the remainder of my credit in New York. We had frightful heat recently, 38 R. [117°F.] in the sun. We are slimming down as a result of the heat and work. I do not know whether I have written about our carriage, the main parts of which are the

2. Undoubtedly much to Seyffardt's disappointment, the Democrats carried the Presidency, Pierce winning over Scott, 1,601,474 votes to 1,386,580. John P. Hale, candidate of the Free Soil Party trailed far behind with 156,147. Michigan followed the national trend, going to Pierce by some 8,000 votes. Seyffardt's anti-Democratic views made it almost inevitable that he would join the ranks of the Republican Party after its formation in the mid 1850s. His later letters, particularly during election years, contain considerable political commentary.

wheels and axle of the rental wagon. Now the bold decision has been made to set an elegant box upon the manure wheels. I am the mailman for two miles around so I may become Postmaster in time. Barck has bought a horse now, too, so now we can get together more often. Now comes the lovely autumn with its cool nights, when one can feel like living again.

1853
William Seyffardt to his Parents.

Titibawassee, October 2.

We went through hard times, but it is better now. Our Mathilde had whooping cough of the worst kind for 8–9 weeks. Also Sophie is coughing hard, but I still do only when I get up. This cough was common here and attacked all the farmers. It was necessary to hire the wife of Deibel, our laborer, during our sickness, and together they receive $140 annually. In order to make up the wages, it is absolutely necessary to put the farm on a larger footing. I must have more land under all circumstances. Prices of products will rise, since we will get 6–8 sawmills in the county. One is being built 2½ miles below me. Our prices now are [per bushel]: wheat $1¼, rye $1, barley $1, oats $.50, Indian corn $.75, potatoes $.50, hay $10 a ton. All of these items are rising in price. But if I have to pay $140 wages and have further help with the harvest, and have only 6–7 acres of winter grain I cannot get along, although I made so much noise that I had to make do on the income from my farm. My intention is to buy 40–80 acres of adjoining land and clear my farm. My harvest this year is 20 tons of hay, 60 bushels rye, 130 bushels potatoes, 70 bushels of Indian corn, 11 bushels buckwheat, 6 bushels apples, vegetables, etc. I am requesting father to ask for $500 credit for me in New York. I was always opposed to large farms before, but when one constantly keeps hired help, one must have work for them.

Your William.

1854
William Seyffardt to his Father.

Titibawassee, April 28.

First, I want to announce that I have bought 40 acres of very good land across from mine. I paid $100 for it, and am connecting it to the mill with a ferry. I decided to go East to buy my machinery, and went to Rochester, N.Y., by way of Detroit, Canada, and the Suspension Bridge (Niagara Falls). The steam engine has 10 horse power and is arranged so that the power can be used in two ways so that if grinding grain does not pay, I will saw wood. This is definitely more profitable. My 9 days' trip cost me $30. The machine, with everything that went with it, cost $2135. There will be 99,000,000 feet of lumber cut this year on the Saginaw and branch streams and 400 ships will be needed to transport it.

I have most of the building material and bricks in place. The freight was lower because of the snow. The mill will be between our house and the river, so that the grain can come by land or water. It is being said that there will be a village here soon. It is 6 miles from here to Amelith and 9 miles to Frankenlust, both German Settlements, and we are negotiating for the building of a road from Amelith to here.

The whole thing amounts to more than I had expected, and I am sorry to have to get so much money from Germany where it is so well invested by you, but I am forced, dear father, to ask for further credit of $500, for I do not like to use a stranger's money. Next January 1, I will receive the rest of the money ($200), which August Frank has from me. How can I express my thanks to you for all the love and goodness which you are continually showing me. Just now in anticipation of all the horrors Europe faces, and which may also shake America, I think of all my loved ones with trepidation. But do not forget, dear father, that there are hearts beating on the other side of the big water, in a country which is younger and more firm than shaky old Europe, who will do their duty with happy hearts. Now farewell, greet dear mother and brother and sisters.

From your faithful son *William.*

1854
Sophie Seyffardt to William Seyffardt's Parents.

Titibawassee, August 18.

I ask you to overlook the first long interruption in our correspondence, for the building of the mill took all of our time. Things are pretty topsy-turvy here, as we had 9–14 men regularly every day and there were headaches in the kitchen-department, as you, dear mother, can imagine. Our farm is as though transformed. It used to be so quiet, and now it is so lively, but I must admit that I miss the pleasant farm life very much. We finally received your package. Sincere thanks for the ring from William's sainted mother. I will save it as a sacred keepsake. Mathilde takes great pleasure in her fat boy [doll]. I will save the pretty garment until she is older and more sensible. She is not well just now, as she is teething. Barck is in agreement to start a little store here, and all that remains is to sell the farm. We would have them near us then and Barck would not have to work so hard. It was an awfully hot summer, 105°F. in the shade. To you, dear parents, most sincere kisses from your

faithful daughter Sophie.

1855
William Seyffardt to his Parents.

Titibawassee, January 17.

On January 13, at nine o'clock at night, we were presented with a little, healthy, 7¾ pound girl, who will be given the name of *Marie* Auguste.

We laughed, father, that you believed that Sophie takes care of the boiler. She only looks out the window to see if steam comes out of the safety-valve, for this shows whether there is more than 80 pounds of steam pressure. Since my engineer, through his carelessness, cost me so much money, in addition to $30 and board and room monthly, I run the machine myself, and find out that my miller stole from me and pocketed the money while I was absent. I chased [him] away, raved, even reached for the gun, the good friend of the backwoodsman. After calm deliberation, I now have an honest miller for $20, Emil Scheuermann is fireman for $15, a man on the farm $12, a girl $1–1¼ a week, W. Seyffardt with undetermined salary as overseer. That my mill is considered worthwhile by speculators is shown by the fact that a N[ew] Y[ork] company made offers to me. Since I cannot have the mill insured, I would sell the whole thing for $15,000, especially since I have too much gall for a miller. You dear father, think that we are saving in the wrong place by having too little help. It is an old story that where the pay is the highest the work is the poorest, because everyone wants to be a gentleman. In the present bad time for

N. York and other large cities there is enough work here. Above us there are 120–150 oxen and 500 men working on 5–6 rivers which flow into the Saginaw. Today, the 22nd of January, the first worthwhile snow in 5 weeks and everyone is jubilant.

Your William.

1855
William Seyffardt to his Parents.

Titibawassee, May 2.

On March 30 I took about 4500 pounds of mill stones on the ice 16 miles from Saginaw to here with two teams. On April 2, I attended Town Meeting, also across the ice [River], and the ticket which was hatched in Barck's store and called dutch ticket completely knocked out the old officers who had eaten at the public trough. Otto Roeser is now justice of the peace. Little Marie is sitting next to me and swinging her feet, so that I can hardly write. There is a small steam boat traveling the river now and I will have it deliver iron from the mill. Barck has rented his farm this year, gets hay for half, the rest for ⅓. He also wants to sell his cattle and invest the proceeds in the store.

1856
Sophie Seyffardt to the Parents in Crefeld.

Titibawassee, January 10.

We celebrated a merry Christmas at Barck's and drove down with the children and Jacobine. The four Scheuermanns were there also, and happiness showed in the eyes of the three brothers to have their sister Emma here also. Yes, they glorified the occasion with a little keg of beer, which Barck and Mr. Jaexen [Jackson] rolled two miles along the snow. Afterward we danced, as William may not go anywhere without his accordion. Jacobine's box finally arrived, and she wept for joy when she saw it. What joy it was to see the pretty clothes for our children and the beautiful collar for me. What work for you, dear mother! Accept our heartfelt thanks for everything. The gold items will be saved until the girls are able to appreciate the value of the keepsakes from their sainted grandmother. We will make a flower bed with father's flower seeds. The mill is doing very well and William has much work. Our Marie will be a year old next Sunday, and she is a strong child but has no teeth yet.

Louis [Seyffardt] should be back from England by now and his bride should be happy. Please tell us the day of the wedding. We had 20° [Reamur? –13°F] of cold for a week and could hardly get the room warm. Sincerest kisses from your

faithful daughter Sophie.

1856
William Seyffardt to his Parents.

Titibawassee, May 15.

A big letter-writing day today, and our Tilde has said: Papa, are you writing to Germany? I would like to know what her idea of Germany is. The little one says quite a bit already. She is very comical and is beginning to climb as recklessly as Tilde. We have a post office now and our address is Post Office Jay, Saginaw Co., Mich. The mail is delivered by a coach, which travels between Saginaw and Midland[3] twice a week. We also have a blacksmith shop, so now our village consists of two homes, three barns, one hotel and one pig sty. I did not include the mill and post office.

As soon as I can, I will buy another quarter section (160 acres). I have done pretty well until now, and I think that prospects are very good. I believe that I wrote to you that I had sold an acre for $50. 400,000,000 feet of fir planks were taken out of Michigan last year, (120,000,000 of it in the Saginaw valley). Average price was $12 per 1,000 feet. It is very cold at present, and we are expecting frost every night. Apple blossoms are ready to open and all trees are filled. All of the peaches froze in northern Michigan last year, and I will not plant any more trees.

Your loving son *William.*

1856
Sophie Seyffardt to the Parents in Crefeld.

Titibawassee, May 15.

We were very glad about the good news. How robust the dear grandfather must be that he can do things at the age of 81. It is getting pretty here now. Everything is getting green, so that

3. Midland, Michigan, on the Titibawassee River about 15 miles northwest of Saginaw.

one feels good after the long winter. I have sown the flower seed, dear father, and am looking forward to the flowers like a child. We even started an asparagus bed 3 years ago, and it has finger-thick asparagus already this year. So we are introducing the German vegetables little by little, while the American lives on cake, meat and potatoes all year. There will be variety in Crefeld, with weddings and baptisms. We will gladly celebrate with them if we know the exact days. Dear Mathilde undoubtedly has her hands full getting the wardrobe nicely in order. Your sincerely loving daughter

Sophie.

1859
William Seyffardt to the Parents in Dietlingen.

Titibawassee, September 18.

For the first time in 8 years there is quite a bit of fever, especially along the rivers. The ground pants for rain, and the plowed land is dusty as ashes. Business is slow, flour is 2½ cts. a pound, and boards can hardly be sold. Sophie is not very lucky with her poultry, for a neighboring dog devoured eggs and young poultry by the dozen. You will be interested to know that we started a Titibawassee quartette. We meet every Saturday and Wednesday from 8 until 11 or 12. At present we are very eager for the trip of the big steamer, The Great Eastern.[4] I would like to see it. We will soon have to get ready for winter. When there is sledding, the winter is very charming. The Seyffardt family has a good sled and Willi drives and crows mightily. It is a good thing my horses are steady. Now farewell and greet Foersters heartily. Your

W. Seyffardt.

1860
William Seyffardt to his Parents, Brothers and Sisters.

Titibawassee, December 24.

After very good business in my mill this winter and the prospect, that by spring I would be out of the hole, we were

4. Seyffardt is probably referring to the maiden voyage of the trans-Atlantic steamer, *The Great Eastern*. Built in 1858 in England, she was 680 feet long and had a gross weight of 18,915 tons. Until early in the 20th century, she was the largest vessel afloat.

frightened out of our sleep by the blood-red glow from our burning mill at 4:30 on the morning of the 20th. In the space of 15 minutes there was no hope of saving anything, for the flames drove us from doors and windows. In half an hour everything was but a heap of rubble. We had to work hard to save our home. Over 10,000 square feet of boards were dragged out of the fire and 10 barrels of flour for me and 40–50 sacks of flour for the customers. Besides the mill, we lost 600 bushels of grain and about 40–50,000 square feet of boards, everything we owned besides the farm. You can imagine that Sophie was very upset; she worked and sacrificed, to keep things together and to save, and now—but what good does it do! Now we must keep our heads.—In this, our time of great need, our friends have proved themselves. As our well being is of concern to you, I will tell you how I stand. First, I am announcing that we will start rebuilding today.

Mortgage on the place	$ 700.00
Obligations to creditors	$1200.00
Credit for the new building	$1100.00
	$3000.00

A very large debt!

The loss has not touched me as much as the sincere sympathy manifest on all sides. The loss of the mill is considered a public misfortune, but the people within a radius of several miles want to rebuild for me, I have only to furnish the boards and shingles. This is a great help and in 6 weeks we can start working again. The machine was damaged very little, the boiler not at all. The sawmill, which has not brought in anything for me will go by the way, one less danger of fire. The fire started because of the extreme carelessness of the fireman. When I think of our mill and work, I could almost despair. After having been helped so strongly by dear father 2 times, it was with a certain feeling of self-assurance that I wrote in my last letter that I would be rid of my greatest worry by next spring. But, head up! The battle shall be waged again for wife and 5 children. Sincere greetings and kisses

Your faithful son and brother
William Seyffardt.

1862
William Seyffardt to his Father.

Post Office Jay, Saginaw, May 16.

To my grief I saw from your letter of April 12, that you take me for a thoughtless person who cannot be advised or helped. If I would not have so much elasticity I would have given in long ago to all the vexations. But what hits me hardest is that you misjudge me. My obligations to you are burdensome to me; therefore I have exchanged 90 acres here for 120 in Saginaw. Believe me, we have deprived ourselves until we were able to make things a bit comfortable for ourselves. It is understandable that we have bad times as a result of the War, but the land is good and wood is always needed. As far as building in Saginaw is concerned, there is time and you need not worry. I did not write sooner because I had a bad fever, and our Willi cut off the first joints of his index finger and middle finger of the left hand. It hurt me more than it did him. It happened at a chopping bench while I was ill and the laborers were away. The boy had hardly any pain.

To your concern about my change of occupation and my not being a merchant, I must say that while I had mills I was primarily a merchant. It is enough that as a result of the destruction of that which I had worked so hard to get, my pride received the hardest blow. Not having the mills insured was a mistake which I made years ago, and I did not have the funds to remedy it. I am determined now to accept any work which I can do from my property at Saginaw. I have no intention of making a complete change. You cannot understand why Schmitz offered me the partnership?[5] The offer according to prospects here is very good. Schmitz is one of my best friends and needs someone in the business on whom he can depend when he travels. Now farewell and be assured that my circumstances, even though not in order at present, are on the way to becoming satisfactory, and that I will start nothing which could endanger them. Be sincerely greeted by your

grateful son Wm. Seyffardt.

5 Seyffardt did not accept the offer of a business partnership, and sixteen months later was expressing regret over this decision.

1862
William Seyffardt to his Father.

Post Office Jay, Saginaw, October 28.

I would have written sooner but was kept from it by the uncertainty, which still exists, as to whether I will be inducted into the army. But it is high time to congratulate you on your birthday, the 18th of November, and to wish you many more and cheerful days in the bosom of your family. After the war has dragged on for 20 months with superhuman sacrifices, the Democrats have tried, step by step, to replace the wonderful successes of the Administration so that the sovereign people of the North will become shoe shiners for the South. It seems as though the majority only counts when the Democrats have it. Saginaw is going ahead rapidly, and prospects are exceeding the keenest expectations. Wood, which sold for $1.50 last year, sells for $2.00, and fabulous gains are made in the salt works. A barrel of salt costs the manufacturer 60 cts., but it costs $3.00 wholesale for cooking salt and $4.00 for coarse salt (produced by evaporation). Woodland has gone up in value 25% in the last two weeks. Farm produce does not keep up with the enormous increase in wholesale groceries and dry goods. At present I am a butcher, but my butchering is confined to three large oxen. I sell a quarter @ 3½ cts. a pound. We had a letter from August Frank last week telling us that he is doing a brilliant business. He suggests that we drop farming after the war. I do not know if he knows our Saginaw situation well. I will correspond with him regarding it, because he is good at figures. Sophie is so busy with her big household that she has asked me to send her sincere congratulations and best wishes to dear mother. I am having hopes again of being able to embrace you some time.

Your faithful son
Wm. Seyffardt.

1863
Sophie Seyffardt to Pastor Frank.

Saginaw, November 9.

It is a long time since I have written to you and I reproach myself, but time flies with all of the work I have. We left the farm in May and moved to Saginaw, but were hardly here for several weeks when Louis and Soepherle became ill with scarlet fever. After that our little Ernst, who after a hard struggle, succumbed to the illness. Oh, it was a hard blow to lose the dear child and I often have such a great longing for our little darling, but he is better off with God than with us. Nane and I were in Bay City several times this summer. Ernst's business is pretty good, and he has paid back quite a bit already. Unfortunately he was drafted but he hopes to become free. If it is not the case, August wrote that he would give him the money to buy himself free. Babo also is in Bay City and he is a pleasant man. He will start a billiard parlor and is rooming with Ernst. We are sending pictures of ourselves with music teacher Zeller, who will be going to Stuttgart. The children look good, and also William is pretty good, but not I. Our Little Soepherle would not sit still, and that is why there is no picture of her. Now I will close, make us glad again soon with a letter. Be sincerely kissed by your faithful daughter

Sophie.

Questions about the Passage

1. Why do you think the Seyffardts write about their financial dealings in detail to their parents?
2. Locate the places in the letters where larger American political events and social concerns are mentioned. Is William or Sophie more interested in these? What other gender differences in their attitudes and activities can you discern?
3. How "American" do you think the Seyffardts become during the course of the letters? Support your answer with evidence from the letters.

Questions about the Argument

1. Although family letters are not usually thought of as arguments, what persuasive techniques can you see in these letters? How do William and Sophie take the needs of their specific audiences in mind? How do they use pathos? Are they concerned about their ethos?
2. What thesis might you propose about the life of German immigrants in eastern Michigan based on these letters? How would you use the letters to support your thesis? You might work on this question in class in small groups and present your ideas to the class.

"The Life Story of an Irish Cook"

About 1900, the managing editor of the magazine *The Independent*, Hamilton Holt (1872–1951), began publishing "lifelets," or brief autobiographical pieces by ordinary Americans, many of them immigrants. Some seventy-five "lifelets" were published, of which sixteen were later published in 1906 as *The Life Stories of Undistinguished Americans as Told by Themselves*. Some of these autobiographical pieces were written by the subjects themselves; others were written up from interviews. In the case of the Irish cook's story, an employer wrote it down. Internal evidence suggests that Ann McNabb arrived in Philadelphia in the early 1850s. The great Potato Famine that killed one sister and sent another to America lasted from 1845 to 1851. About 1.5 million people emigrated from Ireland, many coming to the United States, but a third or more died en route or shortly after arrival. The cook's reason for immigrating was thus both sad and common, but her voice speaks uniquely across the years to us.

> *The cook whose story follows, lived for many years in the home of one of America's best known literary women, who has taken down her conversation in this form.*
>
> I don't know why anybody wants to hear my history. Nothing ever happened to me worth the tellin' except when my mother died. Now she was an extraordinary person. The neighbors all respected her, an' the minister. "Go ask Mrs. McNabb," he'd say to the women in the neighborhood here when they come wantin' advice.
>
> But about me—I was born nigh to Limavaddy; it's a pretty town close to Londonderry. We lived in a peat cabin, but it had a good thatched roof. Mother put on that roof. It isn't a woman's work, but she—was able for it.
>
> There were sivin childher of us. John an' Matthew they went to Australia. Mother was layin' by for five year to get their passage money. They went into the bush. We heard twice from thim and then no more. Not another word and that is forty year gone now—on account of them not reading and writing. Learning isn't cheap in them old countries as it is here, you see. I suppose they're dead now—John would be ninety now—and in heaven. They were honest men. My mother sent Joseph to Londonderry to larn the weaver's trade. My father he never was a steddy worker. He took to the drink early in life. My mother an' me an' Tilly we worked in the field for Squire Varney. Yes,

plowin' an' seedin' and diggin'—any farm work he'd give us. We did men's work, but we didn't get men's pay. No, of course not. In winter we did lace work for a merchant in Londonderry. (Ann still can embroider beautifully.) It was pleasanter nor diggin' after my hands was fit for it. But it took two weeks every year to clean and soften my hands for the needle.

Pay was very small and the twins—that was Maria and Philip—they were too young to work at all. What did we eat? Well, just potatoes. On Sundays, once a month, we'd maybe have a bit of flitch [side of bacon]. When the potatoes rotted—that was the hard times! Oh, yes, I mind the famine years. An' the cornmeal that the 'Mericans sent. The folks said they'd rather starve nor eat it. We didn't know how to cook it. Here I eat corn dodgers and fried mush fast enough.

Maria—she was one of the twins—she died the famine year 5
of the typhus and—well, she sickened of the herbs and roots we eat—we had no potatoes.

Mother said when Maria died, "There's a curse on ould green Ireland and we'll get out of it." So we worked an' saved for four year an' then Squire Varney helped a bit an' we sent Tilly to America. She had always more head than me. She came to Philadelphia and got a place for general housework at Mrs. Bent's. Tilly got but two dollars a week, bein' a greenhorn. But she larned hand over hand, and Mrs. Bent kept no other help and laid out to teach her. She larned her to cook and bake and to wash and do up shirts—all American fashion. Then Tilly axed three dollars a week. Mother always said, "Don't ax a penny more than you're worth. But know your own vally and ax that."

She had no expenses and laid by money enough to bring me out before the year was gone. I sailed from Londonderry. The ship was a sailin' vessel, the "Mary Jane." The passage was $12. You brought your own eating, your tea an' meal, an' most had flitch. There was two big stoves that we cooked on. The steerage was a dirty place and we were eight weeks on the voyage—over time three weeks. The food ran scarce, I tell you, but the captain gave some to us, and them that had plenty was kind to the others. I've heard bad stories of things that went on in the steerage in them old times—smallpox and fevers and starvation and worse. But I saw nothing of them in my ship. The folks were decent and the captain was kind.

When I got here Mrs. Bent let Tilly keep me for two months to teach me—me bein' such a greenhorn. Of course I worked for her. Mr. Bent was foreman then in Spangler's big mills. After two months I got a place. They were nice appearing people enough, but the second day I found out they were Jews. I never had seen a Jew before, so I packed my bag and said to the lady, "I beg your pardon, ma'am, but I can't eat the bread of them as crucified the Saviour." "But," she said, "he was a Jew." So at that I put out. I couldn't hear such talk. Then I got a place for general housework with Mrs. Carr. I got $2 till I learned to cook good, and then $3 and then $4. I was in that house as cook and nurse for twenty-two years. Tilly lived with the Bents till she died, eighteen years. Mr. Bent come to be partner in the mills and got rich, and they moved into a big house in Germantown and kept a lot of help and Tilly was housekeeper. How did we keep our places so long? Well, I think me and Tilly was clean in our work and we was decent, and, of course, we was honest. Nobody living can say that one of the McNabbs ever wronged him of a cent. Mrs. Carr's interests was my interests. I took better care of her things than she did herself, and I loved the childher as if they was my own. She used to tell me my sin was I was stingy. I don't know. The McNabbs are no wasteful folk. I've worn one dress nine year and it looked decent then. Me and Tilly saved till we brought Joseph and Phil over, and they went into Mr. Bent's mills as weaver and spool boy and then they saved, and we all brought out my mother and father. We rented a little house in Kensington [an Irish neighborhood in Philadelphia] for them. There was a parlor in it and kitchen and two bedrooms and bathroom and marble door step, and a bell. That was in '66, and we paid nine dollars a month rent. You'd pay double that now. It took all our savings to furnish it, but Mrs. Bent and Mrs. Carr gave us lots of things to go in. To think of mother having a parlor and marble steps and a bell! They came on the old steamer "Indiana" and got here at night, and we had supper for them and the house all lighted up. Well, you ought to have seen mother's old face! I'll never forget that night if I live to be a hundred. After that mother took in boarders and Joseph and Phil was there. We all put every cent we earned into building associations. So Tilly owned a house when she died and I own this one now. Our ladies told us how to put the money so as to breed more, and we never spent a cent we could save. Joseph pushed on and got big wages and started a flour store, and Phil went to night-school and got a place as clerk. He married a teacher in the Kensington public school. She was a showy miss! Silk dress and feathers in her hat!

Father died soon after he come. The drink here wasn't as wholesome for him as it was in Ireland. Poor father! He was a goodhearted man, but he wasn't worth a penny when he died.

Mother lived to be eighty. She was respected by all Kensington. The night she died she said: "I have much to praise God for. I haven't a child that is dependent on the day's work for the day's victuals. Every one of them owns a roof to cover him."

Joseph did well in his flour store. He has a big one on Market Street now and lives in a pretty house out in West Philadelphia. He's one of the wardens in his church out there and his girls gives teas and goes to reading clubs.

But Phil is the one to go ahead! His daughter Ann—she was named for me, but she calls herself Antoinette—is engaged to a young lawyer in New York. He gave her a diamond engagement ring the other day. And his son, young Phil, is in politics and a member of councils. He makes money hand over hand. He has an automobile and a fur coat, and you see his name at big dinners and him making speeches. No saving of pennies or building associations for Phil.

It was Phil that coaxed me to give up work at Mrs. Carr's and to open my house for boarders here in Kensington. His wife didn't like to hear it said I was working in somebody's kitchen. I've done well with the boarders. I know just how to feed them so as to lay by a little sum every year. I heard that young Phil told some of his friends that he had a queer old aunt up in Kensington who played poor, but had a great store of money hoarded away. He shouldn't have told a story like that. But young folks will be young! I like the boy. He is certainly bringing the family into notice in the world. Last Sunday's paper had his picture and one of the young lady he is going to marry in New York. It called him the young millionaire McNabb. But I judge he's not that. He wanted to borrow the money I have laid by in the old bank at Walnut and Seventh the other day and said he'd double it in a week. No such work as that for me! But the boy certainly is a credit to the family!

Questions about the Passage

1. What is a "greenhorn" (paragraph 6)? Look up the word in a good dictionary.
2. What does the cook's obtaining and then leaving a place in a Jewish house tell you about mid-century Philadelphia and about the cook herself? Can you infer anything about the Jewish family as well?
3. Compare the success in the United States of the McNabb sisters to the brothers. How would you explain the differences? What does the cook think of her brother Phil's wife? Daughter? Son? What do her responses to them tell you about social mobility for Irish immigrants at this time?

Questions about the Argument

1. Like the Seyffardt letters, McNabb's life story was not created as an argument. We can ask, however, what were the rhetorical purposes of the woman who recorded it and Holt who published it?
2. How would you characterize the cook's ethos? How reliable a narrator of her own life do you find her? Defend your answer.

Marie Hall Ets, "An Italian Immigrant in a Missouri Mining Camp"

Rosa Cassettari (1866 or 1867–1943) was an Italian immigrant and a fine storyteller. She told the story of her life to Marie Hall Ets (1893–1984), a social worker, artist, and children's book author. Ets worked as a social worker at the Chicago Commons, a social settlement house where Rosa received aid over the years and where she worked as a cleaning woman. Although Rosa told her life stories to Marie Ets in the 1920s and 1930s, Ets did not publish Rosa's life story until 1970. Rosa emigrated from northern Italy in 1884 to join her abusive husband, Santino, who worked in the iron mines of southwest Missouri. After some years, she escaped with her children to Chicago and married another Italian immigrant, Gionin. The following passage describes her arrival in the mining camp at Union, Missouri, where she was to cook and clean for the miners.

I had never seen houses like these before—nothing but boards. The one where we stopped was larger than the others and had two doors to go in. Me and Santino were going to live in the side we were going in, and Domiana and Masino in the other. There was one large room with a long table and benches and a big cook stove and some shelves with pans and things. Then behind was a little room with an iron-frame bed and straw mattress. Gionin and some of the other men carried in my two chests. Then they came back and put food on the table.

Bread! White bread! Enough for a whole village! And butter to go on it! I ate until I no longer had any pains in my stomach. Then I went back by the stove to watch Gionin. He had built a fire and was making coffee. Never in my life had I made coffee and I would have to learn if I was going to cook for these men in America.

"But it's easy, Rosa," Gionin said, and his eyes smiled into mine. "Just make the water boil and grind the coffee and put it in like this. And always we have plenty of sugar and cream to go in. The German women on the farms taught me that."

When the coffee was on the table Gionin sat down with the others and started telling Francesca [his cousin] the plans he had made for her. Until she and Orlando were married on Sunday she was going to stay with an old Sicilian woman, Angelina, who was like a mother to all the young girls in camp. But after Sunday she and Orlando would live in a shack by themselves and she would do the cooking for another bunch of men. She was going to be married in a little village four miles down the tracks. But before then, on Saturday night, she must go to confession. Enrico, the boss of the iron mine, would go with her and interpret.

"*Santa Maria*! I have to tell my sins to a man not a priest? Bet- 5
ter I don't get married!" Francesca was so comical she made everyone die laughing.

Gionin was laughing too and teasing Orlando about choosing a wife with sins so black that only a priest could hear them. But then he explained. He told how Enrico went in the priest's house with the girls and stood one side of the priest and the girl the other. Then the girl put her hand in the priest's hand and the priest asked the questions in English and Enrico said them in Italian. If the girl *did* make the sin—she did not go to mass on Sunday, or she stole something worth more than a penny—she must squeeze the priest's hand. Enrico couldn't see if she did or didn't. And in the end the priest gave her the penance and that was all.

"God is a dog," muttered Santino. "I'd burn in hell before I'd squeeze the hand of one of those black crows!"

"Listen to Santino!" laughed Pep. "Every Saturday night he's pinching the backside of his fat Annie or of some of those other bad women over Freddy's saloon. But he wouldn't squeeze the hand of a man—even to keep out of hell."

"Man, bah! I spit on all those black crows that wear dresses!"

As soon as I could I went into the bedroom and opened up 10
my chests. I had never expected to see them again. And there inside I found the featherbed and sheets Mamma Lena and Zia Teresa had put in. And I found the little Madonna and the crucifix Don Domenic had blessed. I kissed the bleeding feet of Jesus and said a little prayer. With that crucifix over my bed I would not feel so alone—so afraid. God would help me to be meek. I went into the other room to find a nail and Gionin came back and nailed the crucifix up for me. "Tomorrow, Rosa," he said, "I'll make you a shelf for the little Madonna."

Summer was not yet over but it grew dark early. That little boy, Giorgio, had fallen asleep with his head on the table. So now Domiana went off to her side of the house to open her chests and make her bed. Then some of the men left too. Gionin and Orlando went off to take Francesca to Angelina's. So me, I lighted the lamp in the bedroom and made the bed. Then I sat down on one of my chests and took out my rosary. "*Ave Maria, Mater Dei, ora pro nobis. . . .*"

When everyone else had gone Santino blew out the lamp in the big room and came looking for me. Just inside the door he stopped. It was the crucifix over the bed that stopped him. He started cursing: "God is a dog! God is a pig! Can't a man sleep with his own wife without God watching him from the wall? Take it down, I tell you! Take it down!"

A wife doesn't have to obey her husband when he wants her to do something against God or the Madonna. I held my rosary tighter, waiting for him to come after me and watching for him to tear the crucifix down himself. But he didn't do either. He stood for a while just staring at it. Then without moving his eyes he backed away to the lamp and blew out the light. He was afraid—I could tell by the way he acted—afraid to have Jesus on the cross looking down at him. (But I have to leave that man out of this story. The things he did to me are too bad to tell! I leave him out, that's all!)

The next morning I was up early making a fire in the stove and bringing water from the spring. When Gionin came to show me how to make breakfast he was surprised. He said he was the one chosen to collect the money and buy the food for the men who were going to eat in my house. He said the men wanted me to do the cooking and make their beds and clean their shacks and once every week wash their clothes.

"But I don't know how to cook," I told him.

"Don't worry, Rosa. Angelina will teach you everything—even how to make the spaghetti and ravioli like the people in South Italy. But this morning, Rosa, you take the big sack from the woodshed and go back up that path between the hills to the first farmhouse. That farmer's wife knows you are coming and she will give you some chickens."

"But how can I talk when I don't know English?"

"No use to know English for Mrs. Quigley. The farmers around here speak only German. You just make her understand, that's all. When she starts to give you the rooster, you don't take it."

For breakfast there was white bread again and butter and coffee with cream and sugar and sausages and eggs besides! *Mamma mia*! Did all the poor people in America eat like kings?

When the men had eaten I watched them go off to the sheds for their picks and drills. Most stayed in the open mine, but Santino and a few others went half up the hill and into the tunnel. For a while I couldn't see Gionin, but then I saw him down by the tracks marking empty cars and writing in a notebook. Gionin was more educated than my *paesani* [fellow Italians, countrymen and women]. I was lucky to have him in my house. I liked the way his white teeth were shining under his black mustache when he smiled, and the way his eyes grew kind when he looked into mine. It's funny how you can tell by a man's eyes when he likes you.

For my own breakfast I ate all that I wanted. Then I cleared the table and was washing the dishes when there came a crash that made my ears deaf and shook the whole house. Holy Mary, Mother of God! When I looked out all I could see was a cloud of dust and dirt. Then here came running Domiana with Giorgio. We thought all the men—all the miners—were dead. But when the dust and dirt cleared away we could see the men standing back and watching. It was something they did on purpose. Something that would come again.

Because Angelina was too old to walk four miles down the tracks, I went with Francesca and Enrico on Saturday night and waited outside the priest's house while Francesca made her confession. It was dark when we started home and Enrico walked ahead with his lantern. We had reached the marshy place—almost back at the camp—when suddenly I saw a little flame at one side of the tracks. I stopped and looked. That little flame wasn't burning anything—it was just dancing over the ground.

"Hail Mary Mother of God pray for us now and in the hour of our death!" I said. "Enrico! Enrico! Look! The *fiammetta*!"

Francesca grabbed hold of me and started shaking.

"Sure, it's the *fiammetta*," said Enrico, "but what of it? The *fiammetta* doesn't hurt anything. It's only some gas that comes out of the ground when it's warm and damp. Those people who think it's the evil spirit are foolish—stupid. Come, I'll show you." And there he took his lantern and went after the little flame and put his hand where it was and touched all the places where it had been. And sure enough it didn't hurt him at all. So then me and Francesca tried, and nothing happened to us either.

"I'm going to get those other *Lombardi* and show them too," said Enrico. "If I don't, they will be afraid to pass this place on their way to the lower quarry."

Enrico's real name was Henry but because he could talk in Italian the men all called him Enrico. He was high-educated and was the boss of the mine, but he talked to us poor like we were equal and taught us the things we must know. That was how it was in America. What a pity that all the people of

Bugiarno [her home town, actually Cuggiano] couldn't come to America and learn not to be afraid. They almost died when they saw the *fiammetta* in their fields. In the daytime the priest would come with his holy water and bless all the ground where it had been, but then he would run away. He was afraid too. And the ground where it had been—no one wanted to work there anymore.

"How do you say it in English?" I asked Enrico.

"Will-o'-the-wisp," he said. "But here in America the people know what it is and are not afraid."

As the weeks went by I grew friendly with other Americans 30
too—with old Mr. Miller and his daughter, Miss Mabel, in the store at Union. They were the boss of the store and of the post office, but they were treating me like I was as good as them. "Here's Rosa!" they would say when they saw me come in. "Hello, Rosa! Come in!" And when they saw how much I wanted to speak English they were helping me. And as it grew cold with the winter they made me come in to dry my feet and get warm. And they gave me coffee.

But those saloons in Union were bad. I didn't even want to walk past. Freddy's saloon was the worst. Some of those bad women who lived upstairs were always standing in the window looking out over the half curtain. And Annie, the friend of Santino, always thumbed her nose at me and made faces. She didn't know that I was more happy when he stayed with her than when he came home. Probably she didn't like it that Santino left most of his pay in the pocket of my underskirt so she and his other friends in Freddy's saloon couldn't get it when he was drunk.

Santino had started getting whiskey from some American men who brought it to the camp. More and more he would come home drunk and start beating me. Probably he would like it better if I was not so meek—if I fought with him. But I didn't want to offend God and the Madonna. Gionin couldn't stand it. He would put his head in his hands. Or he would get up and go out. Gionin really loved me—that I knew. And that made me feel not so lonesome. But Gionin couldn't do anything—Santino was my husband.

Questions about the Passage

1. What differences between Italy and America does Rosa point out? What does Rosa like about living in America?
2. How much interaction does Rosa have with non-Italians? How does she see them?

Questions about the Argument

1. What inferences can you draw from this episode about Italian immigration to the United States?
2. Do you think Ets succeeds in conveying a voice and persona for Rosa? If so, how does she achieve this goal?

Hilda Satt Polacheck, "Chicago Sweatshop"

Hilda Satt Polacheck (1882–1967) was born in Poland. When she was nine years old, she emigrated with her mother and siblings to join her father in Chicago, where he had gone about a year earlier. The family was financially comfortable in Poland and even in Chicago because her father was a skilled artisan, a Jewish tombstone carver. When he died less than two years after their arrival in Chicago, the family was penniless. Hilda's mother and her older sister worked to support the family of five children, but the Satts were so poor that Hilda lied about her age and went to work in a knitting factory. In her memoir, she claims she was 14, the legal age to work in 1896, but she was most likely only 13 and had only completed the fourth grade. The passage below begins with her decision to leave school and start working.

Hilda's life was changed profoundly by going to the world-famous settlement house, Hull-House, run by Jane Addams. The house was located a few blocks from Hilda's tenement flat on the near west side of Chicago. At Hull-House, Hilda found cultural and intellectual stimulation to counter the stultifying life of a factory worker. Addams arranged for Hilda to attend the University of Chicago for one term, and her learning there nourished her for the rest of her life.

In the 1950s, Hilda wrote her autobiography but could find no publisher interested in her experiences. Her daughter, Dena J. Polacheck Epstein, a music librarian, edited the manuscript, and a university press published the memoir over twenty years after Hilda's death. Her narrative gives a vivid picture of impoverished immigrant living and working conditions in the late nineteenth and early twentieth centuries, and of her views of trade unions, women's roles, and becoming an American in a diverse city. Her portrait of Hull-House and Jane Addams, whom she adored, are unique—the only account by an immigrant of this institution created to serve immigrants.

> I went to school and told Mrs. Torrance that I was not coming back to school. I shall never forget that leave-taking. I looked at the beloved—yes, beloved—blackboard where I had learned to write my first English words. The bright pictures on the wall, the cutouts pasted on the windows, the desk, all seemed dear to me that day. My desk, at which I had spent the first happy years in America. I had finished the fifth grade at the time. I was fourteen years old.[1] It looked as if this would be the end of my schooling.
>
> Mother shed many tears when I told her that I was going to work. But she realized that there was nothing else to do and she agreed to the plan. It was God's will, she said, and we had to accept it.
>
> The first day that I left the house with my small bundle of lunch under my arm was a day of inner struggle for a little girl. I had mixed emotions in my heart. I was glad that I could help feed the family, but I could not forget that I would not go to school again. I did not realize at the time that it was possible to study away from school and that there were classes at Hull-House.
>
> Of that eventful day, when I went to work for the first time, many memories keep coming to me. It was still dark when we left the house. We walked down what was then Twelfth Street, now known as Roosevelt Road, over many viaducts and a bridge that spanned the Chicago River and the railroad tracks. It was beginning to get light as we approached the river and I could not help comparing the dirty, slimy water with the clear sparkling water of my dear Vistula [a river in her native Poland].
>
> We arrived at State Street and walked down a flight of stairs 5
> to the street below. The factory looked very large and imposing to me. It was a six-story brick building. We got into the elevator, my first elevator ride, and were taken to the fourth floor, I believe. There my name was taken and I presented my

1. She was most likely only 13 and had only finished fourth grade.

working permit. I had become an adult and a worker at the age of fourteen.

I was assigned to a knitting machine and a girl was stationed at my side to teach me the complicated rudiments of knitting. There were about four hundred machines in the room, which covered an entire floor of the building. In front of each machine sat a girl or woman on a high stool. I had no difficulty learning the trade and I was soon able to earn four dollars a week. The work was piecework, and the harder one worked, the more one made. But the pay was so regulated that even the fastest worker could not make over five dollars a week. At that time, however, five dollars would buy food for a family of six. So between my sister's and my pay the family could exist.

We worked from seven thirty in the morning till six in the evening, six days a week. We had a half hour for lunch, which we ate sitting in front of the machine. There were no towels provided for drying hands before eating. Paper towels had not yet been invented. So we brought towels from home.

I had been working there about two weeks when, during the morning, I heard the most agonizing shriek I had ever heard. Soon the power stopped and it became so quiet that our hearts almost stopped beating. Quiet except for the piercing shriek that kept coming from across the room. My sister came up to me and put her arms around me and told me not to be afraid. A girl had caught her hand in the machine. The machine had to be taken apart before the poor girl could be freed. At that time there was no law stipulating that machines had to be equipped with safety devices.

Several months after I started working in the knitting factory, the doors of the toilets were removed so that there was no privacy while performing natural functions. The reason given for this utter lack of consideration was that girls were spending too much time in the toilet. This could not be true, as the girls were eager to make as much money as possible and no one could earn money sitting in the toilet.

Very often a machine would break down, and we had to wait 10
till the repairman came to fix it. Sometimes that would take an hour or more and that time was lost by the worker. That meant less money in the weekly pay envelope. Each machine had about eighty needles, and while running at full speed a needle would jump out of place and break. This was no fault of the

worker, but in addition to losing time to change the needle, we had to pay a penny for it.

During the weeks of getting adjusted to work in the factory I did not go to Hull-House. I was usually so tired in the evening that I was glad to just eat supper, help with the dishes, and go to bed. So for several months I had no idea what Hull-House offered in the way of classes and recreation.

One evening, as my sister and I were leaving the factory, we saw a man at the entrance with his arms full of leaflets. As each girl came out of the building she was handed a leaflet. We read it in front of a lamppost. We were being asked to come to a meeting to help organize a union.[2] My sister and I talked about it all the way home. She was reluctant about going. She was always more cautious than I was. I, however, decided to go to the meeting.

This was my introduction to trade unionism. About one hundred girls and a few men were gathered in a small smoky room. A man called the meeting to order and told us of the advantages of an organized union. He urged us to organize a union. When he had finished his formal talk, he asked if anyone had anything to say. There was a dead silence. And then, impulsively, I rose and said that I had a lot to say. The words came tumbling out of my mouth as if they had been stored within me. I asked the girls why we had to pay for broken needles that were broken accidentally. Why was there only one mechanic to keep all those machines in repair? Why did we not object to having the doors removed from the toilets? Were we not entitled to some privacy and a little decency? That was all the meeting needed; a reminder of real grievances. The union was organized that night.

The next morning when I came to work I was called into the forelady's office and given whatever pay I had coming and was told that I was a troublemaker and that I was to get out and never come back.

The bookkeeper had been sent to the meeting and she had 15
reported the part I had played in helping to organize the union. And so ended my four-year career as a knitter.

While walking to work that morning, I thought it would be fine to work in the union. It would take some of the monotony

2. Probably the Glove Workers Union.

out of the work, for one thing, and it would be good for everybody to have something to say about working conditions. But now my career as a knitter was over and I wondered if there were other unions.

I left the factory, strangely enough, not depressed. I was not sorry for what I had said at the meeting, but I was not impressed with the importance of the trade union movement. I had no idea of the stirring events that were to follow in the days to come. The fact that the first years of my life had been spent in a home where there was no want and where I had never heard of trade unionism or labor troubles of any kind may have had something to do with it.

As I had the whole day before me, I decided to walk downtown. I had heard about the elegant part of State Street, which I had never seen. So far, the only part of State Street that I knew was the sordid, filthy block I had covered each morning and evening. Every house on that block was a house of prostitution. Even early in the morning, as I walked by on my way to work, I saw women and often young girls sitting in the windows or standing in the doorways, beckoning to men who passed by. It was a strange contrast between the two sections of State Street, only one mile apart. One where there was nothing but degradation, and the other where magnificent stores offered all the decencies and even the luxuries of life.

During that one-mile walk all sorts of thoughts kept running through my head. I thought of that speech that the forelady had made to me, telling me that I was ungrateful. What was I supposed to be grateful for? For the privilege of working ten hours a day, six days a week, for four dollars and fifty cents?

Being called a foreign troublemaker stuck in my throat and 20
almost choked me.

I thought of the conversations that Uncle Mischa had had with Father about the conditions of the tailors. You either worked long hours or not at all. And when you did not work, you did not eat.

All of a sudden I was in front of the Marshall Field store. I walked in. To my surprise no one paid any attention to me. No one asked me what I wanted. I wandered about and no one objected. I walked down the aisles, admiring the displays and wondering how many people had the money to buy all those things.

I found myself in front of an elevator and heard the words "Going up." So I went up. When I heard the operator call "Third floor, waiting room," I stepped out and walked to the famous Marshall Field waiting room.

I sank into a luxurious chair and just sat there watching the well-dressed people.

How many times have I thought of that day? Every time I 25
rested between shopping, or when I would meet friends there, that day came back to me. That wonderful room, where people from all over the world met and greeted friends. I have a very warm feeling for that room.

After resting for a while, I decided to find out if there was anything else worth seeing. The thought of looking for a job did not enter my head. For this one day I was a free soul, doing just what I wanted to do. I walked through the book department, looked at the wonderful displays of china and glassware, at silks and satins and velvet.

I left the store and walked down Michigan Avenue and sat on a bench in Grant Park, where I ate my lunch. I looked about me and saw an interesting building down the street. It was the only building on that side of the street. My curiosity was aroused and I walked over. It was the Chicago Art Institute, and it happened to be a free day. I walked in and stood looking at the broad staircase. I wandered from room to room. The pictures looked down from the walls. The statues seemed to greet me. All the sordidness of the world was blotted out. There was only beauty in the world.

As I look back on that day, I wonder how I managed to crowd all the events into one day. I went to the public library next. I was very much impressed with all the marble and inlaid designs. I went up to the fourth floor and found myself in the reference room; there before my eyes was Lake Michigan. It had been about eight years since I had come to Chicago, and this was my first glimpse of the lake. I stood there for a long time, thinking of my father's words. Yes, Lake Michigan was big! I would have to see much more of it. I was almost glad I had been fired from my job.

When I got home that evening and told Mother that I had lost my job, she was understandably disturbed. She was afraid of hunger and cold, not so much for herself as for the rest of us.

Food, coal, clothing, and shelter had become her only interests in life.

Being young, I began to rebel against a life that offered only food and warmth and shelter. There were all those books in the public library, and I wanted to read some of them. There were pictures on the walls of the Art Institute and I wanted to look at them. And I wanted to look at Lake Michigan.

After our meager supper had been eaten, I realized that no matter how meager the meal had been, it still had to be bought and paid for.

I assured Mother that I would find another job soon. I would start to look for one first thing in the morning. I was confident that I would find some work.

Questions about the Passage

1. Why does Hilda go to the union organization meeting? Do you sympathize with her decision? Why was she surprised that she was fired?
2. What reasons does Hilda give, and what other ones might you suggest, for her lack of worry about finding another job?

Questions about the Argument

1. Hilda draws several contrasts in this chapter—between her life at school and her life at work, between her attitude towards the world and her mother's attitude towards it, and between her portion of State Street and the downtown part where the great department store Marshall Field's was located. What purpose do these contrasts serve? What is Hilda's point?
2. Why does Hilda tell us about her visit to downtown Chicago after she was fired?
3. Consider Hilda's ethos. How does she project herself? Do you trust and like her? What strategies does she use to convey her ethos?
4. Who do you think was the audience Hilda had in mind when she wrote about her life? When her daughter sent her mother's work to a publisher, who had become the likely audience? (Hint: Consider the audience for a university press.)

Mary Antin, "Have We Any Right to Regulate Immigration?"

Mary Antin (1881–1949) was born to Jewish parents in the Russian Pale and immigrated to the United States in 1894. Like Hilda Satt Polacheck's father, Mary's father came ahead of the family, hoping to bring his wife and four children to the United States after a few years; unlike Hilda's father, however, Mary's father was not financially successful, and the family's passage was paid for by a Jewish benevolent society. The family lived in the immigrant slums of Boston, but Mary thrived in the public school and showed a special aptitude for writing. Only five years after arriving in the United States, she published her first book, *From Plotzk to Boston* (1899), her translated letters to her uncle in Russia. In 1911 and 1912, Antin published parts of her autobiography, *The Promised Land*, in the *Atlantic Monthly*. The book was a terrific success when it was published in 1912; it was reprinted thirty-three times and sold almost 84,000 copies before her death. Antin's argument for an open immigration policy, *They Who Knock at Our Gates: A Complete Gospel of Immigration*, was also first published serially, in the *American Magazine*, in 1914. Antin ordered her argument as the answers to three questions: "First: A question of principle: Have we any right to regulate immigration? Second: A question of fact: What is the nature of our present immigration? Third: A question of interpretation: Is immigration good for us?" We have reprinted here the heart of her answer to the first question.

> *And these words, which I command thee this day, shall be in thine heart: and thou shalt teach them diligently unto thy children. . . . And thou shalt write them upon the posts of thy house, and on thy gates.*
>
> DEUT. VI, 6, 7, 9.

If I ask an American what is the fundamental American law, and he does not answer me promptly, "That which is contained in the Declaration of Independence," I put him down for a poor citizen. He who is ignorant of the law is likely to disobey it. And there cannot be two minds about the position of the Declaration among our documents of state. What the Mosaic Law is to the Jews, the Declaration is to the American people. It affords us a starting-point in history and defines our mission among the nations. Without it, we should not differ greatly from other nations who have achieved a constitutional form of government and various democratic institutions. What marks us out from other advanced nations is the origin of our liberties in one supreme act of political innovation, prompted by a conscious sense of the dignity of manhood. In other countries advances have been made by favor of hereditary rulers and aristocratic parliaments, each successive reform being grudgingly handed down to the people from above. Not so in America. At one bold stroke we shattered the monarchical tradition, and installed the people in the seats of government, substituting the gospel of the sovereignty of the masses for the superstition of the divine right of kings.

And even more notable than the boldness of the act was the dignity with which it was entered upon. In terms befitting a philosophical discourse, we gave notice to the world that what we were about to do, we would do in the name of humanity, in the conviction that as justice is the end of government so should manhood be its source.

It is this insistence on the philosophic sanction of our revolt that gives the sublime touch to our political performance. Up to the moment of our declaration of independence, our struggle with our English rulers did not differ from other popular struggles against despotic governments. Again and again we respectfully petitioned for redress of specific grievances, as the governed, from time immemorial, have petitioned their governors. But one day we abandoned our suit for petty damages, and instituted a suit for the recovery of our entire human heritage of freedom; and by basing our claim on the fundamental principles of the brotherhood of man and the sovereignty of the masses, we assumed the championship of the oppressed against their oppressors, wherever found.

It was thus, by sinking our particular quarrel with George of England in the universal quarrel of humanity with injustice, that we emerged a distinct nation, with a unique mission in the world. And we revealed ourselves to the world in the Declaration of Independence, even as the Israelites revealed themselves in the Law of Moses. From the Declaration flows our race consciousness, our sense of what is and what is not American. Our laws, our policies, the successive steps of our progress—all must conform to the spirit of the Declaration of Independence, the source of our national being.

The American confession of faith, therefore, is a recital of the 5
doctrines of liberty and equality. A faithful American is one who understands these doctrines and applies them in his life.

It should be easy to pick out the true Americans—the spiritual heirs of the founders of our Republic—by this simple test of loyalty to the principles of the Declaration. To such a test we are put, both as a nation and as individuals, every time we are asked to define our attitude on immigration. Having set up a government on a declaration of the rights of man, it should be our first business to reaffirm that declaration every time we meet a case involving human rights. Now every immigrant who emerges from the steerage presents such a case. For the alien, whatever ethnic or geographic label he carries, in a primary classification of the creatures of the earth, falls in the human family. The fundamental fact of his humanity established, we need only rehearse the articles of our political faith to know what to do with the immigrant. It is written in our basic law that he is entitled to life, liberty, and the pursuit of happiness. There is nothing left for us to do but to open wide our gates and set him on his way to happiness.

That is what we did for a while, when our simple law was fresh in our minds, and the habit of applying it instinctive. Then there arose a fashion of spelling immigration with a capital initial, which so confused the national eye that we began to see a PROBLEM where formerly we had seen a familiar phenomenon of American life; and as a problem requires skillful handling, we called an army of experts in consultation, and the din of their elaborate discussions has filled our ears ever since.

The effect on the nation has been disastrous. In a matter involving our faith as Americans, we have ceased to consult our fundamental law, and have suffered ourselves to be guided by the conflicting reports of commissions and committees, anthropologists, economists, and statisticians, policy-mongers, calamity-howlers, and self-announced prophets. Matters irrelevant to the interests of liberty have taken the first place in the discussion; lobbyists, not patriots, have had the last word. Our American sensibility has become dulled, so that sometimes the cries of the oppressed have not reached our ears unless carried by formal deputations. In a department of government which brings us into daily touch with the nations of the world, we have failed to live up to our national gospel and have not been aware of our backsliding.

What have the experts and statisticians done so to pervert our minds? They have filled volumes with facts and figures, comparing the immigrants of to-day with the immigrants of other days, classifying them as to race, nationality, and culture, tabulating their occupations, analyzing their savings, probing their motives, prophesying their ultimate destiny. But what is there in all this that bears on the right of free men to choose their place of residence? Granted that Sicilians are not Scotchmen, how does that affect the right of a Sicilian to travel in pursuit of happiness? Strip the alien down to his anatomy, you still find a *man*, a creature made in the image of God; and concerning such a one we have definite instructions from the founders of the Republic. And what purpose was served by the bloody tide of the Civil War if it did not wash away the last lingering doubts as to the brotherhood of men of different races?

There is no impropriety in gathering together a mass of sci- 10
entific and sociological data concerning the newcomers, as long as we understand that the knowledge so gained is merely the technical answer to a number of technical questions. Where we have gone wrong is in applying the testimony of our experts to the moral side of the question. By all means register the cephalic index of the alien,—the anthropologist will make something of it at his leisure,—but do not let it determine his right to life, liberty, and the pursuit of happiness.

I do not ask that we remove all restrictions and let the flood of immigration sweep in unchecked. I do ask that such restrictions as we impose shall accord with the loftiest interpretation of our duty as Americans. Now our first duty is to live up to the gospel of liberty, through the political practices devised by our forefathers and modified by their successors, as democratic ideas developed. But political practices require a territory wherein to operate—democracy must have standing-room—so it becomes our next duty to guard our frontiers. For that purpose we maintain two forms of defense: the barbaric devices of army and navy, to ward off hostile mass invasions; and the humane devices of the immigration service, to regulate the influx of peaceable individuals.

We have plenty of examples to copy in our military defenses, but when it comes to the civil branch of our national guard, we dare not borrow foreign models. What our neighbors are doing in the matter of regulating immigration may or may not be right for us. Other nations may be guided chiefly by economic considerations, while we are under spiritual bonds to give first consideration to the moral principles involved. For this, our peculiar American problem, we must seek a characteristically American solution.

What terms of entry may we impose on the immigrant without infringing on his inalienable rights, as defined in our national charter? Just such as we would impose on our own citizens if they proposed to move about the country in companies numbering thousands, with their families and portable belongings. And what would these conditions be? They would be such as are required by public safety, public health, public order. Whatever limits to our personal liberty we are ourselves willing to endure for the sake of the public welfare, we have a right to impose on the stranger from abroad; these, and no others.

Has, then, the newest arrival the same rights as the established citizen? According to the Declaration, yes; the same right to live, to move, to try his luck. More than this he does not claim at the gate of entrance; with less than this we are not authorized to put him off. We do not question the right of an individual foreigner to enter our country on any peaceable errand; why, then, question the rights of a shipload of foreigners? Lumping a thousand men together under the title of immigrants does not deprive them of their humanity and the rights inherent in humanity; or can it be demonstrated that the sum of the rights of a million men is less than the rights of one individual?

15 The Declaration of Independence, like the Ten Commandments, must be taken literally and applied universally. What would have been the civilizing power of the Mosaic Code if the Children of Israel had repudiated it after a few generations? As little virtue is there in the Declaration of Independence if we limit its operation to any geographical sphere or historical period or material situation. How do we belittle the works of our Fathers when we talk as though they wrought for their contemporaries only! It was no great matter to shake off the rule of an absent tyrant, if that is all that the War of the Revolution did. So much had been done many times over, long before the first tree fell under the axe of a New England settler.

Emmaus[1] was fought before Yorktown,[2] and Thermopylæ[3] before Emmaus. It is only as we dwell on the words of Jefferson and Franklin that the deeds of Washington shine out among the deeds of heroes. In the chronicles of the Jews, Moses has a far higher place than the Maccabæan brothers. And notice that Moses owes his immortality to the unbroken succession of generations who were willing to rule their lives by the Law that fell from his lips. The glory of the Jews is not that they received the Law, but that they kept the Law. The glory of the American people must be that the vision vouchsafed to their fathers they in their turn hold up undimmed to the eyes of successive generations.

To maintain our own independence is only to hug that vision to our own bosoms. If we sincerely believe in the elevating power of liberty, we should hasten to extend the reign of liberty over all mankind. The disciples of Jesus did not sit down in Jerusalem and congratulate each other on having found the Saviour. They scattered over the world to spread the tidings far and wide. We Americans, disciples of the goddess Liberty, are saved the trouble of carrying our gospel to the nations, because the nations come to us.

Questions about the Passage

1. How does *The Declaration of Independence*, according to Antin (paragraphs 1–4), make the United States unique?
2. In paragraph 6, how does Antin connect *The Declaration* to immigration?
3. What are Antin's objections to the study and classification of immigrants (paragraphs 8–10)?
4. What limits does Antin impose on immigration (paragraph 13)?
5. What separates the American Revolution from other uprisings against oppression, according to Antin (paragraph 15)?

1. Village near Jerusalem, site of a successful battle fought by the Jewish Maccabees against their Greek occupiers in 164 BCE.
2. The British surrender at Yorktown, Virginia, in 1781 ended the major fighting of the American Revolution.
3. Site of a famous mountain pass battle of the Greeks against the Persian conqueror Xerxes in 480 BCE.

Questions about the Argument

1. Evaluate Antin's extended argument by analogy in this passage. To do so, list the similarities and differences between the compared peoples (ancient Jews, Americans) and their founding documents (Hebrew Bible, *The Declaration of Independence*). Then consider whether the argument is strong. Be prepared to defend your answer.
2. Look up and read all of Deuteronomy 6 from which Antin takes her epigraph. Why do you think Antin chose this passage? How does it contribute to the argument? Think about Antin's original audience and today's readers. How might they differ in their knowledge of the Bible? What might she have assumed that her original readership would conclude from seeing these verses quoted?
3. On your own or in small groups in class, try to turn Antin's argument into one or more syllogisms. Share these with the class for discussion.
4. When we read Antin after September 11, 2001, do we see things differently than she does? Do you think she would have changed her position with the threat of terrorism? Why or why not?

Cartoons on Restriction of Immigration

Visual images, not just written texts, can also be arguments, especially about current issues being debated. Political cartoons are one voice among many in sometimes heated conversations. Editorial cartoons are topical and time-bound. They are very much of the moment. They rely on visual associations, jokes, and allusions. They convey a message economically by careful selection of ideas but with few words. They rely heavily on the use of pathos.

The first pair of cartoons comes from the nineteenth century. In the cartoon in Figure 4-1, published in the 1860s in San Francisco, we see some Americans' "great fear" of immigrants quite literally portrayed. The second cartoon (Figure 4-2), by the great nineteenth-century caricaturist and political cartoonist for *Harper's Weekly*, Thomas Nast, comments on the Chinese Exclusion Act of 1882. This law made Chinese immigrants already in the country ineligible for naturalization and suspended immigration from China for ten years. (Other anti-Chinese immigration laws were passed in 1882 and 1902, and Chinese immigrants did not become eligible for naturalization until 1943.)

More modern concerns are addressed in the second pair of cartoons. Both the Mike Keefe and the Clay Bennett cartoons use the image of the Statue of Liberty. The immediate context of the Keefe cartoon (Figure 4-3), published just before September 11, 2001, was President George W. Bush's support for Mexican President Vicente Fox's proposal that the United States grant legal rights to undocumented Mexican immigrants. The final cartoon by Bennett (Figure 4-4) returns to more general attitudes towards immigration.

Cartoon Pair 1

Figure 4-1: *"The Great Fear of the Period that Uncle Sam May Be Swallowed by Foreigners: The Problem Solved," San Francisco lithograph, 1860s.*

Questions about the Cartoons: Cartoon Pair 1

1. Look at the faces, hats, hair, and clothing of the two figures in the top panel of Figure 4-1. What features of each figure convey their

Figure 4-2: *Thomas Nast, "The New Declaration of Independence,"* Harper's Weekly, *1882.*

nationalities? What impression does each of the figures make on the viewer? Compare the figure on the left to Pat in the Nast cartoon (Figure 4-2). What features do they have in common? How do they differ?

2. Where is the first cartoon (Figure 4-1) set? Note that in the top panel the Pacific Ocean is on the right, and the Atlantic is on the left. Why are the figures so large? Why are east and west apparently reversed?
3. Who is being swallowed in Figure 4-1? What visual clues are given?
4. What happens in the bottom panel of Figure 4-1? What does the figure on the right look like at the end? What impression does he leave the viewer with?
5. Look carefully at the men's clothing, hats, pipes, facial hair, and names in Figure 4-2. Which immigrant groups are they meant to represent?

6. What seems to be the relationship between the men in Figure 4-2? What visual clues does Nast provide about their relationship?
7. Looking at the bottom caption of Figure 4-2, why does Fritz refer to the "Yankee Congress"? What appears to be Fritz and Pat's attitude towards American government, and what do they think of the Chinese Exclusion Act of 1882?
8. Who is the *yellow man* Fritz and Pat refer to in Figure 4-2?

Questions about the Arguments: Cartoon Pair 1

1. Both cartoons employ caricature. Look up *caricature* in the dictionary. In your groups in class, list all the elements that are caricatured in the two cartoons. How might caricature be connected to stereotyping?
2. What are we to think of the first cartoonist's view of the "great fear of the period"? What sort of solution does he present? Does he endorse the fear or question it? Formulate his message as a claim in an argument. Be prepared to defend your answers to your group and to the whole class.
3. In Figure 4-2, who has labeled the Chinese Exclusion Act the "New Declaration of Independence"? How does this label help to frame the cartoon's argument?
4. In Figure 4-2, why do Fritz and Pat feel affected by the law even though they are not Chinese?
5. Why might Nast have chosen the color green to represent Fritz and Pat in Figure 4-2? Human groups have been called red, white, black, brown, and yellow. Have any groups ever been called green? (Hint: Think of the Irish Cook's use of the term "greenhorn.")
6. In your group, decide what claim the Nast cartoon (Figure 4-2) is making.

Questions about the Cartoons: Cartoon Pair 2

1. Look up "The New Colossus" by Emma Lazarus that appears on the base of the Statue of Liberty. What connection does the Statue of Liberty have to immigration? How have immigrants and citizens responded to the statue and the poem?
2. Read each revision of the Lazarus poem. What changes do Keefe (Figure 4-3) and Bennett (Figure 4-4) make?
3. How does each cartoonist portray the statue itself? How do the people relate in size to the statue? Why do we only see the

Cartoon Pair 2

Figure 4-3: *Mike Keefe, "Masses," September 7, 2001.*

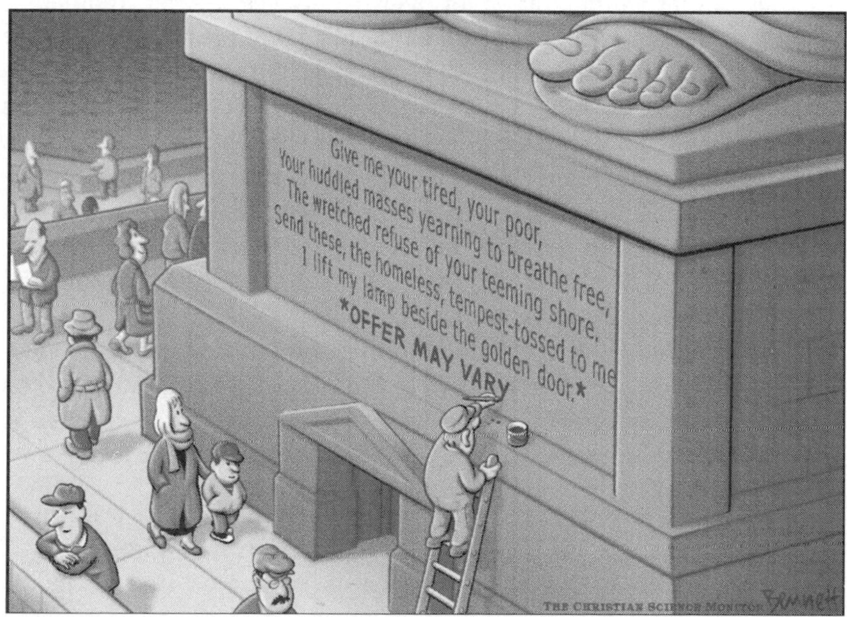

Figure 4-4: *Clay Bennett, "Offer May Vary," January 10, 2002.*

statue's feet in the Bennett cartoon? Why does Keefe's version of the statue cast a shadow? Why is his version of the statue small in relation to its base?
4. Looking at the Keefe cartoon (Figure 4-3), is President Fox "up against" the real inscription on the statue or the revised one? Why does he call it "the statuette of liberty"?

Questions about the Argument: Cartoon Pair 2

1. Are both cartoons making the same argument? Try to formulate the claim or claims.
2. Which set of changes to the Lazarus lines, Keefe's or Bennett's, has the greater impact? Explain your answer.
3. Who is responsible for the changed message on the statues? Are the revised sentiments typical of American opinion? How do the cartoonists intend us to view these sentiments?

Tamar Jacoby, "Too Many Immigrants?"

Tamar Jacoby (1954–) has been writing extensively about justice issues, race relations, and immigration for over twenty years. After completing her B.A. at Yale, she worked on the editorial staff of the *New York Review of Books*, as deputy editor for the *New York Times* Op-Ed page, and as senior editor and justice editor at *Newsweek*. In addition to this journalistic experience, she has been a lecturer at Yale and an instructor at the New School for Social Research. Currently, she is a senior fellow at the Manhattan Institute for Policy Research, a center-right think tank. In addition to her numerous periodical articles, she has recently edited *Reinventing the Melting Pot: The New Immigrants and What It Means to Be American* (2004), a collection of essays from both the left and the right.

"Too Many Immigrants?" was first published in *Commentary*, a neoconservative journal published by the American Jewish Committee. As you read the essay, weigh both Jacoby's qualifications and expertise as an arguer. What strategies does she use to engage you in her argument?

> Of all the issues Americans have had to rethink in the wake of September 11, few seem more baffling than immigration. As polls taken in the following weeks confirmed, the attacks dramatically heightened people's fear of foreigners—not just Muslim foreigners, all foreigners. In one survey, fully two-thirds of the respondents said they wanted to stop any immigration until the war against terror was over. In Congress, the

once marginal Immigration Reform Caucus quadrupled in size virtually overnight, and a roster of sweeping new proposals came to the fore: a six-month moratorium on all visas, shutting the door to foreign students, even militarizing our borders with troops and tanks.

In the end, none of these ideas came close to getting through Congress. On the issue of security, Republicans and Democrats, law-enforcement professionals and civilians alike agreed early on that it was critical to distinguish terrorists from immigrants—and that it was possible to protect the country without isolating it.

The Bush administration and Congress soon came up with similar plans based on the idea that the best defense was to intercept unwanted visitors before they reached the U.S.—when they applied for visas in their home country, were preparing to board a plane, or were first packing a lethal cargo shipment. A bipartisan bill now making its way through Congress calls for better screening of visa applications, enhanced intelligence-sharing among federal agencies, new tamper-proof travel documents with biometric data, and better tracking of the few hundred thousand foreign students already in the U.S.

But the security debate is only one front in a broader struggle over immigration. There is no question that our present policy is defective, and immigration opponents are hoping that the attacks will precipitate an all-out fight about overhauling it. Yet even if the goal is only to secure our borders, Americans are up against some fairly intractable realities.

5 In the aftermath of September 11, for example, there have been calls for tracking not just foreign students but all foreigners already in the country. This is not an unreasonable idea; but it would be next to impossible to implement. Even monitoring the entry and exit of visitors, as the Immigration and Naturalization Service (INS) has been charged with doing, has turned out to be a logistical nightmare—we are talking about a *half-billion* entries and probably an equal number of exits a year. (Of the total, incidentally, by far the largest number are Canadian and Mexican daily commuters, a third are Americans, and only a tiny percentage—fewer than a million a year—are immigrants seeking to make a new life in the U.S.) If collecting this information is difficult, analyzing and acting on it are a distant dream. As for the foreign-born population as a whole, it now

stands at 28 million and growing, with illegal aliens alone estimated at between seven and eight million. It would take years just to identify them, much less find a way to track them all.

To this, the more implacable immigration opponents respond that if we cannot keep track of those already here, we should simply deport them. At the very least, others say, we should move to reduce radically the number we admit from now on, or impose a five- or ten-year moratorium. In the months since September 11, a variety of more and less extreme restrictionists have come together in a loose coalition to push forward such ideas. Although the movement has so far made little headway in Washington, it has become increasingly vocal, gaining a wide audience for its views, and has found a forceful, nationally known spokesman in the former presidential candidate and best-selling author Patrick J. Buchanan.

The coalition itself is a motley assemblage of bedfellows: liberals worried about the impact of large-scale immigration on population growth and the environment, conservatives exercised about porous borders and the shattering of America's common culture, plus a sizable contingent of outright racial demagogues. The best known organization pushing for restriction is the Federation for Immigration Reform, or FAIR, which provided much of the intellectual ammunition for the last big anti-immigration campaign, in the mid-1990s.

FAIR is still the richest and most powerful of the restrictionist groups. In the months since the attacks, a consortium it leads has spent some $300,000 on inflammatory TV ads in Western states where the 2002 mid-term elections will bring immigration issues to the fore; over pictures of the nineteen hijackers, the spots argue that the only way to keep America safe is to reduce immigration severely. But FAIR no longer dominates the debate as it once did, and newer groups are springing up around it.

On one flank are grassroots cells. Scrappier and more populist than FAIR, some consist of no more than an individual with a web page or radio show who has managed to accumulate a regional following; other local organizations have amassed enough strength to influence the politics of their states, particularly in California. On the other flank, and at the national level, FAIR is increasingly being eclipsed by younger, more media-savvy groups like the Center for Immigration Studies (CIS) in Washington and the writers associated with the website VDARE, both of which aim at swaying elite opinion in New York and Washington.

Different groups in the coalition focus on different issues, and 10
each has its own style and way of presenting itself. One organization, Project USA, has devoted itself to putting up roadside billboards—nearly 100 so far, in a dozen states—with provocative messages like, "Tired of sitting in traffic? Every day, another 8,000 immigrants arrive. Every day!!" Those in the more respectable factions spend much energy distancing themselves from the more militant or fanatical, and even those with roughly the same mandate can seem, or sound, very different.

Consider CIS and VDARE. Created in 1985 as a fact-finding arm of FAIR, CIS is today arguably better known and more widely quoted than its parent. The group's executive director, Mark Krikorian, has made himself all but indispensable to anyone interested in immigration issues, sending out daily electronic compendiums of relevant news stories culled from the national press. His organization publishes scholarly papers on every aspect of the issue by a wide circle of respected academic researchers, many of whom would eschew any association with, say, FAIR's exclusionary politics. Along with his director of research, Steven Camarota, Krikorian is also a regular on Capitol Hill, where his restrained, informative testimony is influential with a broad array of elected officials.

VDARE, by contrast, wears its political views on its sleeve—and they are deliberately provocative. Founded a few years ago by the journalist Peter Brimelow, a senior editor at *Forbes* and the author of the best-selling *Alien Nation: Common Sense About America's Immigration Disaster* (1995), VDARE is named after Virginia Dare, "the first English child born in the New World." Kidnapped as an infant and never seen again, Virginia Dare is thought to have eventually married into a local Indian tribe, or to have been killed by it—almost equally unfortunate possibilities in the minds of VDARE's writers, who make no secret of their concern about the way America's original Anglo-Saxon stock is being transformed by immigration.

The overall strength of today's restrictionist movement is hard to gauge. But there is no question that recent developments—both September 11 and the flagging American economy—have significantly boosted its appeal. One Virginia-based organization, Numbers USA, claims that its membership grew from 5,000 to over 30,000 in the weeks after the attacks. Buchanan's *The Death of the West: How Dying Populations and Immigrant Invasions Imperil Our Country and Civilization*[1]—a deliberately confrontational jeremiad—shot to the top of Amazon.com's best-seller list within days of publication, then moved to a perch in the *New York Times* top ten. Nor does it hurt that the anti-immigrant cause boasts advocates at both ends of the political spectrum. Thus, leftists repelled by the likes of Buchanan and Brimelow could read a more congenial statement of the same case in a recent, much-discussed series in the *New York Review of Books* by the distinguished sociologist Christopher Jencks.

To be sure, immigration opponents have also had some significant setbacks. Most notably, the Republican party, which stood staunchly with them in the mid-1990s in California, is now firmly on the other side of the issue—if anything, George W. Bush has become the country's leading advocate for liberalizing immigration law. But there can be no mistaking the depth of public concern over one or another of the questions raised by the restrictionists, and in the event of more attacks or a prolonged downturn, their appeal could surely grow.

In addition to national security, immigration opponents offer 15
arguments principally about three issues: natural resources, economics, and the likelihood that today's newcomers will be successfully absorbed into American society. On the first, restrictionists contend not only that immigrants compete with us and consume our natural resources, to the detriment of the native-born, but that their numbers will eventually overwhelm us, choking the United States to death both demographically and environmentally.

Much of Buchanan's book, for example, is devoted to a discussion of population. As he correctly notes, birth rates in Europe have dropped below replacement level, and populations there are aging. By 2050, he estimates, only 10 percent of the world's people will be of European descent, while Asia, Africa, and Latin America will grow by three to four billion people, yielding "30 to

1. Dunne Books, 320 pp., $25.95.

40 new Mexicos." As the developed countries "die out," huge movements of hungry people from the underdeveloped world will swamp their territory and destroy their culture. "This is not a matter of prophecy," Buchanan asserts, "but of mathematics."

Extrapolating from similar statistics, Christopher Jencks has predicted that the U.S. population may double in size over the next half-century largely as a result of the influx of foreigners. (This is a much faster rate of growth than that foreseen by virtually any other mainstream social scientist.) Jencks imagines a hellish future in which American cities will become all but unlivable and suburban sprawl will decimate the landscape. The effect on our natural resources will be devastating, as the water supply dwindles and our output of carbon dioxide soars. (To put his arguments in perspective, Jencks finds nothing new in this pattern. Immigration has always been disastrous to our ecology, he writes: the Indians who crossed the Bering Strait 13,000 years ago depleted the continent's fauna by overhunting, and many centuries later the germs brought by Europeans laid waste to the Indians.)

Not all the arguments from scarcity are quite so apocalyptic, but all begin and end with the assumption that the size of the pie is fixed, and that continued immigration can only mean less and less for the rest of us. A similar premise underlies the restrictionists' second set of concerns—that immigrants steal jobs from native-born workers, depress Americans' wages, and make disproportionate use of welfare and other government services.

Here, groups like FAIR and CIS focus largely on the portion of the immigrant flow that is poor and ill-educated—not the Indian engineer in Silicon Valley, but the Mexican farmhand with a sixth-grade education. "Although immigrants comprise about 12 percent of America's workforce," CIS reports, "they account for 31 percent of high-school dropouts in the workforce." Not only are poverty rates among these immigrants higher than among the native-born, but, the restrictionists claim, the gap is growing. As for welfare, Krikorian points out that even in the wake of the 1996 reform that denied means-tested benefits to many immigrants, their reliance on some programs—food stamps, for example—still exceeds that of native-born Americans.

The restrictionists' favorite economist is Harvard's George 20
Borjas, the author of a widely read 1999 book, *Heaven's Door*.[2] As it happens, Borjas did not confirm the worst fears about immigrants: they do not, for example, steal Americans' jobs, and today's newcomers are no poorer or less capable than those who came at the turn of the 20th century and ultimately did fine in America. Still, in Borjas's estimation, compared with the native-born of their era, today's immigrants are *relatively* farther behind than, say, the southern Europeans who came a century ago, and even if they do not actually take work away from Americans, they may prompt the native-born to move to other cities and thus adversely affect the larger labor market.

As a result, Borjas contends, the presence of these newcomers works to lower wages, particularly among high-school dropouts. And because of the cost of the government services they consume—whether welfare or public schooling or hospital care—they impose a fiscal drain on a number of states where they settle. In sum, immigrants may be a boon to U.S. business and to the middle class (which benefits from lower prices for the fruit the foreigners pick and from the cheap lawn services they provide), but they are an unfair burden on ordinary working Americans, who must subsidize them with higher taxes.

Borjas's claims have hardly gone unchallenged by economists on either the Right or the Left—including Jagdish Bhagwati in a heated exchange in the *Wall Street Journal*—but he remains a much-quoted figure among restrictionists, who particularly like his appealing-sounding note of concern for the native-born black poor. Borjas's book has also greatly strengthened those who propose that existing immigration policy, which is based mainly on the principle of family unification, be changed to one like Canada's that admits people based on the skills they bring.

This brings us to the third issue that worries the anti-immigration community: the apparent failure, or refusal, of large numbers of newcomers to assimilate successfully into American society, to learn our language, adopt our mores, and embrace American values as their own. To many who harp on this theme—Buchanan, the journalist Georgie Anne Geyer, the more polemical VDARE contributors—it is, frankly, the racial makeup

2. Reviewed by Irwin M. Stelzer in the September 1999 *Commentary*.

of today's influx that is most troublesome. "Racial groups that are different are more difficult to assimilate," Buchanan says flatly, painting a nightmarish picture of newcomers with "no desire to learn English or become citizens." Buchanan and others make much of the influence of multiculturalism and identity politics in shaping the priorities of the immigrant community; his chapter on Mexican immigrants, entitled "La Reconquista," quotes extensively from extremist Chicano activists who want, he says, to "colonize" the United States.

On this point, it should be noted, Buchanan and his followers are hardly alone, and hardly original. Any number of observers who are *favorably* disposed to continued immigration have likewise raised an alarm over the radically divisive and balkanizing effects of multiculturalism and bilingual education. Where they part company with Buchanan is over the degree of danger they perceive—and what should be done about it.[3]

About one thing the restrictionists are surely right: our immi- 25
gration policy is broken. Not only is the INS one of the least efficient and most beleaguered agencies in Washington—at the moment, four million authorized immigrants are waiting, some for a decade or more, for their paperwork to be processed—but official policy, particularly with regard to Mexico, is a hypocritical sham. Even as we claim to limit the flow of migrants, and force thousands to wait their turn for visas, we look the other way as hundreds of thousands enter the country without papers—illegal but welcomed by business as a cheap, pliable labor force. Nor do we have a clear rationale for the selection we end up making from the vast pool of foreigners eager to enter the country.

But here precisely is where the restrictionists' arguments are the least helpful. Take the issue of scarcity. The restrictionists construct their dire scenarios by extrapolating from the current flow of immigrants. But as anyone who follows these matters is aware, nothing is harder to predict than who and how many will come in the future. It is, for example, as easy today as it

3. In *Commentary*, see, for example, Linda Chavez's "Our Hispanic Predicament" (June 1998) and "What To Do About Immigration" (March 1995), and my own "In Asian America" (July–August 2000).

ever was to migrate to the U.S. from Puerto Rico, and wages on the island still lag woefully behind wages here. But the net flow from Puerto Rico stopped long ago, probably because life there improved just enough to change the calculus of hope that had been prodding people to make the trip.

Sooner or later, the same thing will happen in Mexico. No one knows when, but surely one hint of things to come is that population growth is slowing in Mexico, just as it slowed earlier here and in Europe. Over the past three decades, the Mexican fertility rate has dropped from an average 6.5 children per mother to a startling 2.5.

Nor are demographic facts themselves always as straightforward in their implications as the restrictionists assume. True, population is still growing faster in the underdeveloped world than in developed countries. But is this an argument against immigration, or for it? If they are to remain strong, countries *need* population—workers, customers, taxpayers, soldiers. And our own openness to immigrants, together with our proven ability to absorb them, is one of our greatest advantages over Japan and Europe, which face a demographic crisis as their ratio of workers to retirees adversely shifts. The demographer Ben Wattenberg has countered Buchanan with a simple calculation: "If we keep admitting immigrants at our current levels, there will be almost 400 million Americans by 2050. That"—and only that, one might add—"can keep us strong enough to defend and perhaps extend our views and values."

The argument from economics is equally unhelpful. The most commonly heard complaint about foreign workers is that they take jobs from Americans. Not only is this assertion untrue—nobody has found real evidence to support it—but cities and states with the largest immigrant populations (New York, Los Angeles, and others) boast far faster economic growth and lower unemployment than cities and states that do not attract immigrants. In many places, the presence of immigrants seems to reduce unemployment even among native-born blacks—probably because of the way immigrants stimulate economic growth.

Economists looking for a depressive effect on native-born 30
wages have been nearly as disappointed: dozens of studies

over the past two or three decades have found at most modest and probably temporary effects. Even if Borjas is right that a native-born black worker may take home $300 less a year as a result of immigration, this is a fairly small amount of money in the overall scheme of things. More to the point, globalization would have much the same effect on wages, immigrants or no immigrants. Pressed by competition from foreign imports, American manufacturers have had to change production methods and cut costs, including labor costs. If they did not, they would have to go out of business—or move to an underdeveloped country where wages are lower. In either case, the U.S. economy would end up being hurt far more than by the presence of immigrant workers—who expand the U.S. economic pie when they buy shoes and groceries and washing machines from their American neighbors and call American plumbers into their homes.

What about the costs imposed by immigrants, especially by their use of government services? It is true that many immigrants—though far from all—are poorer than native-born Americans, and thus pay less in taxes. It is also true that one small segment of the immigrant population—refugees—tends to be heavily dependent on welfare. As a result, states with large immigrant populations often face chronic fiscal problems.

But that is at the state level, and mostly in high-welfare states like California. If we shift the lens to the federal level, and include the taxes that immigrants remit to the IRS, the calculation comes out very differently: immigrants pay in more than they take out. This is particularly true if one looks at the picture over the course of an immigrant's lifetime. Most come to the U.S. as young adults looking for work—which means they were already educated at home, relieving us of a significant cost. More important, even illegal immigrants generally keep up with payroll taxes, contributing to Social Security though they may never claim benefits. According to Stephen Moore, an economist at the Cato Institute, foreign-born workers are likely to contribute as much as $2 trillion to Social Security over the next 70 years, thus effectively keeping it afloat.

The economic debate often comes down to this sort of war of numbers, but the victories on either side are rarely conclusive. After all, even 28 million immigrants form but a small part of the $12-trillion U.S. economy, and most of the fiscal costs and benefits associated with them are relatively modest. Besides, fiscal calculations are only a small part of the larger economic picture. How do we measure the energy immigrants bring—the pluck and grit and willingness to improvise and innovate?

Not only are immigrants by and large harder-working than the native-born, they generally fill economic niches that would otherwise go wanting. The term economists use for this is "complementarity." If immigrants were exactly like American workers, they would not be particularly valuable to employers. They are needed precisely because they are different: willing or able to do jobs few American workers are willing or able to do. These jobs tend to be either at the lowest rungs of the employment ladder (busboy, chambermaid, line worker in a meat-packing plant) or at the top (nurse, engineer, information-technology worker).

It is no accident that 80 percent of American farmworkers 35
are foreign-born, or that, if there were no immigrants, hotels and restaurants in many cities would have to close their doors. Nor is it an accident that immigrants account for a third of the scientific workforce in Silicon Valley, or that Asian entrepreneurs run a quarter of the companies there. Today's supply of willing laborers from Mexico, China, India, and elsewhere matches our demand in these various sectors, and the result is good for just about everyone—business, workers, and American consumers alike.

To be sure, what is good for business, or even for American consumers, may not ultimately be good for the United States—and this is where the issue of assimilation comes in. "What is a nation?" Buchanan asks. "Is America nothing more than an economic system?" If immigrants do not come to share our values, adopt our heroes, and learn our history as their own, ultimately the nation will not hold. Immigration policy cannot be a suicide pact.

The good news is that assimilation is not going nearly as badly as the restrictionists claim. Though many immigrants start out at the bottom, most eventually join the working poor, if not the middle class. And by the time they have been here twenty years, they generally do as well as or better than the native-born, earning comparable salaries and registering *lower* poverty rates.

Nor is it true that immigrants fail or refuse to learn English. Many more than in previous eras come with a working knowledge of the language—it is hard to avoid it in the world today. Despite the charade that is bilingual education, nearly all high-school students who have been educated in this country—nine out of ten of them, according to one study—prefer English to their native tongue. And by the third generation, even among Hispanics, who are somewhat slower than other immigrants to make the linguistic shift, only 1 percent say they use "more or only Spanish" at home.

Despite the handicaps with which many arrive, the immigrant drive to succeed is as strong as ever. According to one important study of the second generation, newcomers' children work harder than their U.S. classmates, putting in an average of two hours of homework a night compared with the "normal" 30 minutes. They also aspire to higher levels of educational achievement, earn better grades, drop out less frequently—and expect only the best of their new homeland. Nearly two-thirds believe that hard work and accomplishment can triumph over prejudice, and about the same number say there is no better country than the United States. As for the lure of identity politics, one of the most thorough surveys of Hispanics, conducted in 1999 by the *Washington Post*, reported that 84 percent believe it is "important" or "very important" for immigrants "to change so that they blend into the larger society, as in the idea of the melting pot."

There is also bad news. Immigrant America is far from 40
monolithic, and some groups do worse than others both economically and culturally. While fewer than 5 percent of Asian young people use an Asian language with their friends, nearly 45 percent of Latinos sometimes use Spanish. Close to 90 percent of Chinese parents expect their children to finish college; only 55 percent of Mexicans do. Indeed, Mexicans—who account for about a quarter of the foreign-born—lag behind on many measures, including, most worrisomely, education. The average Mexican migrant comes with less than eight years of schooling, and though the second generation is outstripping its parents, it too falls well below American norms, either for other immigrants or for the native-born.

When it comes to absorbing the American common culture, or what has been called patriotic assimilation, there is no question that today's immigrants are at a disadvantage compared with yesterday's. Many Americans themselves no longer know what it means to be American. Our schools teach, at best, a travesty of American history, distorted by political correctness and the excesses of multiculturalism. Popular culture supplies only the crudest, tinniest visions of our national heritage. Even in the wake of September 11, few leaders have tried to evoke more than a fuzzy, feel-good enthusiasm for America. No wonder many immigrants have a hard time making the leap from their culture to ours. We no longer ask it of them.

Still, even if the restrictionists are right about all this, their remedy is unworkable. Given the global economy, given the realities of politics and law enforcement in the United States, we are not going to stop—or significantly reduce—the flow of immigrant workers into the country any time soon. Businesses that rely on imported labor would not stomach it; as it is, they object vociferously whenever the INS tries to enforce the law. Nor are American citizens prepared to live with the kinds of draconian measures that would be needed to implement a significant cutback or time-out. Even in the wake of the attacks, there is little will to require that immigrants carry ID cards, let alone to erect the equivalent of a Berlin Wall along the Rio Grande. In sum, if many immigrants among us are failing to adopt our common culture, we will have to look elsewhere than to the restrictionists for a solution.

What, then, is to be done? As things stand today, American immigration policy and American law are perilously out of sync with reality—the reality of the market. Consider the Mexican case, not the only telling one but the most dramatic.

People born in Mexico now account for roughly 10 percent of the U.S. workforce, and the market for their labor is a highly efficient one. Very few recent Mexican migrants are unemployed; even modest economic upturns or downturns have a perceptible impact on the number trying to enter illegally, as word quickly spreads from workers in California or Kansas back to home villages in Mexico. This precise coordination of supply and demand has been drawing roughly 300,000 Mexicans over the border each year, although, even including minors and elderly parents, the INS officially admits only half that many.

One does not have to be a free-market enthusiast to find this 45
discrepancy absurd, and worse. Not only does it criminalize badly needed laborers and productive economic activity. It also makes an ass of the law and insidiously corrupts American values, encouraging illegal hiring and discrimination against even lawful Mexican migrants.

Neither a moratorium nor a reduction in official quotas would eliminate this thriving labor exchange—on the contrary, it would only exacerbate the mismatch. Instead, we should move in the opposite direction from what the restrictionists demand, bringing the number we admit more into line with the reality of the market. The rationale for whom we ought to let in, what we should encourage and reward, is work.

This, as it happens, is precisely the direction in which President Bush was moving before September 11. A package of reforms he floated in July, arrived at in negotiations with Mexican president Vicente Fox, would have significantly expanded the number of visas for Mexican workers. The President's impulse may have been partisan—to woo Latino voters—but he stumbled onto the basis for an immigration policy that would at once serve America's interests and reflect its values. He put the core idea plainly, and got it exactly right: "If somebody is willing to offer a job others in America aren't willing to do, we ought to welcome that person to the country."

Compared with this, any other criterion for immigration policy—family reunification, country of origin, or skill level—sinks into irrelevancy. It makes no sense at all that three-quarters of the permanent visas available today should be based on family ties, while only one-quarter are employment-related. As for the Canadian-style notion of making skill the decisive factor, admitting engineers and college professors but closing the door to farmworkers, not only does this smack of a very un-American elitism but it disregards our all too palpable economic needs at the low end of the labor market.

The problem is that there is at present virtually no legal path into the U.S. for unskilled migrant laborers; unless they have relatives here, they have no choice but to come illicitly. If we accept the President's idea that immigration policy should be based on work, we ought to enshrine it in a program that makes it possible for those who want to work, and who can find a job, to come lawfully. The program ought to be big enough to meet market needs: the number of visas available the first year should match the number of people who now sneak in against the law, and in future years it should follow the natural rise and fall of supply and demand. At the same time, the new regime ought to be accompanied by serious enforcement measures to ensure that workers use this pipeline rather than continuing to come illegally outside it.

Such a policy makes sound economic sense—and also would 50
provide a huge boost for immigrant absorption and assimilation. By definition, the undocumented are effectively barred from assimilating. Most cannot drive legally in the U.S., or, in many states, get regular care in a hospital. Nor, in most places, can they send their children to college. An indelible caste line separates them from other Americans—no matter how long they stay, how much they contribute, or how ardently they and their children strive to assimilate. If we want newcomers to belong, we should admit them legally, and find a fair means of regularizing the status of those who are already here illicitly.

But rerouting the illegal flow into legal channels will not by itself guarantee assimilation—particularly not if, as the President and Congress have suggested, we insist that workers go home when the job is done. In keeping with the traditional Republican approach to immigration, the President's reform package included a proposal for a guest-worker program, and before September 11, both Democrats and Republicans had endorsed the idea. If we want to encourage assimilation, however, such a system would only be counter-productive.

The cautionary model in this case is Germany, which for years admitted unskilled foreigners exclusively as temporary guest workers, holding out virtually no hope that either they or their children could become German citizens. As it happened, many of these migrants remained in Germany long after the work they were imported for had disappeared. But today, nearly 40 years later, most of them still have not assimilated, and they remain, poorly educated and widely despised, on the margins of German society. Clearly, if what we hope to encourage is the putting-down of roots, any new visa program must give participants a shot at membership in the American body politic.

But how we hand out visas is only the first step in a policy aimed at encouraging immigrant absorption. Other steps would have to include the provision of basic services like instruction in English, civics classes, naturalization programs—and also counseling in more practical matters like how to navigate the American banking system. (Many newcomers, even when they start making money, are at sea in the world of credit cards, credit histories, mortgage applications, and the like.) All these nuts-and-bolts services are as essential as the larger tasks, from overhauling the teaching of American history to eliminating counterproductive programs like bilingual education and ethnic entitlements that only breed separatism and alienation.

There can be no gainsaying the risks America runs in remaining open to new immigrants. The security perils, though real enough, are the least worrisome. Legalizing the flow of needed workers and providing them with papers will help keep track of who is here and also help prevent those who wish to do us harm from entering in the first place. The more daring, long-term gamble lies in continuing to admit millions of foreigners who may or may not make it here or find a way to fit in. This is, as Buchanan rightly states, "a decision we can never undo."

Still, it is an experiment we have tried before—repeatedly. 55
The result has never come out exactly as predicted, and the process has always been a wrenching one. But as experiments go, it has not only succeeded on its own terms; it has made us the wonder of the world. It can do so again—but only if we stop denying reality and resolve instead to meet the challenge head-on.

Questions about the Passage

1. Working in groups, outline the article's three main sections. What title would you give to each section? Now briefly summarize the main points of each section. For the first section, be sure to explain why immigration has become an important issue since September 11. How have various groups favoring restriction of immigration proposed doing so? Explain the argument based on national security, on natural resources, on economics, and on the failure of immigrants to assimilate.

For the second section, briefly summarize Jacoby's refutations of the arguments from scarcity, from economics, and from failure to integrate.

For the third section, explain what the criteria for entering the country *should not be*, according to Jacoby. What *should be* the criterion for entering the country? Why is Germany not a good model for U.S. policy? What services should be provided for immigrants once they have entered the country?

2. Now use the outline/summary you formulated in question 1 to initiate a class discussion of each section of Jacoby's argument. Where do you agree with her? Where do you disagree? Where would you like additional information?
3. Do a Web search of the organizations listed in paragraphs 7–10. Does Jacoby characterize these organizations fairly?
4. In paragraph 6, how does Jacoby differentiate the positions of the "more implacable immigration opponents" from the "less extreme restrictionists"? What claims do Patrick Buchanan, Christopher Jencks, and George Borjas make? What view does she take of each writer?
5. For each of the following phrases Jacoby uses, first provide the denotative meaning and then explore their connotations: "motley assemblage of bedfellows" (paragraph 7); "grassroots cells" and "scrappier and more populist" (paragraph 9); "exclusionary politics" (paragraph 11); "deliberately provocative" (paragraph 12); "radically divisive and balkanizing effects of multiculturalism and bilingual education" (paragraph 24).
6. Why does Jacoby focus on Mexican immigration to the United States? Why are Mexican immigrants of special interest to her and to other writers on immigration?

Questions about the Argument

1. How does Jacoby use the phrases you investigated in question 5 above to construct her ethos and to persuade us? Think about synonyms she might have used for these phrases and try to figure out why she chose the ones she did.
2. What qualifies Jacoby to write about this topic? How would you describe her ethos? Is she fair-minded, balanced, biased in favor of one position, partisan, or some other word? Defend your choice with evidence from the text, including the phrases from question 5 above.

3. In what ways is *Commentary* an appropriate forum for her argument? Use the Web to discover what you can about its readership and editorial policy.
4. Locate the assumptions on which she bases her argument. Do you agree with them?
5. Does Jacoby clearly and fairly present the issues and problems raised by restrictionists? Explain your response.
6. How effectively does she refute the positions that restrictionists take?
7. What is her proposal/solution? Does it adequately address the complexity of the issues? Where does Jacoby herself stand on the restrictionist–open immigration spectrum?
8. Jacoby uses two examples of argument by analogy in paragraphs 27 and 55. Do you accept them as valid analogies? Why or why not?
9. Evaluate the strengths and weaknesses of this argument. Do you think Jacoby's argumentative strategies (for example, the way she structures her argument, her use of evidence, and her descriptions of the restrictionists) would help you to write an effective argument?

Writing Assignments

Conversations

1. Imagine a roundtable discussion among the immigrants we have read in this chapter: William and Sophie Seyffardt, Ann McNabb (the Irish cook), Rosa Cassettari, and Hilda Satt Polacheck. Each speaks of his or her experiences in the United States. What views of their lives do they have in common? On what issues do they differ?
2. Lyman Beecher, Mary Antin, and Tamar Jacoby are guests on a serious television news program. Each participant makes a case for or against restricting immigration to the United States, both in their own day, in the case of Beecher and Antin, and today. What issues are of importance to each of them? For example, does Beecher focus as much on economic issues as Jacoby does? Is Antin concerned with immigrants learning English? On what, if any, issues do they agree? Where do they disagree? What parallels between the past and present do they draw?

3. Sophie Seyffardt, Rosa Cassettari, and Hilda Satt Polacheck meet for coffee to discuss their experiences as women immigrants. How do they imagine their lives in their home countries would have been? How have their experiences been different in the United States? They should focus especially on work and family ties in their discussion.

Writing Sequence: Making a Case For or Against Open Immigration

1. In a brief paper, compare and contrast the immigrant narratives in this chapter, looking at the immigrants' adjustment to American society and at their contributions to the United States.
2. Using the conclusions from the primary source accounts you drew in question 1 as evidence, make a case for or against open-door immigration. You may also use the cartoons as evidence.
3. Summarize Antin's argument for open-door immigration. Be sure you include each step of the argument she builds.
4. How does the case you made in question 2 from the immigrants' narratives support or oppose Antin's argument? Write your own essay in which you argue for or against Antin and use the immigrant accounts as support for your own case.

CHAPTER

5

From the Immigrant Experience to Immigration Theory

As we jump forward in time to read the late twentieth-century narratives of Bharati Mukherjee from India, Bong Hwan Kim from Korea, and the Gembremariams from Eritrea, we find we have many questions: Are the experiences of these latest immigrants similar to those of earlier immigrants? How do they "fit in"? How do they see themselves? How much of their culture have they left behind? How American have they become? Do the metaphors that have been used to describe the way immigrants have integrated into American society shed any light on the process: Melting pot? Salad bowl? Mosaic?

To answer these questions, we turn to the writings of several social scientists, sociologists, and anthropologists who propose models to explain complicated human interactions. These writers question earlier models and challenge each other. For example, Milton Gordon's classic study *Assimilation in American Life* (1964) identifies three major trends in assimilation theory: Anglo-conformity, which requires rejection of the immigrants' home culture and adoption of the customs and core principles of the Anglo-Saxon core group; the "melting pot," which posits a "biological merger" of immigrants with the core Anglo-Saxon group and a "blending of their respective cultures into a new indigenous American type"; and "cultural pluralism," which argues for political and economic integration alongside retention of significant home society cultural customs. Though Gordon finds some validity in each of these theories, he argues that there is a still existing "maintenance of the structurally separate subsocieties of the three major religions and the racial and quasi-racial groups, and even vestiges of the nationality groupings, along with a massive trend toward acculturation of all groups—particularly their native-born—to American culture patterns." Gordon identifies this trend as "structural pluralism."

In a recent book, *Remaking the American Mainstream: Assimilation and Contemporary Immigration* (2003), Richard Alba and his co-author, Victor Nee, acknowledge in their first chapter that older formulations of the assimilation model take too much for granted: for example, "the seeming inevitability of assimilation, which is presented as the natural end point of incorporation into American Society"; another objection is to elevating "a particular cultural model, that of middle-class Protestant whites of British ancestry, to the normative standard by which other groups are to be assessed and towards which they should aspire." Other difficulties with the older assimilation model include that it fails to allow for the impact of an immigrant group on the larger society or for the positive effect that an ethnic group might have on the adjustment process of new immigrants. At the same time that they admit the limitations of earlier assimilation theories, Alba and Nee carefully distinguish the research on the assimilation of immigrant groups they are doing from two other models of immigration, "segmented" or "downward" assimilation and transnationalism.

"Segmented" assimilationists focus on the second generation, granting that some ethnic groups forge ahead, clearly upwardly mobile and assimilating well. What concerns Alejandro Portes and Rubén Rumbaut in *Legacies: The Story of the Immigrant Second Generation* (2001) is the downwardly mobile group that seems "poised for a path of blocked aspirations" and that might constitute a "new rainbow underclass" by mid-century. Portes and Rumbaut carefully examine the causes and conditions for such a trajectory.

Theorists of transnationalism, like the authors of *Nations Unbound: Transnational Projects, Postcolonial Predicaments, and Deterritorialized Nation-States* (1994), distinguish immigrants and migrants from "transnationals." Immigrants are traditionally seen as "those who have come to stay" and migrants as transient workers. Transnationals "develop networks, activities, patterns of living, and ideologies that span their home and the host society." Where the immigrant becomes deeply involved with the new country, having cut off ties with the old, the transnational has much more back and forth communication with home. Alba and Nee note that transnationalists see the opportunities afforded by technology, globalization, and air travel as making it "feasible for immigrants and perhaps the second and later generations to maintain significant relationships with their homeland. . . ."

As you read about the models of immigration that follow, we hope you will take the opportunity to engage these writers in conversation and to test their ideas. Do you agree that failure of the second generation to assimilate may lead to a "rainbow underclass" rather than a "rich mosaic" (the term Portes and Rumbaut use for immigrant incorporation into American society)? Can you apply Alba's model to the narratives we have read? Does the transnational model apply only to recent immigrants? Or do elements of earlier narratives point to some transnational characteristics? Try to make your reading of the theory a truly interactive process.

We also encourage you to collect and record immigrant narratives yourself (see Writing Sequence One). Not only are such oral histories a valuable way to preserve the immigrant experiences of your friends and families, but they also provide a service to the elderly and those with poor English skills who may have difficulty in recording their memories. Such stories, considered along with the narratives your class has read, can also help you challenge or confirm the immigration theories.

Bharati Mukherjee, "Two Ways to Belong in America"

Born in Calcutta, India, Bharati Mukherjee (1940–) came to the United States to study at the University of Iowa's Writing Workshop. She received an MFA in 1963 and a Ph.D. in 1969. From 1966–78 she taught at McGill University in Montreal, Canada, and then returned to the United States where she has been a professor of English at the University of California, Berkeley, since 1987. She left Canada because, as she told an interviewer for the California Alumni Association (June 2004), she had been "thrown out of hotel lobbies . . . , told to move to the back of a Greyhound bus, and spat upon."

Mukherjee's novels and short stories reflect her experience of living in two cultures. For example, the heroine of *Tiger's Daughter* returns to India and sees it through new lenses acquired in the West. Other characters, like Dimple in *Wife* and the heroine of *Jasmine*, must try to reconcile their Indian cultural background with their experiences as immigrants in the United States. Despite Mukherjee's acknowledgment of dual cultures, she rejects being labeled an Asian American writer. In an article by Nicholas A. Basbane, Mukherjee, now a U.S. citizen, is quoted as maintaining, "I am an American writer of Indian origin . . . because my whole life has been lived here, and I write about the people who are immigrants going through the process of making a home here. . . . I write in the tradition of immigrant experience rather than nostalgia and expatriation." At the same time, she notes (in her interview for the California Alumni Association) a "two-way transformation" going on where immigrants must resolve conflicts over "how much original culture to let go and how much American culture to embrace." She adds, "As I see it, over time—and often in spite of the immigrant's best efforts—the inherited and the adopted values fuse together." For America, too, there is "a healthy mongrelization of heritages and values going on."

> This is a tale of two sisters from Calcutta, Mira and Bharati, who have lived in the United States for some 35 years, but who find themselves on different sides in the current debate over the status of immigrants. I am an American citizen and she is not. I am moved that thousands of long-term residents are finally taking the oath of citizenship. She is not.
>
> Mira arrived in Detroit in 1960 to study child psychology and pre-school education. I followed her a year later to study creative writing at the University of Iowa. When we left India, we were almost identical in appearance and attitude. We dressed alike, in saris; we expressed identical views on politics, social issues, love and marriage in the same Calcutta convent-school accent. We would endure our two years in America, secure our degrees, then return to India to marry the grooms of our father's choosing.
>
> Instead, Mira married an Indian student in 1962 who was getting his business administration degree at Wayne State University. They soon acquired the labor certifications necessary for the green card of hassle-free residence and employment.
>
> Mira still lives in Detroit, works in the Southfield, Mich., school system, and has become nationally recognized for her contributions in the fields of pre-school education and parent-teacher relationships. After 36 years as a legal immigrant in this country, she clings passionately to her Indian citizenship and hopes to go home to India when she retires.
>
> In Iowa City in 1963, I married a fellow student, an American 5
> of Canadian parentage. Because of the accident of his North Dakota birth, I bypassed labor-certification requirements and the race-related "quota" system that favored the applicant's country of origin over his or her merit. I was prepared for (and even welcomed) the emotional strain that came with marrying

outside my ethnic community. In 33 years of marriage, we have lived in every part of North America. By choosing a husband who was not my father's selection, I was opting for fluidity, self-invention, blue jeans and T-shirts, and renouncing 3,000 years (at least) of caste-observant, "pure culture" marriage in the Mukherjee family. My books have often been read as unapologetic (and in some quarters overenthusiastic) texts for cultural and psychological "mongrelization." It's a word I celebrate.

Mira and I have stayed sisterly close by phone. In our regular Sunday morning conversations, we are unguardedly affectionate. I am her only blood relative on this continent. We expect to see each other through the looming crises of aging and ill health without being asked. Long before Vice President Gore's "Citizenship U.S.A." drive, we'd had our polite arguments over the ethics of retaining an overseas citizenship while expecting the permanent protection and economic benefits that come with living and working in America.

Like well-raised sisters, we never said what was really on our minds, but we probably pitied one another. She, for the lack of structure in my life, the erasure of Indianness, the absence of an unvarying daily core. I, for the narrowness of her perspective, her uninvolvement with the mythic depths or the superficial pop culture of this society. But, now, with the scapegoating of "aliens" (documented or illegal) on the increase, and the targeting of long-term legal immigrants like Mira for new scrutiny and new self-consciousness, she and I find ourselves unable to maintain the same polite discretion. We were always unacknowledged adversaries, and we are now, more than ever, sisters.

"I feel used," Mira raged on the phone the other night. "I feel manipulated and discarded. This is such an unfair way to treat a person who was invited to stay and work here because of her talent. My employer went to the I.N.S. and petitioned for the labor certification. For over 30 years, I've invested my creativity and professional skills into the improvement of *this* country's pre-school system. I've obeyed all the rules, I've paid my taxes, I love my work, I love my students, I love the friends I've made. How dare America now change its rules in midstream? If America wants to make new rules curtailing benefits of legal immigrants, they should apply only to immigrants who arrive after those rules are already in place."

To my ears, it sounded like the description of a long-enduring, comfortable yet loveless marriage, without risk or recklessness. Have we the right to demand, and to expect, that we be loved? (That, to me, is the subtext of the arguments by immigration advocates.) My sister is an expatriate, professionally generous and creative, socially courteous and gracious, and that's as far as her Americanization can go. She is here to maintain an identity, not to transform it.

I asked her if she would follow the example of others 10
who have decided to become citizens because of the anti-immigration bills in Congress. And here, she surprised me. "If America wants to play the manipulative game, I'll play it too," she snapped. "I'll become a U.S. citizen for now, then change back to Indian when I'm ready to go home. I feel some kind of irrational attachment to India that I don't to America. Until all this hysteria against legal immigrants, I was totally happy. Having my green card meant I could visit any place in the world I wanted to and then come back to a job that's satisfying and that I do very well."

In one family, from two sisters alike as peas in a pod, there could not be a wider divergence of immigrant experience. America spoke to me—I married it—I embraced the demotion from expatriate aristocrat to immigrant nobody, surrendering those thousands of years of "pure culture," the saris, the delightfully accented English. She retained them all. Which of us is the freak?

Mira's voice, I realize, is the voice not just of the immigrant South Asian community but of an immigrant community of the millions who have stayed rooted in one job, one city, one house, one ancestral culture, one cuisine, for the entirety of their productive years. She speaks for greater numbers than I possibly can. Only the fluency of her English and the anger, rather than fear, born of confidence from her education, differentiate her from the seamstresses, the domestics, the technicians, the shop owners, the millions of hard-working but effectively silenced documented immigrants as well as their less fortunate "illegal" brothers and sisters.

Nearly 20 years ago, when I was living in my husband's ancestral homeland of Canada, I was always well-employed but never allowed to feel part of the local Quebec or larger Canadian society. Then, through a Green Paper that invited a national referendum on the unwanted side effects of "nontraditional" immigration, the Government officially turned against its immigrant communities, particularly those from South Asia.

I felt then the same sense of betrayal that Mira feels now. I will never forget the pain of that sudden turning, and the casual racist outbursts the Green Paper elicited. That sense of betrayal had its desired effect and drove me, and thousands like me, from the country.

Mira and I differ, however, in the ways in which we hope to 15
interact with the country that we have chosen to live in. She is happier to live in America as expatriate Indian than as an immigrant American. I need to feel like a part of the community I have adopted (as I tried to feel in Canada as well). I need to put roots down, to vote and make the difference that I can. The price that the immigrant willingly pays, and that the exile avoids, is the trauma of self-transformation.

Questions about the Passage

1. How does Mukherjee describe Mira and Bharati as they leave India? Why do you think she refers to them both in the third person? How did their paths differ once they came to the United States? Have the paths they each took affected their "sisterly closeness" (paragraph 6)? Why does Mukherjee think they "probably pitied one another" (paragraph 7)? Why were they "unable to maintain the same polite discretion"? Why were they "always unacknowledged adversaries" and "now, more than ever, sisters"?
2. In paragraphs 11 and 12, how does Mukherjee characterize the wide divergence of the sisters' immigrant experience? In paragraph 15, why does she say that Mira "is happier to live in America as expatriate Indian than as an immigrant American"? What does "expatriate" mean? What does "exile" mean? How does Mukherjee view her sister's choice? What is your view of each sister's choice?

Questions about the Argument

1. Can Mukherjee speak with authority about her sister's experience? Why or why not?
2. Would you expect Mukherjee's audience to be unsympathetic, neutral, or sympathetic to Bharati? To Mira? Why?

3. Mukherjee concludes her article with the following statement: "The price that the immigrant willingly pays, and the exile avoids, is the trauma of self-transformation." Is she making a value judgment here? If so, what is it? Can this statement be read as an argumentative claim? If so, outline the argument she is making.
4. How does Mukherjee use pathos in describing both Mira's and Bharati's experience? Is it effective?

Bong Hwan Kim, "As American as Possible"

In April 1992, following the verdict acquitting white police officers of beating black motorist Rodney King, Los Angeles exploded in a violent and destructive riot with many fatalities. The riot illustrated the animosities and misunderstandings between Korean Americans, African Americans, Latinos, and whites. Approximately 2,300 Korean American businesses were damaged or destroyed by looting. University of California Berkeley Asian American Studies professor Elaine H. Kim and California State University Los Angeles sociologist Eui-Young Yu conducted about 100 interviews of Korean Americans in Los Angeles. They hoped to portray Korean Americans as they were, rather than as the stereotyped hysterical shopkeeper seen on television news. In their 1996 published collection of thirty-eight oral histories, Bong Hwan Kim's account is placed last.

Bong Hwan Kim was born in Korea in 1958 and came to the United States as a toddler in 1962. His account of his upbringing in New Jersey and his work as a community activist in Los Angeles illustrate many of the issues facing Asian immigrants. As he describes in the following reading, Kim, after an important visit to Korea, moved to Oakland, California, where he began to work for the Korean American community as the director of the Korean Community Center of the East Bay in 1982. In 1988, Kim moved to Los Angeles to become the director of the Korean Youth Center, later called the Korean Youth and Community Center, which was the position he held when he was interviewed by Elaine H. Kim (no relation) in 1992, 1993, and 1995. Bong Hwan Kim is currently the executive director of the MultiCultural Collaborative, a Los Angeles organization devoted to strengthening collaboration between ethnic and racial community groups to advance social justice and equity. In July 2004, he writes: "My experience in navigating the racial fault lines in Los Angeles is just one of countless stories which play out in disenfranchised communities throughout America. I hope that others can learn and be inspired to work for social change—just as I have been inspired by so many others who have and continue to fight for the real American dream of equality and justice for all."

I am always amazed at how pervasive the stereotype of Asian Americans as a model minority is. When European Americans start up conversations with me at airports, they invariably assume that I am an engineer or have something to do with computers. When I tell them I work with Korean American gangsters in Los Angeles, they get this blank look of total bewilderment on their faces. It's so far from their expectation of what I am supposed to be. I am very conscious of the way people perceive me just based on what I look like.

For the past thirteen years, I have been working for Korean American organizations in California, first for the Korean Community Center of the East Bay in Oakland, and now at the Korean Youth and Community Center (KYCC) in Los Angeles. When I was growing up in New Jersey, I never imagined that this kind of work would be possible. And I didn't dream that I could feel so at home with being a person of color in America. Throughout my childhood, I associated mostly with whites, but all through my adult working life, I've associated mostly with people of color, both professionally and personally. My current work on behalf of poor and immigrant communities often pits me against homeowners' associations, which are predominantly white, and white business leaders, who have the most access to political power and economic resources.

At this moment, it's hard for me to imagine having to live and work exclusively among people who thought the way people thought when I was back in New Jersey. To tell the truth, now that I know how much better I feel working in racially diverse groups, I am uncomfortable in a group of all white folks. Having grown up with white folks, I think I got to know "white culture" pretty well. I have to admit that I have a stereotype in my mind of white folks who have little contact with people of color still believing they're superior. I feel a strong kinship with other people of color because of the experiences I have had growing up as a Korean American in this society.

The Bergenfield, New Jersey, community where I was raised was a blue collar town of about 40,000 people, mostly Irish and

Italian Americans. I lived a schizophrenic existence. I had one life in the family, where I felt warmth, closeness, love, and protection, and another life outside—school, friends, television, the feeling that you were on your own. I accepted that my parents would not be able to help me much.

I can remember clearly my first childhood memory about 5
difference. I had been in the U.S. for maybe a year. It was the first day of kindergarten, and I was very excited about being able to have lunch at school. All morning, I could think only of the lunch that was waiting for me in my desk. My mother had made *kimpap* [rice balls rolled up in dried seaweed] and wrapped it all up in aluminum foil. I was eagerly looking forward to having that special treat. I could hardly wait for lunch time. When the lunch bell rang, I happily took out my foil-wrapped *kimpap*. But all the other kids pointed and gawked. "What is *that*? How could you eat *that*?" they shrieked. I don't remember whether I ate my lunch or not, but I told my mother I would only bring tuna or peanut butter sandwiches for lunch after that.

As a child you are sensitive; you don't want to be different. You want to be like the other kids. I was made to understand that I was different, and that the difference was negative. They made fun of my face. They called me "flat face." When I got older, they called me "chink" or "jap" or said "remember Pearl Harbor." In all cases, it made me feel terrible. I would get angry and get into fights. In high school, even the guys I hung around with on a regular basis, would say, "You're just a chink" when they got angry. Later, they would say they didn't mean it, but that was not much consolation. When you are angry, your true perceptions and emotions come out. The rest is a façade.

They used to say, "We consider you to be just like us. You don't *seem* Korean." That would give rise to such mixed feelings in me. I wanted to believe that I was no different from my white classmates. It was painful to be reminded that I was different, which people did when they wanted to put me in my place, as if I should be grateful to them for allowing me to be their friend.

Part of growing up in America meant denying your cultural and ethnic identity, and part of that meant negating your parents. I still loved them, but I knew they were not going to be able to help me outside the home. Once when I was small and had fought with a kid who called me a "chink," I ran to my mother. She would say, "Just tell them to *shut up*." Or my parents would say that the people who did things like that were just "uneducated." "You have to study hard to become an educated person so that you will rise above all that," they would advise. I didn't really study hard. Maybe I knew somehow that studying hard alone does not take anyone "above all that."

I was a kind of natural athlete, and I enjoyed every kind of sport. My parents encouraged my interest in sports, indulging and nurturing all my boyish enthusiasms by sparing no expense whenever I needed equipment. Probably sports saved me from complete lack of self-esteem as an Asian growing up in New Jersey in the early and mid-1960s. Through sports, I got lots of positive feedback and was able to make friends with white boys, who respected my athletic abilities even though I was Asian. In high school, I was elected captain of the football team, and my girlfriend was captain of the cheerleaders. I was not particularly good in school. My parents were upset, but I didn't pay much attention to them.

I grew up thinking that "American" meant "white," and 10
whatever was not American and not white was not good. I wanted to be as American as possible. I drank a lot and tried to be cool. I convinced myself that I *was* "American," whatever that meant, even though I wasn't white. But I was always hounded by a nagging sense of inadequacy, by the sense that I was less than a man, which I kept trying to compensate for by pursuing sports.

I tried to avoid the few other Asians at school. The guys were pretty much nerds, the studious type—Chinese Americans who played tennis. One of them played golf, but they weren't into the macho sports that get you accepted. When I met another Korean guy in college who was athletic, I was guarded and rejecting. It's strange: if I had met him at the Korean church, I probably would have befriended him, because the church was a familiar environment that felt like an extension of my family, so there wasn't that strong backdrop of white male standards to measure people against.

Back then, I thought of white women as the epitome of womanhood. But at the same time that I viewed white women as ideal, I knew that they viewed Asian men as less than ideal.

I clearly remember wanting to avoid Korean and Asian women. I had the feeling that I was superior to them. I know now that I avoided them because they reminded me of my own inadequacy as an Asian male. At the same time, the Asian woman was probably trying to avoid me, because I reminded her of her inadequacies vis-à-vis white people.

Thinking back to how pervasive that feeling of wanting to belong to whatever was popular or cool at the time, I realize that I should have been with other people who were on the fringes, like the artist types, who rejected social conventions and didn't care what was popular or cool. If I had gotten to know them, I probably would have had a much more meaningful experience then and much better memories now. But you have to be confident to enjoy being on the fringes.

When I got to college, sports failed to be a way of leveraging acceptance into circles I would not otherwise be allowed in because of my race. I was thrown into a kind of identity crisis. I tried to imagine what I might be doing in ten years, to think about the kind of life I would be living in this society, but I just drew a blank. Now I realize that I was facing the knowledge that you can't really participate in society if your humanity and your sexual identity are always in question. You are just too distracted to find a goal, much less focus on it. I became very depressed. I hated even getting up in the mornings. Finally, I dropped out of school. All the while, I knew underneath that I'd have to reconcile myself someday, to try to figure out where I could fit in a culture that never sanctioned my identity as a public possibility. What helped me get out of my depression was going to Korea. I went there hoping to find something to make me feel more whole. Being in Korea somehow gave me a sense of freedom I had never really felt in America. It was a physical space in this world where I would not be rejected simply because of what I looked like, where I did not have to always look over my shoulder, wondering if someone was out to get me for being different. Being in Korea also made me love my parents even more. I could imagine where they came from and what they experienced. I began to understand and appreciate their sacrifice and love and what parental support means. Visiting Korea didn't provide answers about the meaning of life, but it gave me a sense of comfort and belonging, the feeling that there was somewhere in this world that validated that part of me that I knew was real but that few others outside my immediate family ever recognized.

After spending a year in Korea, I returned to finish college, 15
and then I packed up and just headed for California. I had always wanted to go to the West Coast, not only because of the mystique of California "freedom" but also because I heard that Asian Americans had a stronger presence there. I wasn't much into career planning; I still have trouble planning my life over five-year time spans. I wasn't looking forward to getting a job in the mainstream labor market, but I was anxious to find out what the "real world" was like. In California, I had the opportunity to work in the Korean American community and be accepted for what I was. I met Asian Americans of all kinds, and I learned to appreciate Korean American women.

When I was young, the places where I could be a full human being were at home with my family, at the Korean church, and in Korea. It makes sense that I work in the Korean American community now. But I don't think that self-ghettoization is a good thing. In Los Angeles, I run into many Koreans my age who deliberately segregate themselves from non-Koreans. America should not be a society where people don't want to associate with each other. My optimistic side says that this is a transition period in which we are moving away from old paradigms in favor of creating something new, although I have no concrete reasons to be optimistic, what with the current immigrant bashing and backlash against people of color.

Three years ago, I would not have guessed that anti-immigrant sentiment would be this strong. Opportunistic politicians are appealing to majority white voters by simplistically pinning the blame for the nation's social and economic problems on immigrants, most of whom are Asian and Latino. That way, they can also maintain their traditional constituencies. If the current House and Senate version of the welfare reform bill goes through, legal immigrants would be cut off from most government services. Most recently, a government-sanctioned private commission on immigration reform headed by ex-Congressperson Barbara Jordan has been calling for a major overhaul of immigration policy to cut back the number of immigrants allowed into the country by one-third and to eliminate the fifth preference, which gives priority to family members.

At the same time, social services for the poor are being cut back. We are going to be forced to rethink traditional approaches to community development, unless a major tax reform is approved by voters, which is highly unlikely in the current climate. In some respects, Korean and other Asian American communities are relatively better off than other communities of color, given Asians' strong belief in self-help and relatively lesser reliance on agency services. But being relatively better off in a world where most people around you are continuing to sink into poverty will eventually wear you out also.

Asian Americans are juxtaposed between white "haves" and black and brown "have-nots," and we are classified as model minorities in that context to justify the unequal distribution of wealth and power. Asian American successes in education have been used as a rationale to do away with affirmative action programs for African Americans and Latinos. Instead of allowing ourselves to be used as a rationale for dismantling these programs, we need to assert our own opinions and positions in the public policy arena, not only for the benefit of African Americans and Latinos but also for the Asian Pacific American poor, who are being swept into conceptual invisibility by the pervasive stereotypes of Asian American "success." It doesn't benefit us for whites to believe we are smart or "better" than other people of color. Instead of mutely accepting a designated place in the social hierarchy, we must work toward a completely different social structure based not on hierarchy but on social justice and equality, as espoused in the U.S. Constitution.

The stereotype of Asians as goody-goody conformists is so 20
pervasive. Immigrant Korean parents often view themselves as sacrificial lambs, believing that even though they'll go to their graves as deaf, dumb, and blind, they are doing it so that their children can achieve the so-called American dream. Their kids work incredibly hard, knowing that only they can vindicate their parents for their sacrifice. In the end, they may think that as Korean Americans with college degrees they are fulfilling their parents' expectations according to the myth of the American dream. But instead, they become the target of resentment from all sides: white resentment and fear of Asian yellow peril takeover and black and brown resentment because of the per-

ception that Asian Americans are honorary white people unconcerned about social justice issues.

People don't realize that a large percentage of Asian immigrants are from the middle classes of their homelands. When they come to the U.S., they suffer socioeconomic decline but, ironically, this decline is perceived as achievement. The Southeast Asian refugees who didn't come from the middle class share a lot in common with Spanish-speaking working-class immigrants. Those Asians who don't conform to the model minority stereotype are invisible in the mainstream society. There are going to be more and more Korean American high school dropouts and juvenile delinquents succumbing to urban deterioration. There's only so much that the much-touted "family values" can do to defend against these pressures. The family unit can't operate all alone, in a vacuum, indefinitely.

We can't dismiss what happened to Korean Americans during the 1992 Los Angeles riots as a fluke or an aberration in a social system that is otherwise basically working fine. Institutional neglect of urban poverty and lack of effective political leadership allowed the social environment to degenerate to the point where Korean Americans could be scapegoated for conditions that we neither created nor had any control over. I continue to remind Korean Americans that unless those conditions are changed, such a thing could recur.

At the time of the riots, African American communities were politically strong but economically frustrated, Asian American communities were economically stronger and politically invisible, and Latino communities were both politically and economically disenfranchised. Ultimately, we need a multiracial coalition that supports true equality and enfranchisement. The toughest part will be convincing those with the most that even if a redistribution of power means no gains for them in the short term, the society as a whole will be better for everyone in the long term.

Every issue comes down to a convoluted configuration of class and race. I can see myself taking the Central American side in the future on affordable housing, playgrounds, social services as opposed to high-rise office buildings proposed by Korean developers.

It's hard to imagine what happened in April 1992 as a Latino-Korean conflict. Many Korean merchants feel lingering resentment at the role Central Americans played as looters. The traditional Korean love-hate relationship with the poor spills over into attitudes toward Latinos. Like many Latinos, Koreans are immigrants from a homeland decimated by colonial subjugation and U.S. cultural imperialism. As struggling immigrants, they have much to share: I often see working-class Koreans working side by side with Latino laborers, speaking a combination of Korean and Spanish, eating spicy foods together. But the majority of Korean immigrants want desperately to regard themselves as belonging to the middle class, as better than Latinos, whom they believe they have to exploit in a capitalist society.

After the riots, KYCC worked to organize neighborhood-based focus groups between Central Americans and Korean Americans, with the goal of putting together a multiracial planning council in Koreatown. We hired a community organizer who was active in the movement against the military dictatorship in El Salvador to conduct block-by-block canvassing in the neighborhoods. This project required a delicate balancing of Central American street vendors who might be exiled fighters against fascism in their homelands with Koreatown's richest and most capitalistic developers. It failed because KYCC lacked an infrastructure within the Central American community. We have begun to address ways to build coalitions by revising our organization mission statement to incorporate *all* Koreatown residents—many of whom are Latinos—as our constituency.

We also worked to ensure fairness to both Korean and African American communities by responding to the African American community's call to reduce the number of liquor stores while at the same time being mindful that the ruined Korean merchants need to regain a means of livelihood. We set up a liquor store conversion project to help burnt-out Korean and African American liquor merchants establish other businesses that would serve community needs. We were able to get the city council to waive costly sewage hookup fees for conversion of liquor stores to laundromats and other businesses. Another avenue we have been pursuing is technical assistance to help liquor store owners improve their sales of nonliquor items, thereby reducing their dependence on liquor sales. If you compare a Korean immigrant-owned store to, say, a

7-Eleven Store, you see how poorly managed the Korean store is. In the 7-Eleven, each item is located in exactly the same place, so that the delivery man knows exactly where to go. Most immigrant merchants don't keep inventory, so when a shelf space gets emptied, they just put anything in there. We're working with the Korean American Grocers Association to help them provide better technical assistance to their members. Many merchants know that dependence on liquor sales is unhealthy for the community and for them. Poor people who don't have cars rely on the local convenience store for things like produce and dairy products. And liquor sales are a magnet for crime, for residents and merchants alike.

I think that all our strategies have to have a fundamental economic base. People in South Central don't want to talk about improving race relations between African Americans and Asian immigrants unless you're talking about jobs. That redefines how we should approach improving relationships. There are people who still focus on trying to get people to know each other better, which is OK if you are dealing with mostly middle class people in various organizations and institutions. But if you really want to get to the root of a problem, you have to talk about economic development. You have to address the deep, institutional inequities that give rise to violence among people.

I hope that the riots had a profound impact on Korean American community perceptions of our own needs. There had not been a collective longing for leadership before. People were fighting over credit and titles. It was bad, but the community was doing all right economically, and that's all that seemed to matter. The American dream of Korean immigrants was based on economic rather than political wants. That's the desire that capitalism engenders, both in Korea and in the U.S. Korean Americans played by the rules of the game that were already set up. The rhetoric in the U.S. is about inclusiveness, about everyone, no matter what color, being rewarded for working hard and minding his or her own business. The ideals are great, but the reality is about political powerlessness for people of color in a hostile and racist environment.

What stands between Korean Americans and the promise of 30
the American dream is racism. For immigrants of color, the prerequisite for becoming American has been leaving your

culture by the door. But you can give up your culture and still not be accepted. You'll be hated instead, in a society that blames you whether you "succeed" or "fail" in your efforts to attain the American dream. I think it's a trap. We have to ask ourselves, What do we have to give up? What if there's no "there" to enter into after you have given everything up?

It's crucial for Korean Americans to participate in the decisions that affect our lives. That's why we have programs to help Korean immigrants become U.S. citizens and campaigns to get people registered to vote. We also have leadership development internship programs for Korean American youth, because they can serve as bridges between the immigrant families and the society at large, and because they could become key agents of change in our community in the future.

I can't understand why so many young Korean Americans have conservative values, why they give themselves up to the status quo. It's disheartening that so many of them want to go into the legal profession, which in my view is the upholder *par excellence* of the status quo. It's all about manipulating the rules of the game, which implies accepting the rules of the game and becoming part of a network of colleagues whose power and privileges are dependent on locking lay people out of even knowing the code words or the logic that lawyers monopolize.

To many Koreans and Korean Americans, leadership is equated with social status, professional qualifications, and advanced degrees. That's why attorneys and academics with no record of involvement in the community can be so quickly accepted as spokespeople. Many Korean immigrants are only interested in the person's credentials, not in her or his track record. Perhaps it's a holdover from Korean Confucianism, which places so much emphasis on social status.

The people that I admire the most are those who are committed to social equality and justice and have attained a position of influence to make a difference both within their own community as well as the public dialogue, but, most importantly, go about their work in a humble fashion. This is not to say that I measure up to those standards. But those are the standards I aspire to and by which I assess the effectiveness of others as well.

The powerful have to be held accountable. I distrust power, 35
no matter what color or how well-intentioned. I don't buy this

American individualism stuff. Individual success stories don't translate into well being for the Korean community as a whole. If we accept the rules of the game as they are, we are doomed. The game should be about creating a humane and just society, where people can provide their unique perspectives and do their part to build a better world. Korean Americans could be an enrichment instead of a "problem" that needs solving. I want to believe that those who have been on the outside can bring that outsider perspective in and transform America.

Questions about the Passage

1. What is the usual stereotype of Asian Americans as Kim encountered it, both growing up in the 1960s and 1970s and in the 1990s?
2. What does Kim mean by "as American as possible"? Why did he want to be "as American as possible"?
3. What was Kim's response to visiting Korea? Why was it an important step in his life?
4. What is Kim's assessment of the causes of the 1992 L.A. riot?
5. Why do you think that Kim rejected "another Korean guy in college who was athletic" (paragraph 11)?
6. Why do you think Kim is opposed to "self-ghettoization" (paragraph 16) for Korean Americans?

Questions about the Argument

1. Kim refers to himself as a "person of color." What does he mean? Do you consider Korean Americans to be people of color? What ideological and rhetorical purposes does the use of this phrase serve?
2. Why did Kim give up bringing Korean food to school? What did he lose by this decision? Why does the editor put this story early in Kim's life story?
3. Kim is puzzled by the "conservative values" of many young Korean Americans (paragraph 32). Do you think he is being fair when he criticizes the young people hoping to become lawyers or academics? How does this comment contribute to his ethos?
4. Consider other critical statements that Kim makes about Koreans Americans and about himself. How do his criticisms affect our sense of him and his positions?
5. Which, if any, of Kim's points can be applied to other immigrant groups in the United States? Be as specific as you can in your answer.

Tesfai and Lem Lem Gembremariam, "From Eritrea to Washington, DC"

From July 1986 to March 1987, writer and oral historian Al Santoli (1949–) traveled across the country interviewing immigrants and refugees who came from all over the world. Among those whose stories Santoli recorded are Tesfai and Lem Lem Gebremariam, a husband and wife from Eritrea. The couple was living in suburban Washington, DC, in Hyattsville, Maryland, with their two young children. Tesfai, who was 31 when interviewed, and Lem Lem, then 24, arrived in the United States in 1984. Both are Christians and had been members of the Eritrean Liberation Front (ELF), the rebel guerilla fighters who opposed Ethiopian rule in Eritrea, an Eastern African country annexed by Ethiopia in 1962. In the 1970s and 1980s, Eritrea suffered from a terrible famine as well as the prolonged warfare against the Soviet-supported Ethiopian state ruled by a Marxist junta called the Derge. In the ELF, both Tesfai and Lem Lem received some medical training and served as health care workers in Eritrea. But in 1981, they decided to become refugees in neighboring Sudan because of the in-fighting between ELF and a Marxist guerilla group, the Eritrean People's Liberation Front (EPLF). Years after the couple left Eritrea, it became independent from Ethiopia—in 1993. In the Sudan, they were eventually awarded refugee status by the United Nations and then by the American government. At the time of the interview, Tesfai worked as a nurse's assistant at a psychiatric hospital, which was paying for his training as a medical-lab technician; Lem Lem had a job as a hotel chambermaid. Santoli spoke with them in their one-bedroom apartment as their 1-year-old son Jerome and 5-year-old daughter Adiam played near them.

> TESFAI: In my village, I can trace my family back almost twenty grandfathers. They descended from the man who originally camped on the land. Their sons and grandsons all married and raised their families in the same village area.
>
> As a boy, I helped my father on the farm. We had two oxen to pull the plow in our field. Our enemies were wild animals. If we left any livestock outside after dark, hyenas would attack them. Foxes liked to kill lambs and baby goats. I carried a big stick to chase the wild animals away.
>
> To work the land is very hard. Since we were surrounded by mountains, the way we made fertilizer was to break stones and

crush the rocks into powder. We mixed this with the wastes from cattle. This is how we grew most of our food.

Eritreans don't like to take assistance from society. It is no shame to be helped by your brothers or sisters, but to depend on outsiders is like being a beggar. Your family will be shamed.

We arrived in Washington, D. C., from the refugee camps in 5
Sudan in August 1984. My wife was five months pregnant with our youngest child. Right away, we asked friends how to find work. We said, "If there is a job available, we will do it."

LEM LEM: The second week we were here, the Convention Center hired us. For six days, Tesfai and I worked together, busing tables. After that, I found a full-time job at the Ramada Inn. But, three months later, I had to stop working when the baby was born. The children were too young for me to be away from them.

TESFAI: At that time, we had to take public assistance for the family, because we couldn't afford to pay the $4,000 or $5,000 hospital bill. We didn't have insurance, and I was attending a medical-assistant training program without bringing home a paycheck. This caused great conflict. I told myself, "We need to take the money to pay the rent. But if we take it, I feel completely worthless."

Immediately after finishing my training, I found a job at Saint Elizabeth Psychiatric Hospital. My job has been to take care of the more than one hundred Cubans who came during the Mariel boatlift. They are kept in a separate part of the hospital, because they need a lot of help. Some are very tough guys, some are crazy. Many were criminals—some were thieves, others were into drugs. Some killed people.

It's ironic that in Eritrea, for many years, my wife and I were fighting for our freedom against Cuban soldiers. Now that we have freedom in this country, I am taking care of Cubans. And even though I didn't have time to take advanced English classes, I was sent to Spanish classes by the hospital.

Now, most days I attend medical-laboratory-technician 10
classes in Washington from 8:00 A.M. until 2:20 in the afternoon. Then I get into my car and drive for a half-hour to Saint Elizabeth Hospital. I work until 11:30 P.M. By midnight I am home.

It's very difficult to live this way. But my wife and I don't have any second thoughts about our jobs. We have rent to pay and two young children. Our baby, Jerome, is fourteen months. And our daughter, Adiam, started kindergarten this year. She is very American. When we arrived here, she was only three years old, so she doesn't know much about Ethiopia. She plays with American children and speaks perfect English. When we go to the shopping center, we don't know some foods. Adiam tells us everything, because she sees them advertised on TV.

LEM LEM: Now that the baby is a little older, I'm back at the Ramada Inn doing housekeeping. And some evenings I work part-time at the Westin Hotel. Two jobs, twelve hours a day. It's very hard being on my feet all that time.

TESFAI: She is also trying to attend English classes and to complete her high-school equivalency. Lem Lem was just a young teen-ager when she had to flee her parents' home in Asmara to escape the Derge's soldiers. Even before she escaped, schools were closed, because the Derge were killing and arresting students.

Since the Derge took power, thousands of refugees have fled Eritrea. The United States accepts relatively few people from Ethiopia each year. But there are ten times that many Eritreans in Sudan who need to be resettled.

I know some people who were rejected by American immi- 15
gration officers and killed themselves on the same day. They made up their minds that they had to live in America. They failed the immigration hearing because the [Eritrean resistance] Fronts had also fought against the previous Ethiopian regime, which the U.S. supported. So these rejected refugees went off and committed suicide. They didn't have any alternatives.

LEM LEM: Most Ethiopians accepted to the United States are from the cities and have some schooling. Many poor farmers from Eritrea can't flee to Sudan, because the Derge army blocks their escape. Even when some of these people do manage to reach Sudan, they refuse to leave Africa. They still feel very connected to their land and families they left behind. They say, "If we go to America, we are lost."

TESFAI: The people who come from cities like Asmara have European influence. The Italians dominated Eritrea from 1890 until World War II. Then we had self-rule as an autonomous province until 1962. And until 1977 the U.S. Navy had a base very near Asmara. The Americans were well liked. Some Eritreans worked on the base. And Americans came to bars in the city. A lot of the music we heard on the radio was disco music, like Aretha Franklin and James Brown.

LEM LEM: Many Eritreans who escaped to Sudan are Christians, who don't feel comfortable in a Moslem country. Refugee life is especially hard for women. In Asmara, we dressed similar to Americans. Countryside women wear traditional white dresses with embroidered designs. But in Sudan, all women must be covered head to toe like Moslems and wear shawls over their faces. Men are always shouting at them.

* * * * *

TESFAI: My wife and I registered as refugees through the United Nations. UN officials introduced us to the American Joint Voluntary Agency office, where we were interviewed to see if we qualified for acceptance to America. After we passed the JVA interview, we were sent to the American immigration officers.

We knew that they looked unfavorably on former members 20
of the Front. [Because some members had embraced Marxism and had been trained by the Soviet bloc during Haile Selassie's rule.] But I told them the truth, that I had been a fighter. I had done nothing to be ashamed of. Fortunately, we were accepted and began a four-month orientation program.

We had three hours of classes every day about life in America and the English language. For those of us who already knew English, we had classes on culture: how to ride a subway, how to use a shopping center, and many other necessary activities in this country. Those classes were very helpful, because in our country there are no large supermarkets and we don't have refrigerators to keep food fresh or frozen for long periods of time. We go to small shops and bargain over prices with the merchants. And in the countryside, we grow most of our food. We only need to buy little things, like coffee, sugar, or oil, which are not very expensive. A nickel's worth of salt can last you three or four months.

Besides attending classes, I continued working in the clinic until we departed for the States in August 1984. We were informed in Khartoum that we were going to Washington, D.C., and given the address of our sponsor, the International Rescue Committee.

As we flew into New York at night, we saw the harbor lights from the plane's window. The city lights reminded us of Asmara. The most difficult part of our arrival was that we didn't have relatives to greet us. It was after midnight when our connecting flight arrived in Washington. Only Mr. Canh, a Vietnamese representative of the IRC, was at the airport to welcome us. He drove us to a hotel in Washington. We were so exhausted from the long trip and the time change that we rested the entire first day.

On the second day, we went to the IRC office. We were so happy to meet some Eritrean friends there who we had known in Sudan. They were waiting to apply for jobs. Afterwards, they invited us to their apartments. We had lunch at one place and dinner at another friend's home. They told us how to get around the city, how to use the bus. I told them, "Our main concern is finding any kind of work."

LEM LEM: Even though we had the orientation about American 25
life in Sudan, we still felt a little awkward in Washington. We spoke enough English to understand what people said, but it was difficult for Americans to understand us because of our accent. [Laughs]

We moved into this apartment complex in Hyattsville. We are just a short bus ride from Washington, and many of our friends were already living in this apartment complex. When we first moved in, they helped us to find furniture. They brought us a dining-room set, a king-size bed and a small bed for our daughter, a sofa for the living room, and enough cooking and kitchen materials. Since then, little by little, we've been buying what we need to decorate the apartment.

In the beginning, one friend or another would drive us to the store to buy whatever food we needed. In our culture, we like to have a lot of relatives or friends eating together. The way Eritreans eat, we cook a big bowl of spiced beans or chicken or lamb stew. We then cover a large round tray with a kind of soft, thin pancake called *enjira*. On the *enjira* we serve the main courses of food, with smaller pieces of *enjira* on the side. Everyone shares the meal, eating with their hands by using pieces of *enjira* to pick up the food, like a small sandwich.

TESFAI: I have come to like American food, but it took time, because the spices and texture of Ethiopian food are very different. After living here for two years, we have shifted our expectations and feel more comfortable being a part of this society. It's true that we went through many changes, trying to forget about life in our country before the war and adjusting to this life style. Living in a large apartment complex, my wife and I working different shifts, sharing responsibility for the children—this is a big change from how we lived before.

In Ethiopia, we don't feel good when little children, like my daughter, play outside without parents' being with them. But it is common for children in the apartment complex to play in the large parking lot by themselves. We have good communication with the neighbors, and we keep an eye on each other's kids.

LEM LEM: In our country, families usually have between five and ten children. In the cities, the wife stays home to take care of the children most of the time, maybe one percent of the women hold regular jobs. But in the countryside, wives cannot stay home, they have to work on the farms. When the husband cultivates the land with the oxen, the wife follows behind, planting the seeds, and women have to do all the housework and cleaning. Men never cook, only do the outdoor jobs. Inside the home, women have equal rights, but in public, men have the dominant role in our culture.

TESFAI: I came from a big family, nine brothers and sisters. My mother always helped my father grow food during the planting season and she helped cut the crops at harvest. They worked side by side.

LEM LEM: But in the city, my mother didn't have an outside job. The only women who work are nurses, teachers, and bankers. People in Asmara wouldn't understand if I told them that I was working in the hotels here doing housekeeping.

TESFAI: We have both worked hard for the two years we have lived here. The rent hasn't been too high, so we've been able to save a little money for each of the children's college education, little by little. Our son, Jerome, was born here, so he is automatically an American citizen. The rest of us must wait five years from the date we arrived to apply for American citizenship. For now we are mostly concerned with working and trying to save.

My wife and I leave for work or school at the same time in the morning. But with the shifts we work, we see each other for only a short time in the evening and early morning. When I get home from the hospital and Lem Lem gets home from her second job at night, we go right to sleep. We are so tired. The only time we get to talk is in the morning, when we are driving in the car.

LEM LEM: Sometimes the hotel work slows down, but the Ramada is usually busy. I try to put in a few extra hours at the Westin when I'm not in school. On Mondays, I attend GED class for my high-school diploma. And on Tuesday and Thursday, I have English as a Second Language classes.

TESFAI: Working in the hotels, she gets paid more than $7 an hour. She makes more money than I do. In hospitals, if you're not a registered nurse, the pay isn't much at all. But when I finish technical school, work will pay a lot better.

For more than one year, I've been a psychiatric aide for Cuban Marielitos. It was sad that, when ordinary people tried to escape from Cuba, Castro opened all of his jails and mixed in these prisoners. They have caused trouble. Some have killed people, some are on drugs, others are thieves. I always have to keep an eye on them. You never know if they are going to hit somebody.

Most of them had spent ten or fifteen years in prison, so it's hard to do anything with them. They were given a lot of drugs in the Cuban prisons. Even though they are criminals, when they tell me stories about their lives, I cry. I understand that they are dangerous, but they've had a very bad life in Cuba. I try to treat them like human beings who have a mother and brothers, so it is not too bad.

I am very grateful to the hospital for sending me to a private medical school. I chose the eighteen-month medical-laboratory-technician course. When I complete the program,

I can get a job with doctors or hospitals anywhere. The only problem is finding time to study. Right after classes, I drive straight to my job. When the patients are quiet and sleeping, I am able to do some reading.

40 Right now it is a hectic and difficult life for my wife and me. But this is not uncommon for many Ethiopian refugees. When they first come, many are discouraged. They have difficulty finding a job commensurate with their educations. They see some crime; some people have things stolen. We don't like drugs in Eritrea, and I have heard a lot about drugs since we've been here. But I don't know any Eritreans who use them.

Ethiopians like to work. If we have to be home, off work, for two weeks or a month, we get upset. We like to spend money and appreciate that we have to earn it.

A new car costs at least $6,000, and we like to have a good car. It's kind of a competitive attitude.

Whenever new people from Ethiopia arrive in our apartment complex, we give them a party and try to make them feel welcome. We try to help by inviting them to come by if they have any questions. But after a while everybody is working and has their separate lives, so they drift apart.

LEM LEM: I know some people who have very troubled minds. They worry about paying the rent, they don't have a car, they cannot go to school, and they're very far away from their families.

45 Sometimes I have communicated with my younger brother and sister, who are still in Asmara. They are asking me to bring them to England or America. But how can I help them? They are in Eritrea studying Marxism-Leninism in high school now. They don't believe in that, but this is one way that the Communists are trying to erase our traditions, our culture. I am worried that the Derge will force them into the army. I have told my sister that, even though there are still many refugees, it is a big problem for a young woman to try to escape to Sudan now.

TESFAI: There are still Eritrean Fronts fighting against the Derge and the Soviets. In the countryside, the Ethiopian government continues to force farmers into collectives. Many people are still dying because of these policies, even though the world seems to have forgotten them.

Tonight a friend called on the telephone to tell us that her mother died in Ethiopia. We are going to her apartment this evening with three or four other families so she will not have to be alone. We will stay until late, then come home for a little rest before we go to work in the morning.

In Eritrea when somebody dies, a member of the family will notify all of the people in the surrounding area. Everybody takes time from what they are doing to come to the home. For two weeks, day and night, some friends help to cook and do the housework to make it easier on the family. In the evenings, other friends and relatives bring food from their homes for everyone to eat together. They make jokes and everybody laughs, even though they are very sad. Guests stay until around 1:00 A.M. so the family won't have to cry alone.

Now, in America, we try to do the same thing, but only for three or four days. In American culture, people are too busy.

No matter how long we live in America, we remain very concerned about our families back in Ethiopia. Our parents are always on our minds. If any friend's father or mother dies, we are all deeply touched. We cry and shout just like a baby, because it is like death twice over. First is the actual death. Second is the fact that we cannot be with them, even for the funeral. We are far away from home, but we always hope to be reunited with our families.

We would like our children to grow up in America. That is our decision. They have a chance to get a good education. And to live in any other country as a refugee we would have problems being accepted. Everybody says, "You are foreigners."

In America, we have the same rights as everyone. It's true that my wife and I have to work very hard; to be an American, you have to work hard. But nobody asks us, "Where are you from?" They can tell when they hear me speak that I was not born here. My accent is still very noticeable. But nobody makes a big deal out of it. This is our chance to live.

Questions about the Passage

1. How much of Eritrean culture are the Gebremariams able to maintain in the United States? What aspects seem to be the most important to them?

2. What sort of generalizations do they make about their fellow Eritrean immigrants?
3. What are their responses to immigrants from other countries?
4. What are their goals in their new lives as immigrants? What do they appreciate about America? What do they dislike?

Questions about the Argument

1. The Gebremariams make many statements about themselves, Eritrea, and the United States. On what knowledge or evidence do they base their opinions? How reliable do you find their descriptions and analyses? Why do you find them more or less reliable?
2. Based on what they say in their interview, do you think the Gebremariams will succeed as Americans? Do you think they will return to Eritrea after it becomes independent from Ethiopia? Make a case for your answer using evidence from the text.

Richard D. Alba, "Assimilation's Quiet Tide"

Richard Alba (1942–) received both his A.B. and Ph.D. from Columbia University. As he moved up the academic ranks, he became an assistant professor of sociology at CUNY and then at Cornell, and associate professor and then distinguished professor of sociology and public policy at SUNY. He has headed the Center for Social and Demographic Analysis at SUNY since 1981. A prolific writer of books and articles in sociology journals and newspapers, Alba has focused on group boundaries and group structure.

His work on immigration investigates how ethnic identities of European immigrants have attenuated over time. The article we have included as an example of Alba's views on assimilation (published in 1995 in *Public Policy*) describes various factors that have increased the attenuation of ethnic identity.

> Assimilation has become America's dirty little secret. Although once the subject of avid discussion and debate, the idea has fallen into disrepute, replaced by the slogans of multiculturalism. At best, assimilation is considered of dubious relevance for contemporary minorities, who are believed

to want to remain outside the fabled "melting pot" and to be, in any event, not wholly acceptable to white America.

However, assimilation was, and is, a reality for the majority of the descendants of earlier waves of immigration from Europe. Of course, it does have its varieties and degrees. Among Americans descended from the immigrants of the nineteenth and early twentieth centuries, assimilation is better viewed as a direction, rather than an accomplished end state.

Assimilation need not imply the obliteration of all traces of ethnic origins, nor require that every member of a group be assimilated to the same degree. That ethnic communities continue to exist in many cities and that many individuals identify with their ethnic ancestry do not indicate that assimilation is a myth. What, then, does assimilation mean when applied to American ethnic groups derived from European immigration?

It refers, above all, to long-term processes that have whittled away at the social foundations for ethnic distinctions. These processes have brought about a rough parity of opportunities to attain such socioeconomic goods as educational credentials and prestigious jobs, loosened the ties between ethnicity and specific economic niches, diminished cultural differences that serve to signal ethnic membership to others and to sustain ethnic solidarity, shifted residence away from central-city ethnic neighborhoods to ethnically intermixed suburbs, and, finally, fostered relatively easy social intermixing across ethnic lines, resulting ultimately in high rates of ethnic intermarriage and ethnically mixed ancestry.

The assimilation associated with these outcomes should 5
not be viewed as imposed upon resistant individuals seeking to protect their cultural identities—a common image of assimilation in recent, largely negative, discourse—nor as self-consciously embraced by individuals seeking to disappear into the mainstream (though, in both instances, there may be some who fit the description).

Rather, it is, in general, the perhaps unintended, cumulative byproduct of choices made by individuals seeking to take advantage of opportunities to improve their social situations. For many white ethnics, these opportunities opened especially in the period following World War II, due to more favorable attitudes towards groups such as Jews and Italians, the expansion of higher education and middle-class and upper-middle-class employment, and the mushrooming growth of housing in suburban communities.

The decision to make use of these opportunities sometimes has greater impact on the following generations than on the one responsible for them. When socially mobile families forsake the old neighborhood, where the stamp of ethnic ways on everyday life could be taken for granted, for a suburb, it is the children who grow up in a multi-ethnic, or even non-ethnic, environment.

What's in a Name

The rising tide of assimilation is illustrated by data from the most recent U.S. census (1990). A first sign is given by responses to the ancestry question, which appeared for the first time in the 1980 census. From the 1980 to the 1990 census, there were surprising changes in the way ancestries were reported. In contrast to the racial- and Hispanic-origin data collected by the census, the distributions of responses across European-ancestry categories underwent sharp alterations, which appear to correlate strongly with the specific ancestry examples offered on the census questionnaire. These ancestry examples were listed immediately below the question, and their influence on the resulting responses implies that many whites are suggestible when it comes to the way they describe their ancestry.

For instance, in 1980, "English" was among the first examples given, and 49.6 million Americans claimed English ancestry; in 1990, it was omitted from the list of examples, and the number who identified themselves as of English ancestry fell to 32.7 million, a decline of one-third. Similarly, in 1990, German and Italian were the first two ancestry examples given; though both were also listed in 1980, their positions were not as prominent. Both ancestry groups increased in number by about 20 percent between the two censuses, an increase substantially larger than that for European-ancestry categories in general. Such shifts suggest that ethnic ancestry is not a firmly anchored self-concept for many Americans, and alert us to the need to take ancestry data with a dose of caution, for the "Germans" and "Italians" of 1990 have changed in unknown ways from the "Germans" and "Italians" of 1980.

Increasing Socioeconomic Parity

Historically, one of the most important moorings of ethnicity 10
has been the concentration of different ethnic groups in specific socioeconomic strata. This brings the members of an ethnic group together by circumstances other than ethnicity and gives them common material and other interests arising from their shared situations. As Nathan Glazer and Daniel Patrick Moynihan explained in their seminal book, *Beyond the Melting Pot*, "to name an occupational group or a class is very much the same thing as naming an ethnic group."

However, in recent years, there has been a growing and impressive convergence in the average socioeconomic opportunities for members of white ethnic groups. Convergence here means that the disadvantages that were once quite evident for some groups of mainly peasant origins in Europe, such as the Italians, have largely faded, and their socioeconomic attainments increasingly resemble, if not even surpass, those of the average white American.

This phenomenon is quite demonstrable for education (a convenient indicator because its level is, for the great majority, fixed by the age of 25), but it is hardly limited to this sphere. Tables 5-1 and 5-2 present the educational attainments of

Table 5-1
Educational Attainment by Ethnic Ancestry—Men

	Cohort born 1956–1965		*Cohort born 1916–1925*	
	% attended college	% completed bachelor's degree	% attended college	% completed bachelor's degree
All non-Hisp. white	55.9	25.5	34.6	16.2
Solely British	66.3	31.8	46.6	23.5
German	57.6	25.9	35.2	16.0
Irish	59.4	26.5	33.8	15.4
French	52.6	21.9	32.4	14.4
Italian	61.9	30.2	25.8	12.1
Polish	61.4	32.9	29.2	14.2
All southern and eastern European	64.4	33.8	32.2	16.0

Source: 1-in-1000 Public Use Microdata Sample of the 1990 Census.

younger and older cohorts for the major European-ancestry categories. The data compiled in the table are limited to "non-Hispanic whites" (a population overwhelmingly of European ancestry) and to individuals born in the United States, thus avoiding any confounding with the characteristics of immigrants themselves. Though the data cannot tell us about the quality of education received, the evidence of convergence is strong.

To evaluate changes, two comparison groups are presented: one contains all non-Hispanic whites and the other individuals whose ancestry is solely from the British Isles (exclusive of the Republic of Ireland). The latter is commonly viewed as one of America's privileged ethnic groups. The other groups presented are the largest non-British groups, divided between the early-arriving groups from northern and western Europe (Germans, Irish, French, in order of size), and the later-arriving groups from southern and eastern Europe (Italians, Poles, and a separate category containing all individuals with ancestry from southern and/or eastern Europe).

In the case of each ancestry category, individuals are included in the tabulations regardless of whether their ancestry is solely or partly from the category. Limiting tabulations to

Table 5-2
Educational Attainment by Ethnic Ancestry—Women

	Cohort born 1956–1965		*Cohort born 1916–1925*	
	% attended college	% completed bachelor's degree	% attended college	% completed bachelor's degree
All non-Hisp. white	57.7	24.6	25.1	8.7
Solely British	66.3	31.5	38.1	15.7
German	60.7	24.8	25.8	9.2
Irish	60.4	25.0	24.0	7.7
French	56.2	20.3	26.5	9.9
Italian	61.2	27.8	16.5	4.9
Polish	62.2	29.4	14.4	3.8
All southern and eastern European	64.1	31.8	19.3	6.1

Source: 1-in-1000 Public Use Microdata Sample of the 1990 Census.

individuals with ancestry exclusively from one category would, in effect, eliminate one of the important mechanisms of assimilation—growing up in an ethnically mixed family.

15 The groups from southern and eastern Europe are often regarded as the acid test of assimilation because of the relative recency of their arrival and the prominence of their ethnicity in American cities. For the men of these groups who were born between 1916 and 1925, moderate disadvantages are evident when they are compared to the average non-Hispanic white or to men of German, Irish, and French ancestries; the disadvantage appears more substantial when compared to men of exclusively British ancestry. For instance, only a quarter to a third of Italian and Polish men attended college, compared to almost half of the British men. About one in eight Italians and Poles completed bachelor's degrees, compared to nearly one in four British men.

In the cohort born between 1956 and 1965 (whose education was largely complete by the time of the 1990 census), the southern and eastern Europeans have just about pulled even with the British men and are ahead of the average white and the men of other northern- and western-European origins. The figures for southern and eastern Europeans in general and for Poles may be affected by the extraordinary accomplishments of Jewish men (who are nevertheless minorities of these categories), but the same argument cannot be made in the case of the Italians.

The process of convergence is also quite striking among women. For predominantly rural immigrant groups, like the Italians and Poles, the education of daughters was of secondary importance compared to the education of sons. In the older cohort, British women had rates of college attendance and graduation more than twice those of their Italian and Polish contemporaries. This disparity has been largely eradicated in the younger cohort: Italian and Polish women are slightly behind British women in college attendance and graduation but tied with, if not slightly ahead of, the average non-Hispanic white woman as well as those of German, Irish, and French ancestries. The younger women in the general southern- and eastern-European category have above-average educational attainments that are similar to those of British women; this parity represents a marked improvement over their situation in the older cohort.

Decline of European Mother Tongues

Declines in overt cultural differences are a second component of assimilatory change. In census data, these are measurable in terms of the languages spoken in the home. Communication in a mother tongue marks a social boundary, which includes those who share the same ethnic origin and can speak its language and excludes all others. In addition, many aspects of ethnic culture that are embedded in a mother tongue are diminished or lost as exposure and fluency wane.

All available evidence reveals a powerful pattern of conversion to English monolingualism within three generations, from which only a small minority of any group escapes (a pattern first established by the sociologist Calvin Veltman). Consequently, the use in the home of European mother tongues (other than Spanish), and even exposure to them, have dropped off quite precipitously among those with southern- and eastern-European ancestries. Many older members of these groups spoke these languages in the immigrant homes and communities where they grew up. Data collected by the Census Bureau's Current Population Survey in the late 1970s show that three-quarters of southern- and eastern-European ethnics born in the United States before 1930 grew up in homes where a language other than English was spoken.

The situation for younger members of these and other 20
groups, as depicted in the 1990 census, is presented in Table 5-3 (which omits the English-speaking ethnic categories). The

Table 5-3
Language at Home by Ethnic Ancestry

	Cohort born 1976–1985	*Cohort born 1916–1925*
	% speak other than English	% speak other than English
All non-Hisp. white	3.5	6.1
German	2.2	2.9
French	3.3	13.4
Italian	4.0	19.4
Polish	3.5	24.2
All southern and eastern European	5.1	19.8

Source: 1-in-1000 Public Use Microdata Sample of the 1990 Census.

younger cohort contains individuals who were between the ages of five and fourteen in 1990 (the census does not record the language of children under the age of five). In general, 95 percent or more of the children in each ethnic category speak only English at home. There are scarcely differences to be noted among the categories, except perhaps for the slightly higher percentage of German children who speak English only.

Speaking a mother tongue at home is more common among the older members of these groups. Germans are still an exception, testifying to the deep impact of wartime hostility on the survival of German culture in the United States. For the Italians, Poles, and other southern and eastern Europeans, about 20 percent of their older members continue to speak a mother tongue, presumably on a daily basis. The figure is nearly as high for the French. Of course, still higher percentages spoke mother tongues during their childhoods. A major transition in language is evidently underway.

Qualifiers, however, should not be overlooked here. Perhaps fluency in a language is not required for it to serve an ethnic purpose; the use of words and phrases from a mother tongue, interspersed in English conversation, can signal an ethnic loyalty to others. This sort of knowledge cannot be measured from census data, but it does seem plausible that, where languages cease to be everyday means of communication, knowledge of words and phrases will drop off, too. Also, it is impossible to measure from census data the number of individuals who acquire a mother tongue through schooling or other formal instruction. Yet, given the generally sorry record of Americans' mastery of foreign languages, one would not want to depend too much on this source for cultural support.

The Declining Ethnic Neighborhood

Educational and occupational mobility and language acculturation, combined with the potent catalyst of competition with racial and new immigrant minorities over urban turf, have spurred residential changes. These have brought many white ethnics out of inner-city ethnic neighborhoods and into suburban settings, where ethnic residential concentrations tend to be diluted, if they exist at all. As a result of the continued visibility of surviving ethnic neighborhoods, some of which have become meccas for those seeking an "authentic" ethnic experience, the magnitude and implications of residential shifts are less appreciated than they should be.

In depicting residential shifts, I will switch from the trends in aggregate national census samples to the changes in a single but special geographic context, the Greater New York metropolitan region. This broad swath of cities and suburbs, covering 23 densely settled counties stretching from the Hudson Valley and Long Island in New York to the New Jersey shore, was home to 17 million people in 1990. Examining residential patterns in a single region avoids the risk of decontextualizing residential situations and losing sight of their location in relation to ethnic communities. No doubt due to the New York region's historic role as a gateway for immigrants, white ethnic communities continue to play a visible role in its ethnic geography. If such communities are important anywhere, they are sure to be so here.

Three large groups—Germans, Irish, and Italians—are used 25
to trace residential patterns. Each has between two and three million members in the region, according to both 1980 and 1990 census data, and has figured in significant ways in the region's ethnic neighborhoods in the past. However, based on their histories and the results of past investigations (such as *Beyond the Melting Pot*), the Germans could be expected to be the least residentially distinctive (i.e., with the fewest ethnic areas), while the Italians should be the most.

In fact, all of these groups are now found mainly in the suburban parts of the region, where ethnic residential concentrations are demonstrably thinner (though not nonexistent). By 1980, the Germans and Irish were already disproportionately located in suburbs: roughly three-quarters of both were outside central cities, compared to two-thirds of all non-Hispanic whites (but just one-quarter of Hispanics and nonwhites). Moreover, in suburbia, the residential distributions of the Germans and Irish are barely distinguishable from that of other non-Hispanic whites. In other words, these groups are residentially intermixed.

The Italians present a different, but more dynamic, picture. In 1980, they were slightly less likely to be found in suburbs than the average white (64 percent versus 66 percent), but during the 1980s their numbers in large cities fell while rising in the suburbs. By 1990, 70 percent resided in suburbs. While they were still not as suburbanized as the Germans and Irish, they were more so than the average non-Hispanic white. For the Italians, too, suburban residence means a greater probability of living in an ethnically diverse community.

Ethnic Exodus

This picture gains further credibility when it is taken to the level of specific ethnic neighborhoods. To accomplish this, John Logan, Kyle Crowder, and I have identified the region's ethnic neighborhoods in 1980 and 1990 census data as clusters of census tracts where any of the three groups has an above-average concentration (operationally defined as 35 percent or more of the population).

For the Germans and Irish, these neighborhoods are, generally speaking, few and small; only tiny fractions of each group could be considered to reside in them (just 4 percent of the Irish in 1990, for instance). For the Italians, however, there are a number of these neighborhoods, some of which are quite large and most of which take on familiar outlines, identifiable with well-known Italian areas (such as Brooklyn's Bensonhurst). Nevertheless, it is still the case that just a minority of the group—a quarter in both 1980 and 1990—resides in Italian neighborhoods.

The Italian neighborhoods, moreover, underwent substan- 30
tial changes during the 1980s. The outflow of Italians from the region's large cities especially drained inner-city ethnic neighborhoods. Bensonhurst was the largest contiguous Italian area in 1980, home to nearly 150,000 persons of Italian ancestry. By 1990, it had shrunk in its Italian population to less than 100,000, while also diminishing in spatial extent. Most other inner-city Italian neighborhoods also lost population, though not on such a dramatic scale. In effect, this outflow removed Italians from their most ethnic neighborhoods.

The suburban areas with growing numbers of Italians are very different in character. In the first place, the great majority of suburban Italians reside outside of anything resembling an ethnic neighborhood. Moreover, population growth bypassed inner-suburban ethnic neighborhoods, such as the Italian areas of Yonkers, and insofar as growth was funneled into outer-suburban areas of Italian concentration, these are not very ethnic, as measured for example by the number of residents who are intermarried.

In sum, even in the New York region, the ethnic mosaic *par excellence*, trends favor the further residential assimilation of white ethnic groups. The Irish, long a prominent ethnic group in the region, are already residentially intermixed. The Italians, some of whose ethnic communities are still conspicuous, reside mostly in non-ethnic areas, and their continuing suburbanization is eroding the most ethnic Italian neighborhoods.

The Intermarriage Melting Pot

Intermarriage is usually regarded, with justification, as the litmus test of assimilation. This remains true even if marriage can no longer be taken for granted as a lifetime commitment. A high rate of intermarriage signals that individuals of putatively different ethnic backgrounds no longer perceive social and cultural differences significant enough to create a barrier to a long-term union. In this sense, intermarriage could be said to test the salience, and even the existence, of a social boundary between ethnic categories. Moreover, intermarriage carries obvious and profound implications for the familial and, more broadly, the social contexts in which the next generation will be raised. Its significance in this respect is not much diminished by a high rate of divorce because the children of divorces usually carry on close relationships with both sides of their families.

Among whites, intermarriage has advanced to the point where a substantial majority of marriages involve some degree of ethnic intermixing. In 1990 census data, more than half (56 percent) of whites have spouses whose ethnic backgrounds do not overlap with their own at all (included in this count are spouses whose ethnic ancestries are described as just "American" or in some other non-ethnic way). Only one-fifth have spouses with identical ethnic backgrounds. The remainder, not quite one-quarter, have spouses whose ancestries overlap their own in some respect but differ in some other. Of necessity, one or both partners in these marriages have mixed ancestry (as when, for instance, a German-Irish groom takes an Irish-Italian bride).

Intermarriage has had an especially deep impact on the 35
groups from southern and eastern Europe. This is partly because their smaller size (in comparison, say, with the German ancestry group) makes them more vulnerable to what is called "out-marriage." It may also be due to their concentration

in regions of the nation where ethnic diversity is greater among whites (the Northeast compared to the South, for instance), increasing the likelihood that they will have close relationships with individuals of diverse backgrounds.

Intermarriage patterns are displayed in Table 5-4 for the seven largest ancestry categories of whites. It shows that, among those aged 25 to 34 in 1990, a majority of each category had married unambiguously outside of it, with out-marriage being more common among the smaller ethnic groups.

For the large, long-established categories (English, Germans, and Irish), marriages to individuals whose ancestry is partly from the group figure prominently in the pattern and help explain why the incidence of unambiguous out-marriage is not greater. Perhaps some of these marriages, where there is an ethnic ingredient in common, deserve to be viewed as in-group marriages. However, in the majority of cases, both spouses have ethnically mixed ancestry and share only one ethnic element in common. Thus, they should probably be viewed as akin to intermarriages, even if not so in the strictest sense.

Intermarriage has attained, by any standard, very high levels among the Italians and Poles, the two groups in the table from southern and eastern Europe. Close to three-quarters of the younger Italians have spouses without Italian ancestry; for Poles, the equivalent figure is higher still. However, marriages

Table 5-4
Marriage Patterns of Major Ancestry Groups

	Cohort born 1956–1965 Spouse's ancestry			*Cohort born 1916–1925 Spouse's ancestry*		
Ancestry groups (in order of size)	% entirely from group	% partly from group	% not from group	% entirely from group	% partly from group	% not from group
German	22.6	25.6	51.8	26.3	21.3	52.4
Irish	12.7	22.4	64.9	20.1	21.0	58.9
English	17.7	20.4	61.9	24.0	24.7	51.2
Italian	15.0	11.7	73.3	49.2	2.4	48.3
French	12.1	10.0	77.9	13.2	13.0	73.9
Scots/ Scots-Irish	7.0	10.8	82.1	11.9	12.8	75.4
Polish	7.6	8.3	84.1	36.0	3.9	60.1

Source: 1-in-1000 Public Use Microdata Sample of the 1990 Census.

involving spouses who both have some ancestry from these groups is higher than it would be if marriage were "random" with respect to ancestry, and there is some sign that the increase in intermarriage may be leveling off. A likely forecast is that intermarriage will continue at high levels but that a significant minority of each of these groups will continue to look within for marriage partners.

The rising tide of intermarriage is sweeping over religious barriers as well. This is demonstrated most tellingly by the surge of intermarriage among Jews since the 1960s. Data from the 1990 National Jewish Population Survey reveal that 57 percent of Jews marrying since 1985 have married partners raised in other religions. Just two decades earlier, the figure had been only 11 percent. The consequences of Jewish-Gentile intermarriage are still debatable, at least in principle, because of the possibilities of the non-Jewish spouse converting or of the children being raised as Jewish. However, the data suggest that neither possibility characterizes a majority of intermarried couples. Besides, even if these possibilities were the rule, they do not diminish the import of the fact that religious origins are playing a lesser role in the choice of a spouse than they once did.

An obvious consequence of intermarriage is ethnically 40
mixed ancestry, which holds potentially profound implications for ethnic groups. Though the mere fact of mixed ancestry is certainly no bar to ethnic feelings and loyalties, it is likely to reduce their intensity, especially because most individuals with mixed ancestry are raised with limited exposure to ethnic cultures in their most robust form.

Marriage Across Racial Lines

What is unfolding among whites through intermarriage resembles, then, the proverbial melting pot, but with mainly European ingredients to this point. It is still the case that just a small proportion of marriages by whites (2 percent) are contracted with Hispanics or with nonwhites. The vast majority of their intermarriages, in other words, involve individuals of European ancestries only (the most notable exception being the nontrivial fraction of whites who claim some American-Indian ancestry, typically mixed with European).

Lower rates of racial intermarriage are partly a result of residential segregation, which particularly affects blacks and new immigrant groups, and partly a consequence of the reluctance of many whites, the largest pool of potential marriage partners, to accept a nonwhite or Hispanic spouse. No doubt, there is also a greater desire on the part of many minority-group members to find husbands and wives from their own groups. For the new immigrant groups, from the Caribbean, Latin America, and Asia, the overall intermarriage rate is also driven down by their concentration in the first and second generations, where intermarriage tends to be lower in general.

The extreme case is that of African Americans ("non-Hispanic blacks" in census terminology). According to 1990 census data, just 4 percent of African Americans have married outside their group. However, this figure hides an important and long-standing gender discrepancy: intermarriage is considerably more prevalent among black men than among black women (6 percent versus 2 percent). For both sexes, most intermarriage takes place with non-Hispanic white partners.

Hispanics on the whole exhibit considerably higher, but still modest, levels of intermarriage, even in the second generation. Seventy percent of U.S.-born Hispanics are married to other Hispanics, mostly to individuals of the same national origin. In the Hispanic case, there is no gender gap in intermarriage. Its frequency does, however, vary considerably by specific group, and the total for Hispanics overall is influenced especially by the high rate of endogamy on the part of the largest Hispanic group, Mexican Americans.

Intermarriage is only a bit more common among U.S.-born 45
Asians overall, two-thirds of whom marry other Asians. As with Hispanics, this total disguises substantial variation by specific national origin and is heavily affected by a high level of endogamy in one group, Japanese Americans, who form the largest contingent among U.S.-born Asian adults.

American Indians bracket the intermarriage spectrum at the high end. More than half have married outside the American-Indian population; the great majority of their intermarriages are to non-Hispanic whites. However, since American Indians represent less than 1 percent of the national population, their intermarriage tendency does not have a great influence on the total pattern.

The predominantly European cast to the contemporary melting of ethnic lines through intermarriage may be changing, at least to some degree. One indication is the higher-than-average frequency of marriage to Hispanics or nonwhites on the part of younger non-Hispanic whites. Among those in the 25 to 34 age group, close to 4 percent have married minority-group members; though still low in absolute terms, this figure represents a measurable increase over past levels.

Rising intermarriage with racial minorities is having its most dramatic effects among African Americans, as the demographer Matthijs Kalmijn first documented (in the September 1993 issue of the journal *Social Forces*) with an analysis of marriages for the two-decade period following the Supreme Court's 1967 invalidation of the last anti-miscegenation law. In 1990 census data, 10 percent of 25- to 34-year-old black men have intermarried, most with white women. This figure, while obviously not high, nevertheless represents a stunning upward shift from the historical level. The change has not been as striking for black women, but the level of intermarriage has risen among younger black women to nearly 4 percent.

Intermarriage involving members of groups from new immigration is virtually certain to increase in the near future, as the ranks of their second- and third-generation adults swell. Yet, whether marriage across social boundaries defined by non-European ancestries will attain the acceptability—indeed the unremarkableness—that intermarriage appears to have attained in the case of European ancestries remains to be seen.

Assimilation's Continuing Relevance

The assimilation trends tracked by the census can, to be sure, 50
appear somewhat crude, lacking the nuanced *chiaroscuro* of personal experience where ethnicity may still be present. Nevertheless, taken together, these trends convincingly show that the social bases for ethnic distinctiveness are eroding among Americans of European ancestry. Indeed, the erosion would continue even if the trends were to come to a halt. As older, currently more ethnic generations are replaced by their children and grandchildren, who are less ethnic on average, the groups as a whole become less ethnic.

Decline, however, does not mean disappearance, certainly not in the foreseeable future. The overall picture is mixed, with the proportions of the different elements—i.e., "assimilated" versus "ethnic," to portray them in their extremes—shifting in the assimilated direction.

A larger question, and an unanswerable one for the moment, concerns the relevance of the European-American experience of assimilation for non-European minorities. Even if one narrows the question by accepting that assimilation is probably most relevant for immigrant groups, as opposed to those whose entry to American society was coerced by enslavement or conquest, the conditions of contemporary immigration are sufficiently different from those prevalent in the past that generalizations based on earlier experience are open to doubt.

Currently, we lack good theories and hard-and-fast empirical knowledge about the genesis of European-American assimilation. To what extent does it reflect persisting forces in American society—the lure of opportunities in the mainstream economy, for instance, or the permeability of ethnic boundaries in a society populated largely by immigration? To what extent is it the product of historically unique events and conditions, such as the period of economic expansion following World War II or the virtual shutdown of immigration after 1930, which prevented the renewal of ethnic communities through continuing immigration? To what extent is it restricted to those with European ancestry and white skin? Without answers to these questions, we will have to wait to observe the trajectories of new immigrant groups to assess the ultimate relevance of assimilation for them. Yet, one has to suspect that assimilation is far from a spent force.

Questions about the Passage

1. Carefully examine Alba's word choices in paragraph 1: "America's dirty little secret," "slogans of multiculturalism," and the "fabled 'melting pot.'" What do these phrases reveal about Alba's attitude towards some of those who disagree with him?
2. Paragraphs 1–7 are essentially an extended definition of assimilation. Working in groups, summarize this material in a paragraph, explaining exactly what assimilation is and is not.
3. Alba uses subtitles to divide his article into its important parts. In your class groups, explain briefly and clearly what each section says.

4. Look at each table Alba includes and prepare an explanation of the material it presents for the class. What conclusions can you draw from these tables? Are they the same conclusions as Alba's?

Questions about the Argument

1. Describe Alba's ethos. In addition to his credentials and experience, how might his use of statistical data contribute to his credibility? Look carefully, for example, at his interpretation of the data in paragraphs 12–17.
2. What kind of audience do you think Alba is writing for? Try to examine a copy of *The Public Interest* or locate its Web page to see what else you can discern about his audience. What does the fact that Alba explains the tables he uses (paragraphs 12–17) tell you about what kind of audience he imagines?
3. Locate the argumentative claim Alba makes early in the article. Does he qualify it in any way? List the reasons (subclaims) he gives to support his claim and examine the evidence he supplies for each reason. Does he use a clear logical framework? Is his argument convincing? Is there any place you think it is weak?
4. Does Alba acknowledge the arguments of those who disagree with him? If so, how does he bring them up? How does he refute them? How might Alba's argument factor into the debate, begun in Chapter 4, about how open immigration should be?

Alejandro Portes and Rubén Rumbaut, "Not Everyone Is Chosen"

Alejandro Portes (1944–) and Rubén Rumbaut (1949–) have collaborated extensively in their work on immigration. The titles of the following joint works chart the course of their interests: *Immigrant America: A Portrait* (1990); *Ethnicities: Children of Immigrants in America* (2001); and *Legacies: The Story of the Immigrant Second Generation* (2004). Portes, who is Cuban born, has had a particular interest in Third World poverty and in the way immigrants adapt to American society. His academic background includes a B.A. from Creighton University and an M.A. and Ph.D. from the University of Wisconsin at Madison. His academic career has taken him from the University of Texas, where he was an assistant professor of sociology, to the University of Texas at Austin as associate professor, and to Duke as professor. He is currently at Johns Hopkins.

Rubén Rumbaut's career trajectory has led him from degrees in sociology from Washington University (B.A.) and Brandeis (M.A. and Ph.D.) to his current position as a professor of sociology at Michigan State. His particular research interests include intergenerational relations and what he calls the 1.5 as well as the second and 2.5 generations.

The following selection from Chapter 3 of *Legacies: The Story of the Immigrant Second Generation* presents some of the contributing factors that, according to Portes and Rumbaut, lead to segmented assimilation.

> The story of how a foreign minority comes to terms with its new social surroundings and is eventually absorbed into the mainstream of the host society is the cloth from which numerous sociological and economic theories have been fashioned.[1] For the most part, this story has been told in optimistic tones and with an emphasis on the eventual integration of the newcomers. In other words, increasing contact over time is expected to end in the gradual merging of foreigners and natives, and the speed of the process depends on how close descendants of immigrants come to resemble the mainstream population.
>
> For this reason, the notion of assimilation became the master concept in both social theory and public discourse to designate the expected path to be followed by foreign groups in America. The concept conveys a factual prediction about the final outcome of the encounters between foreign minorities and the native majority and, simultaneously, an assertion of a socially desirable goal.[2] More than half a century ago, sociologists Lloyd Warner and Leo Srole introduced their study of an American city as "part of the magnificent story of the adjustment of ethnic groups to American life" and went on to predict that "oncoming generations of new ethnics will . . . climb to the same heights."[3] In reality, the process is neither as simple nor as inevitable. To begin with, both the immigrant population

1. Alba, Richard D., and Victor Nee, "Rethinking Assimilation Theory for a New Era of Immigration." *International Migration Review* 1997;31(4):826–874.
2. Alba and Nee, "Rethinking Assimilation Theory for a New Era of Immigration"; Gordon, Milton M., *Assimilation in American Life: The Role of Race, Religion, and National Origins*, New York: Oxford University Press, 1971.
3. Warner, W. Lloyd, and Leo Srole, *The Social Systems of American Ethnic Groups*, New Haven, CT: Yale University Press, 1945: p.2.

and the host society are heterogeneous. Immigrants, even those of the same nationality, are frequently divided by social class, the timing of their arrival, and their generation. American society is not homogeneous either. Depending on the timing of their arrival and context of reception, immigrants can find themselves confronting diametrically different situations, and hence the course of their assimilation can lead to a number of different outcomes.

There are groups among today's second generation that are slated for a smooth transition into the mainstream and for whom ethnicity will soon be a matter of personal choice. They, like descendants of earlier Europeans, will identify with their ancestry on occasion and when convenient. There are others for whom their ethnicity will be a source of strength and who will muscle their way up, socially and economically, on the basis of their own communities' networks and resources. There are still others whose ethnicity will be neither a matter of choice nor a source of progress but a mark of subordination. These children are at risk of joining the masses of the dispossessed, compounding the spectacle of inequality and despair in America's inner cities. The prospect that members of today's second generation will join those at the bottom of society—a new rainbow underclass—has more than a purely academic interest, for it can affect the life chances of millions of Americans and the quality of life in the cities and communities where they concentrate.

Hence, while assimilation may still represent the master concept in the study of today's immigrants, the process is subject to too many contingencies and affected by too many variables to render the image of a relatively uniform and straightforward path credible. Instead, the present second generation is better defined as undergoing a process of *segmented assimilation* where outcomes vary across immigrant minorities and where rapid integration and acceptance into the American mainstream represent just one possible alternative. Why this is so is a complex story depending on a number of factors, among which four can be considered decisive: 1) the history of the immigrant first generation; 2) the pace of acculturation among parents and children and its bearing on normative integration; 3) the barriers, cultural and economic, confronted by second-generation youth in their quest for successful adaptation; and 4) the family and community resources for confronting these barriers. This chapter provides a theoretical description of each of these factors and their expected consequences as a way of fleshing out the concept of segmented assimilation and paving the way for the analysis of its diverse aspects in later chapters.

How Immigrants Are Received: Modes of Incorporation and Their Consequences

It stands to reason that the adaptation of second-generation 5
youths is conditioned by what happens to their parents and that the latter's economic performance and social status are likely to vary. In contrast to journalistic and political characterizations of immigrants as a uniform population, every scholarly analysis of the subject begins by emphasizing their great diversity.[4] Today's immigrants differ along three fundamental dimensions: 1) their individual features, including their age, education, occupational skills, wealth, and knowledge of English; 2) the social environment that receives them, including the policies of the host government, the attitudes of the native population, and the presence and size of a co-ethnic community; and 3) their family structure.

The skills that immigrants bring along in the form of education, job experience, and language knowledge are referred to as their *human capital* and play a decisive role in their economic adaptation. The economic attainment of immigrants does not entirely depend on human capital, however, because its utilization is contingent on the context in which they are incorporated. Yet, by and large, educated immigrants are in a much better competitive position and are more likely to succeed occupationally and economically in their new environment. The same is true of those with extensive occupational experience.[5]

4. For earlier European immigrants, see Kraut, Alan M., *The Huddled Masses: The Immigrant in American Society, 1880–1921,* Arlington Heights, IL: Harlan Davidson, 1982; Rosenblum, Gerald, *Immigrant Workers: Their Impact on American Labor Radicalism,* Basic Books: 1973. For contemporary immigrants, see Portes, Alejandro, and Rubén Rumbaut, *Immigrant America: A Portrait,* 2nd ed., Berkeley, CA: University of California Press, 1996.
5. Jensen, Leif, and Yoshimi Chitose, *The New Immigration: Implications for Poverty and Public Assistance Utilization,* New York: Greenwood, 1989; Portes, Alejandro, and Min Zhou, "Self-Employment and the Earnings of Immigrants," *American Sociological Review* 1996;61:219–230.

On arrival, however, immigrant workers and entrepreneurs do not confront American society as a level playing field where only their education and work experience count. Instead, a number of contextual factors shape the way in which they can put their skills to use. The policies of the receiving government represent the first such factor confronting newcomers. Although a continuum of possible governmental responses exists, the basic options are exclusion, passive acceptance, or active encouragement. When enforced, exclusion precludes immigration or forces immigrants into a wholly underground and disadvantaged existence. The second alternative is defined by the act of granting immigrants legal access to the country without any additional effort on the part of authorities to facilitate their adaptation. This neutral stance places newcomers under the protection of the law but does not grant them any special concessions to compensate for their unfamiliarity with their new environment. Most economically motivated immigration to the United States in recent years has taken place under this alternative. A third governmental option occurs when authorities take active steps to encourage a particular inflow or facilitate its resettlement. At various times during the last century, the U.S. government was directly involved in the recruitment of different categories of foreign workers and professionals deemed to be in short supply. During the last 30 years or so, active governmental support and assistance has been granted only to selected refugee flows, arriving mostly in the aftermath of communist takeovers during the cold war.[6] Government support is important because it gives newcomers access to an array of resources that do not exist for other immigrants. This edge provides refugees who have high levels of human capital with a chance for rapid upward mobility. It also improves the economic condition of those from modest backgrounds by providing job apprenticeships and direct economic assistance.

6. Gold, Steven J., *Refugee Communities: A Comparative Field Study,* Newbury Park, CA: Sage Publications, 1992; Zolberg, Aristide, Astri Shurke, and Sergio Aguayo, "International Factors in the Formation of Refugee Movements," *International Migration Review* 1986;20:151–169; Rumbaut, Rubén G., "The Structure of Refuge: Southeast Asian Refugees in the United States, 1975–1985," *International Review of Comparative Public Policy* 1989;1:97–129; Rumbaut, Rubén G., "A Legacy of War: Refugees from Vietnam, Laos, and Cambodia," in Silvia Pedraza and Rubén G. Rumbaut (eds.), *Origins and Destinies: Immigration, Race, and Ethnicity in America,* Belmont, CA: Wadsworth, 1996:315–333.

The second contextual factor is the host society and its reception of newcomers. A well-established sociological principle holds that the more similar new minorities are in terms of physical appearance, class background, language, and religion to society's mainstream, the more favorable their reception and the more rapid their integration. For this reason, educated immigrants from northwestern Europe face little difficulty in gaining access to U.S. middle- and upper-class circles and are readily able to deploy their educational and work skills to their advantage.[7] Though race is in appearance a personal trait, in reality it inheres in the values and prejudices of the culture so that individuals with the same physical appearance can be treated very differently depending on the social context in which they find themselves.

In America, race is a paramount criterion of social acceptance that can overwhelm the influence of class background, religion, or language. Regardless of their class origin or knowledge of English, nonwhite immigrants face greater obstacles in gaining access to the white middle-class mainstream and may receive lower returns for their education and work experience. A racial gradient continues to exist in U.S. culture so that the darker a person's skin is, the greater is the social distance from dominant groups and the more difficult it is to make his or her personal qualifications count.[8] This social context and its differential evaluation of newcomers account, for example, for the generally favorable reception accorded to Irish immigrants in northeastern U.S. cities and the much greater barriers faced by Haitian immigrants in the same areas, despite the fact that

7. By 1945, Warner and Srole were already able to design a hierarchy of American ethnic groups with while English-speaking Protestants at the top. They predicted that the more ethnic groups departed from this standard, the longer they would take to assimilate in American society. See Warner and Srole, *The Social Systems*. See also Portes and Rumbaut, *Immigrant America*, ch.4.
8. Portes and Rumbaut, *Immigrant America*, ch.4; Waters, Mary C., "West Indian Immigrants, African Americans, and Whites in the Workplace: Different Perspectives on American Race Relations," Paper presented at the American Sociological Association Annual Meeting, August 1994, Los Angeles; Tienda, Marta, and Haya Stier, "The Wages of Race: Color and Employment Opportunity in Chicago's Inner City," in Silvia Pedraza and Rubén G. Rumbaut (eds.), *Origins and Destinies: Immigration, Race, and Ethnicity in America*, Belmont, CA: Wadsworth, 1996:417–431.

many Haitians are legal immigrants and many Irish are actually undocumented.[9]

The immigrant community's own compatriots represent the 10
third and most immediate context of reception. In some cases, no such community exists, and newcomers must confront the challenges of adaptation by themselves. More common, however, is the arrival of immigrants into places where a community of their conationals already exists. Such communities can cushion the impact of a foreign culture and provide assistance for finding jobs. Help with immediate living needs, such as housing, places to shop, and schools for the children, also flow through these co-ethnic networks.[10]

This regularity in the process of adaptation conceals, however, significant differences among the ethnic communities that immigrants join. While all such communities help their own, they do so within the limits of their own information and resources. For purposes of future socioeconomic mobility, the central difference is whether the co-ethnic group is mainly composed of working-class persons or contains a significant professional and entrepreneurial element. For newcomers in working-class communities, the natural thing to do is to follow the path of earlier arrivals into the host labor market. The help that ethnic communities can offer for securing employment in these situations is constrained by the kind of jobs held by their more established members. In this fashion, immigrants with considerable human capital can be channeled to below-average occupations as a function of the co-ethnic context that they encounter and the "help" that its members can provide.[11]

9. Stepick, Alex, *Pride against Prejudice: Haitians in the United States*, Allyn & Bacon, 1998; Tumulty, Karen, "When Irish Eyes Are Hiding, " *Los Angeles Times*, 29 Jan., 1989: A-1.

10. On the role of social networks in the onset and adaptation process of immigrants, see Massey, Douglas S., "Understanding Mexican Migration to the United States," *American Journal of Sociology* 1987;92:1372–1403; Roberts, Bryan, "Socially Expected Durations and the Economic Adjustment of Immigrants," in Alejandro Portes (ed.), *The Economic Sociology of Immigration*, New York: Russell Sage Foundation, 1995; Zhou, Min, *Chinatown: The Socioeconomic Potential of an Urban Enclave*, Philadelphia: Temple University Press, 1992.

11. Rumbaut, Rubén G., "Origins and Destinies: Immigration to the United States since World War II," *Sociologial Forum 9* 1994;4:583–621; Mahler, Sarah J., *American Dreaming: Immigrant Life on the Margins*, Princeton: Princeton University Press, 1995.

On the contrary, immigrants fortunate enough to join more advantaged ethnic communities can translate their education and occupational skills into economic returns, even when still unfamiliar with the new language and culture. The main feature of this situation—where a substantial number of conationals holds professional occupations or are independent entrepreneurs—is that the support of ethnic networks does not come at the cost of accepting a working-class lifestyle or outlook. Instead, these networks open a whole range of possibilities—from employment in the outside labor market to jobs within the ethnic community—that make full use of the immigrants' potential.[12]

Jointly, these three levels of reception—governmental, societal, and communal—comprise the mode of incorporation of a particular immigrant group. These modes condition the extent to which immigrant human capital can be brought into play to promote successful economic and social adaptation. No matter how motivated and ambitious immigrants are, their future prospects will be dim if government officials persecute them, natives consistently discriminate against them, and their own community has only minimum resources to offer.

A third dimension of importance for second-generation adaptation is the composition of the immigrant family, in particular the extent to which it includes both biological parents. Immigrant family composition varies significantly across nationalities, reflecting both different cultures and social structures in sending countries and patterns of arrival in the United States. Different modes of incorporation, in particular the outlook of authorities and strength of co-ethnic communities, can affect family composition by facilitating family reunification and reinforcing cultural norms. In turn, family contexts can be expected to affect various second-generation outcomes, even after taking parental human capital and modes of incorporation into account.

Summarizing this discussion, Table 5-5 presents a profile of 15
the human capital, modes of incorporation, and family contexts of several of the largest immigrant groups arriving in the United States during the last two decades. These are also the

12. Portes, Alejandro, "The Social Origins of the Cuban Enclave of Miami," *Sociological Perspectives* 1987;30:340–372; Gold, *Refugee Communities.*

groups best represented in our study, so these profiles provide a set of preliminary expectations concerning parental adaptation and subsequent second-generation outcomes. Specifically, we expect parental human capital, in the form of education and occupational skills, to positively affect their own socioeconomic attainment. In turn, achieved parental status and family composition will affect the pace and character of second-generation acculturation and subsequent adaptation outcomes. Modes of incorporation are expected to significantly affect the socioeconomic attainment of first-generation parents and to influence their family structure. The importance of these contextual variables may even extend beyond the first generation to directly affect second-generation outcomes. This is one of the main questions to be examined in the following chapters.

Acculturation and Role Reversal

In the family of José María Argüelles, a 40-year old Nicaraguan immigrant in Miami, power has drifted steadily away from him and his wife and toward their two teenage sons. José María does not speak English and has only a high school education. His and his wife's lack of permanent immigration papers means that they have been dependent on a string of odd menial jobs, like dishwashing and house cleaning, for survival. However, they have remained in the United States long enough for their children to grow up and learn the language. At 19, Pepe Argüelles already holds a waiter's job at a good restaurant and drives a better car than his parents. His younger brother, Luis, has been drifting toward a local gang dealing drugs, but the money that he brings home helps pay the rent and meet other urgent needs when his father is out of a job. José María feels powerless to discipline Luis or guide the future of their sons. "It's too late to send them back to Nicaragua," he says. "Here, they know English and know their way around far better than us . . . all that their mother and I can do is pray."[13]

13. Fernández-Kelly, Patricia, CILS project interview in southern Florida, 1995.

Table 5-5
Immigrant Nationalities and Their Modes of Incorporation, 1990

Nationality	*Size*	*Status Characteristics*[1]			
		Median Age	College Graduates (%)[3]	Poverty Rate (%)[4]	Median Family Income ($)[4]
Mexican	4,298,014	29.9	3.5	29.7	21,585
Filipino	912,674	38.8	43.0	5.9	47,794
Cuban	736,971	49.0	15.6	14.7	32,007
Chinese					
People's Republic	529,837	40.5	30.9	15.7	34,225
Taiwan	244,102	33.2	62.2	16.7	45,325
Hong Kong	147,131	30.3	46.8	12.7	49,618
Korean	568,397	34.9	34.4	15.6	33,406
Vietnamese	543,262	30.3	16.0	25.5	30,496
Dominican	347,858	33.6	7.5	30.0	19,694
Jamaican	334,140	35.7	14.9	12.1	34,338
Colombian	286,124	35.3	15.5	15.3	30,342
Haitian	225,393	34.6	11.8	21.7	25,556
Laotian	171,577	27.0	5.1	40.3	19,671
Nicaraguan	168,659	30.0	14.6	24.4	24,416
Cambodian	118,833	29.0	5.5	38.4	19,043

1. U.S. Bureau of the Census. *The Foreign-Born Population of the United States* (Washington, D.C.: U.S. Department of Commerce, 1993).
2. Typology based on past studies of individual nationalities.
3. Persons 25 years of age or over.
4. Annual figures (1989).
5. Children under 18 residing with both biological parents.
6. Percent of households headed by women with no husband present.

Family Structure		Mode of Incorporation[2]		
Both Parents Present (%)[5]	Female Head (%)[6]	Governmental[7]	Societal[8]	Co-ethnic Community[9]
73	14	Hostile	Prejudiced	Working class, concentrated
78	15	Neutral	Neutral to prejudiced	Professional, dispersed
72	16	Favorable to hostile	Neutral to prejudiced	Entrepreneurial, concentrated
87	8			
81	10	Neutral	Prejudiced	Professional/ entrepreneurial, concentrated
84	10			
87	11	Neutral	Prejudiced	Entrepreneurial, concentrated
73	15	Favorable	Prejudiced	Entrepreneurial/ working class, concentrated
47	41	Neutral	Prejudiced	Working class, concentrated
53	35	Neutral	Prejudiced	Professional/working class, dispersed
65	21	Hostile to neutral	Prejudiced	Professional/working class, dispersed
56	28	Hostile	Prejudiced	Working class, concentrated
81	12	Favorable	Prejudiced	Poor, concentrated
66	21	Hostile	Prejudiced	Professional/working class, concentrated
71	24	Favorable	Prejudiced	Poor, concentrated

7. Favorable reception accorded to groups composed of legal refugees and asylees; neutral reception to groups of legal immigrants; hostile reception to groups suspected to harbor large numbers of unauthorized immigrants or being involved in the drug trade, becoming targets of deportation by U. S. immigrant authorities.
8. Prejudiced reception accorded to nonwhite immigrants and to those with perceived involvement in the drug trade; neutral to groups defined as mostly white.
9. Concentrated ethnic communities are those that have large and highly visible concentration in at least one metropolitan area.

One of the most poignant aspects of immigrants' adaptation to a new society is that children can become, in a very real sense, their parents' parents. This role reversal occurs when children's acculturation has moved so far ahead of their parents' that key family decisions become dependent on the children's knowledge. Because they speak the language and know the culture better, second-generation youths are often able to define the situation for themselves, prematurely freeing themselves from parental control.

Role reversal was a familiar event among offspring of working-class European immigrants at the beginning of the twentieth century, and it was often seen as part of the normal process of assimilation to America. Children of Italian, Russian, and Polish laborers raced past their parents to take jobs in the expanding industrial economy of the time, set themselves up in business, or claw their way into the corporate world.[14] Today, second-generation Latins and Asians are repeating the story but with an important twist. For reasons that we will see in detail later on, the social and economic context that allowed their European predecessors to move up and out of their families exists no more. In its place, a number of novel barriers to successful adaptation have emerged, making role reversal a warning sign of possible downward assimilation. Freed from parental control at a premature age, the options available to second-generation youths can be different and sometimes more dangerous than those available to children of Europeans earlier in the century.

Role reversal, like modes of incorporation, is not a uniform process. Instead, systematic differences exist among immigrant families and communities. It is possible to think of these differences as a continuum ranging from situations where parental authority is preserved to those where it is thoroughly undermined by generational gaps in acculturation. The process of acculturation is the first step toward assimilation, as both immigrant parents and children learn the new language and normative lifestyles. Yet the rates at which they do

14. Child, Irvin L., *Italian or American? The Second Generation in Conflict,* New York: Russell & Russell, 1970; Alba, Richard D., *Italian Americans: Into the Twilight of Ethnicity,* Englewood Cliffs, NJ: Prentice-Hall, 1985; Gans, Herbert J., "Second Generation Decline: Scenarios for the Economic and Ethnic Futures of the Post-1965 Immigrant, *Ethnic and Racial Studies* 1992;15:173–192.

so and the extent to which this learning combines with retention of the home culture varies, with significant consequences for second-generation adaptation.[15] Table 5-6 presents a typology of possible situations depending on the acculturative gaps across generations and the children's insertion in the ethnic community.

Three of the outcomes portrayed in this figure are especially 20
important. *Dissonant acculturation* takes place when children's learning of the English language and American ways and simultaneous loss of the immigrant culture outstrip their parents'. This is the situation leading to role reversal, especially when parents lack other means to maneuver in the host society without help from their children. *Consonant acculturation* is the opposite situation, where the learning process and gradual abandonment of the home language and culture occur at roughly the same pace across generations. This situation is most common when immigrant parents possess enough human capital to accompany the cultural evolution of their children and monitor it. Finally, *selective acculturation* takes place when the learning process of both generations is embedded in a co-ethnic community of sufficient size and institutional diversity to slow down the cultural shift and promote partial retention of the parents' home language and norms. This third option is associated with a relative lack of intergenerational conflict, the presence of many co-ethnics among children's friends, and the achievement of full bilingualism in the second generation.[16]

Dissonant acculturation does not necessarily lead to downward assimilation, but it undercuts parental authority and places children at risk. Consonant acculturation does not guarantee success because parents' and children's striving for acceptance into the American mainstream may be blocked by discrimination. Still, consonant acculturation lays the basis for parental guidance and mutual intergenerational support in

15. Gordon, *Assimilation in American Life*; Rumbaut, Rubén G., "Assimilation and Its Discontents: Between Rhetoric and Reality," *International Migration Review* 1997;31(4):923–96; Rumbaut, Rubén G., "Ties That Bind: Immigration and Immigrant Families in the United States," in Alan Booth et al. (eds.), *Immigration and the Family: Research and Policy on U.S. Immigrants*, Mahwah, NJ: Lawrence Eribaum Associates, 1997:3–46.

16. This typology has been presented and discussed in greater detail in Portes and Rumbaut, *Immigrant America*, ch.7.

Table 5-6
Types of Acculturation Across Generations

Children's Learning of English and American Customs	Parents' Learning of English and American Customs	Children's Insertion into Ethnic Community	Parents' Insertion into Ethnic Community	Type	Expected Outcomes
+	+	–	–	Consonant acculturation	Joint search for integration into American mainstream; rapid shift to English monolingualism among children
–	–	+	+	Consonant resistance to acculturation	Isolation within the ethnic community: likely to return to home country
+	–	–	+	Dissonant acculturation (I)	Rupture of family ties and children's abandonment of ethnic community; limited bilingualism or English monolingualism among children
+	–	–	–	Dissonant acculturation (II)	Loss of parental authority and of parental languages; role reversal and intergenerational conflict
+	+	+	+	Selective acculturation	Preservation of parental authority; little or no intergenerational conflict; fluent bilingualism among children

Adapted from Alejandro Portes and Rubén G. Rumbaut, *Immigrant America, a Portrait*, 2d ed. (Berkeley: University of California Press, 1996), p. 242.

confronting external challenges. Lastly, selective acculturation offers the most solid basis for preservation of parental authority along with the strongest bulwark against effects of external discrimination. This happens because individuals and families do not face the strains of acculturation alone but rather within the framework of their own communities. This situation slows down the process while placing the acquisition of new cultural knowledge and language within a supportive context.

Types of acculturation do not occur in a vacuum but are conditioned by the variables discussed previously, namely parental socioeconomic achievement, family composition, and modes of incorporation. When parents have greater resources—in the form of higher education, economic status, intact families, or the support of strong co-ethnic communities—intergenerational acculturation tends to shift toward the consonant or selective modes. Parent-child conflict is reduced, and children are less prone to feel embarrassed by their parents' ways. On the other hand, parents whose educational and economic resources are modest, and especially those who are socially isolated, are more likely to experience dissonant acculturation and role reversal.

Questions about the Passage

1. What do the authors mean in paragraph 1 when they say the notion of assimilation "became the master concept"? To what degree do they accept this master concept in paragraph 4? How do they challenge this view in terms of the present second generation? What do they mean by "segmented assimilation"?
2. Other important terms you should define for yourself are "human capital" (paragraph 6); "modes of incorporation" (paragraph 13); "role reversal" (paragraphs 17–19); "acculturation," whether "dissonant," "consonant," or "selective" (paragraphs 20–21).
3. Carefully examine the tables that are used to explain both modes of incorporation (Table 5-5) and acculturation (Table 5-6). Do the data come from reliable sources? In Table 5-5, which group has the greatest percentage of college graduates? Which the highest poverty rate? Which has the highest number of both parents present? Which the lowest? Why do you think the European immigrants about whom Alba speaks are not included in this list?

4. In Table 5-6, how important is the acquisition of English in determining the type of acculturation? Which configuration of factors predicts the least amount of acculturation to American society?

Questions about the Argument

1. What credentials and experience enable Portes and Rumbaut to speak authoritatively about this topic? Is their source of data in Tables 5-5 and 5-6 also authoritative?
2. Who do you think is the audience of this Portes/Rumbaut book? How can you tell?
3. What is the authors' claim? Do they supply adequate reasons for challenging assimilation's "master claim"?
4. In paragraph 15, how do the authors use Table 5-5 to help make their case?
5. By the end of the reading, admittedly only a section of the introductory chapter, are you convinced that there is a case to be made for segmented assimilation? Why or why not? Can you foresee any public policy discussions that might arise from this material? For example, how might those wishing to curtail bilingual programs or restrict immigrant numbers make use of this material? As you think about this question, recall Antin's objection to the study and classification of immigrants. Should the statistical results of such studies be used to support proposals about immigration policy?

Nina Glick Schiller, Linda Basch, and Cristina Blanc-Szanton, "Transnationalism"

Coming from an anthropology background, Nina Glick Schiller, Linda Basch, and Cristina Blanc-Szanton have co-authored several works on transnationalism, including *Nations Unbound: Transnational Projects and Deterritorialized Nation States* (1999). Schiller's background is primarily academic. After earning her B.A. at New York University and her Ph.D. at Columbia, she is currently a professor of anthropology at the University of New Hampshire. Basch is the executive director of the National Council for Research on Women. She came to this position through both administrative and academic pathways. First, she was a program director for the U.N. Institute for Training and Research. After receiving her Ph.D. in anthropology at New York University, she taught there, became dean of arts and sciences at Manhattan College and vice president of academic affairs at Wagner College. Blanc-Szanton was affiliated with the Southern Asian Institute at Columbia University. She is now at the International Center for Research, Practice, and Policy Analysis in New York.

We have selected the following discussion of transnationalism from "Transnationalism: A New Analytic Framework for Understanding Migration," the introduction to an entire issue of the *Annals of the New York Academy of Sciences* devoted to the topic.

> Our earlier conceptions of immigrant and migrant no longer suffice. The word *immigrant* evokes images of permanent rupture, of the uprooted, the abandonment of old patterns and the painful learning of a new language and culture. Now, a new kind of migrating population is emerging, composed of those whose networks, activities and patterns of life encompass both their host and home societies. Their lives cut across national boundaries and bring two societies into a single social field.
>
> In this book we argue that a new conceptualization is needed in order to come to terms with the experience and consciousness of this new migrant population. We call this new conceptualization, "transnationalism," and describe the new type of migrants as transmigrants. We have defined transnationalism as the processes by which immigrants build social fields that link together their country of origin and their country of settlement. Immigrants who build such social fields are designated "transmigrants." Transmigrants develop and maintain multiple relations—familial, economic, social, organizational, religious, and political that span borders. Transmigrants take actions, make decisions, and feel concerns, and develop identities within social networks that connect them to two or more societies simultaneously (Basch, Glick Schiller and Blanc-Szanton n.d.).[1]

1. The term "transnational" has long been used to describe corporations that have major financial operations in more than one country and a significant organizational presence in several countries simultaneously. The growth of transnational corporations has been accompanied by the relocation of populations. It therefore seems appropriate to use the term "transnational" as a description for both the sectors of migrating populations who maintain a simultaneous presence in two or more societies and for the relations these migrants establish. In 1986 the American Academy of Political and Social Science employed the term as the theme of a conference publication entitled *From foreign workers to settlers?—Transnational migration and the emergence of a new minority.* The conference papers dwelt more on the effect on public policy of this type of migration, but did so without developing the concept of transnational migration.

The following vignettes based on our observations of migrants from Haiti, the eastern Caribbean, and the Philippines now living in New York allow a glimpse of the complexities and intricacies of transmigrant experience and identity that, we believe, calls for a new analytical framework.

The ten men sat around a living room on Long Island. The occasion was a meeting of their regional association. Each member of the association had pledged to send $10.00 a month to support an older person living in their home town in Haiti. They came from different class backgrounds in Haiti, although all were fairly successful in New York. But one of the members, a successful doctor, expressed dissatisfaction—although he has a lucrative practice, a comfortable life style in New York and a household in his hometown which he visits every year "no matter what." As he stated it, "I'm making money and I am not happy. Life has no meaning."

His speech about his emotional state was a preamble to his 5
making an ambitious proposal to his hometown association. He called on his fellow members to join him in the building of a sports complex for the youth in their hometown. He indicated that he already had bought the land which he would donate and he would also donate $4,000–5,000 for the building and called on others to assist in the construction. He had given no thought to maintaining the building or staffing it.

The doctor was not alone in his aspirations to make a mark back home in a way that maintains or asserts status both in Haiti and among his personal networks in New York. There were more than 20 Haitian hometown associations in New York in 1988. Their memberships were composed of people who have lived in New York for many years. Many of them undertook large scale projects back "home," projects which often are grand rather than practical. For example, an ambulance was sent to a town with no gasoline supply and no hospital.

These associations differ dramatically in the activities and audience from hometown associations of earlier immigrants whose main, if not only, thrust of activity was to help the newcomers face social welfare issues in the new land. Russian Jewish immigrants in the beginning of the 20th century, for example, founded "landsman" associations to provide their members with burial funds and assist the poor and orphaned in the United States. In contrast, the members of Haitian hometown associations, much as the participants in similar Filipino and Grenadian and Vincentian associations, are part of a social system whose networks are based in two or more nation states and who maintain activities, identities and statuses in several social locations.

Approximately 200 well-dressed Grenadian immigrants, mostly from urban areas in Grenada and presently employed in white collar jobs in New York, gathered in a Grenadian-owned catering hall in Brooklyn to hear the Grenadian Minister of Agriculture and Development. The Minister shared with Grenada's "constituency in New York" his plans for agricultural development in Grenada and encouraged them to become part of this effort.

By being addressed and acting as Grenadian nationals, these immigrants were resisting incorporation into the bottom of the racial order in the United States that categorizes them as "black," much as Haitians do when they construct hometown associations or meet as members of the Haitian diaspora to discuss the situation in Haiti.

By having their views elicited by a government minister 10
from home, the Grenadians were exercising a status as Grenadian leaders, a social status generally unavailable to them in the racially stratified environment of New York. Their perceptions of themselves as Grenadian "leaders" were further activated by the minister's suggestion that these migrants have the power to convince their relatives at home that agricultural work, generally demeaned as a productive activity, is worthwhile and important.

But the Minister was also addressing the migrants as Grenadian ethnics in New York when he asked them to try to assist in introducing Grenadian agricultural goods to the United States market by using their connections in New York within the fledgling Caribbean American Chamber of Commerce to which many of them belonged. And of particular significance, the organizers of this meeting, who had each been in the United States a minimum of ten years, were as involved in the local politics of New York City as in Grenada. In fact, they were able to transfer—and build on—the political capital they gained in New York to Grenada, and vice versa. Grenada's ambassador to the United Nations has been a leader in the New York Caribbean community for 20 years. And so often did these political actors travel between Grenada and New York, that it became difficult for the anthropologist to recall where she had last seen them.

Well-established Filipino migrants are also periodically visited by representatives of the Philippines government urging transnational activities including strong encouragement to reinvest their American earnings into Philippine agriculture. The role of the Philippines state in contributing to the construction of transnational migrant fields extends even further.

At a desk, an employee was helping a customer close her box and complete the listing of items it contains. We were in the offices of a company in New Jersey (the only company where boxes can be delivered directly to the warehouse rather than being picked up for delivery). A regular flow of such boxes leaves every day from seven to eight major Filipino shipping companies. Anything can be sent back door-to-door and with limited taxes—appliances, electronic equipment and the like—as long as it fits the weight and size prescriptions defining a *Balikbayan* box.

President Marcos had created the term *balikbayan* (literally homecomers) during a major national speech encouraging immigrants to visit their home country once a year during the holidays. He developed economic and legal means to facilitate their return and allowed each of them to bring yearly two *Balikbayan* boxes duty-free. Mrs. Aquino restated her concern for the numerous silent "heroes and heroines of the Philippines." She then enabled them to purchase gifts of up to $1,000 duty-free upon entering the Philippines. Contracting for overseas labor and the system of sending remittances, so very important now for the country's economy, has been similarly institutionalized. The existence of transnational migration is thus officially sanctioned and highly regulated by the Philippine state.

15 We thus see how the transnational social field is in part composed of family ties sustained through economic disbursements and gifts. At the same time this field is sustained by a system of legalized exchanges, structured and officially sanctioned by the Philippine state.

As these examples show, transnational migrants arrive in their new country of residence with certain practices and concepts constructed at home. They belong to certain more or less politicized populations and hold particular class affiliations. They then engage in complex activities across national borders that create, shape and potentially transform their identities. . . . This is not to say that this phenomenon has not been observed by others. However, an adequate framework for understanding this phenomenon or its implications has yet to be constructed. Building on our own research with transmigrants from Haiti, the English-speaking Caribbean, and the Philippines[2] as well as the earlier observations of others, we seek in this paper to develop such a framework.

Questions about the Passage

1. Why do the authors call their opening examples "vignettes"? Is using narratives in this way an effective writing tactic?
2. In paragraph 1, how do the authors distinguish between immigrants and migrants? What definition of "transmigrants" is given in paragraph 2?
3. Compare and contrast the Haitian group meeting on Long Island (paragraphs 4–6) and hometown associations of earlier immigrants (paragraph 7).
4. What do the Grenadian migrants gain by being addressed by the Grenadian Minister of Agriculture (paragraphs 8–11)?
5. What are *Balikbayan* boxes? Of what benefit are they to both the Philippines and Filipino migrants (paragraphs 12–15)?
6. Think back over the Alba article and the Portes/Rumbaut selection. How do the immigrants they describe differ from the transmigrants described here? Look back at the narratives told or written by immigrants. Do any of these immigrants share some of the characteristics of transmigrants?

Questions about the Argument

1. These authors have been trained as anthropologists rather than sociologists. How do the two disciplines differ? Do you think their approach to their material differs from that of Alba or Portes/Rumbaut?

2. A fuller development of the themes in this article can be found in our book, *Rethinking Migration, Ethnicity, Race, and Nationalism in Transnational Perspective* (Basch, Glick Schiller, and Blanc-Szanton, forthcoming). See also Glick Schiller and Fouron (1990) and Basch et al. (forthcoming).

2. What kind of audience is likely to read the annals of the New York Academy of Sciences? Try examining the table of contents of several volumes to determine the answer, paying particular attention to topics and authors.
3. Do all three vignettes that the authors provide support their assertion that these migrants are "part of a social system whose networks are based in two or more nation states and who maintain activities, identities and statuses in several social locations" (paragraph 7)?
4. In paragraph 9, the authors claim, "Being addressed and acting as Grenadian nationals, these immigrants were resisting incorporation into the bottom of the racial order in the United States that characterizes them as 'black' . . . ." After reading paragraphs 8–11 carefully, explain what the authors mean. Is the claim warranted by the example?
5. Is the claim made in paragraph 15 a valid conclusion from the Filipino vignette? Does the claim in paragraph 16 derive logically from all three vignettes? Which kind of logical thinking is being used?
6. Do you think studies of transnationalism such as this can be used to bolster a claim for or against restricting immigration? Why or why not?

Writing Assignments

Conversations

1. Imagine a panel discussion among the immigrants whose narratives we read in this chapter. The discussion should be led by Mukherjee, who asks if the immigrants see themselves as immigrants or expatriates. How do they categorize themselves? How might Mira, Mukerjee's sister, respond to this discussion? Do any of the immigrants see themselves returning to their countries of origin? To what degree have they had to—or wanted to—abandon elements of their ethnic heritage?
2. Having read Alba, Portes and Rumbaut, and Schiller, Basch, and Blanc-Szanton, you have the opportunity to join them in an online chatroom. Because this is a chatroom, discussion is fairly informal but respectful. What questions do you ask these writers? How do they respond? How do they interact with each other?

3. At the end of a conference on immigration, the theorists we have read in this chapter get together informally to discuss their ideas. Record their questions and answers. Consider, for example, a question from the assimilationists and segmented assimilationists to the transnationalists: What do you think will happen in the second and third generations to new immigrants of today? A question from the transnationlists might be: What does your theory say about people who do not succeed in the the assimilation task?
4. Choose an immigrant from either Chapter 4 or Chapter 5. What would that person say to the theorists of immigration? What would the immigrant find they got right? Got wrong? How would the theorists respond?

Writing Sequence One: Constructing an Oral History

1. In a short paper, examine the pros and cons of using each of the following forms of immigrant narrative drawn from the examples in the book: letters, memoir, autobiography (entire life story), transcription with editing of stories, oral history, and anthropologists' vignettes. You may also include "Maria's Story" and "Carmen's Story" in Chapter 6, which are oral histories with interpretation.
2. Take an oral history of an immigrant—a family member, friend, or other person your instructor may help you locate. You might also work in teams of two or even three to conduct interviews. Here is a general outline of the oral history process:
   a. Formulate your question(s) or issue(s) in class, either in your interview teams, in small groups, or as a class. What sorts of information do you wish to know? Interview questions need to be open (not closed, yes/no questions). For example, ask what the person's childhood was like, not whether it was a happy childhood.
   b. Select your interviewee. Try to connect before the interviewing process begins either in person, via telephone or email, or, if need be, by letter. Schedule your interview and confirm it a day or so in advance.
   c. Conduct background research about the interviewee's era, home country, and so on.
   d. Prepare interview questions, a life history form on which to record basic information such as date and place of birth, and a

release form (giving you permission to use the information you receive). Check equipment (audio tape or video recorder, tapes, extension cords).

e. Conduct the interview (perhaps one student asks questions; another the operates tape recorder and takes notes).

f. As soon as possible after the interview, write up the interview. Be sure to label tapes and other materials, such as photographs or letters, you receive from the interviewee.

g. Decide on follow-up questions and conduct additional interviews if needed and if time allows.

3. Write the interview up in the narrative form you prefer. You may choose any of the forms you explored in question 1. If your class has an electronic space, post your papers for others to read, comment on, and draw conclusions from. See Research Topics in Appendix A for more uses of this database. You may also make short in-class presentations of your oral histories.
4. Write one to two pages explaining and defending your choice of narrative form for your oral history.

Writing Sequence Two: Choosing an Immigration Theory

1. Summarize the three models found in this chapter (assimilation, segmented assimilation, and transnationalism), highlighting their strengths and weaknesses.
2. Locate at least two immigrant narratives that illustrate or exemplify each model. You may use the same narrative to illustrate more than one model. You may also use your own oral history narrative written for Writing Sequence One or others written by your classmates. Briefly explain how each narrative illustrates the model.
3. Choose the immigration model that you find most convincing. Make a case for your choice as the best model of what happens to immigrants after they arrive in the United States. Use immigrant narratives to support your claim. You may use any narratives appearing in the book as well as your own or other students' oral histories.

CHAPTER

6

From Argument to Public Policy: The Case of Hispanic Immigration

We end this casebook with a hot button topic, Hispanic immigration, that should recall earlier periods of American history where immigration issues—for example, which ethnic groups should be allowed to enter the United States, in what numbers, and under what conditions—have been similarly controversial.

Our central text is "The Hispanic Challenge," first appearing in *Foreign Policy* (March/April 2004), in which Samuel P. Huntington urges us to embark upon a national debate about this issue. He warns that "continuation of this large immigration (without improved assimilation) could divide the United States into a country of two languages and two cultures." He admonishes: "Americans should not let that change happen unless they are convinced that this new nation would be a better one."

Immediate responses to this piece and to the subsequent publication of the book from which it was taken, *Who Are We? The Challenges of America's National Identity* (2004), have been generally, though not entirely, negative, and we have included a sampling of these responses. This is a debate in which we can all engage, and, as Huntington reminds us in his reply to his critics (*Foreign Policy*, May/June 2004), it should be possible to have it without acrimony, keeping in mind that "the last refuge of those unable to make reasoned arguments based on facts and logic is to resort to slander and name-calling."

One form of contribution to the conversation about Hispanic immigration is visual. The issue of *Foreign Policy* in which Huntington's essay appears features a photograph of a young man, apparently Hispanic, with his hand over his heart. The photo's caption reads: "José, Can You See?" Magazine covers are meant to sell the issue, so we may legitimately ask what audience is being courted and what message is being sent. Another take on the issue of Hispanic immigrant life is found in the Lalo Alcaraz cartoon we reprint in this chapter; we may ask here how caricature and stereotypes can be used to convey a particular idea.

Just as we have threaded immigrant narratives throughout this casebook, we have also continued the practice in this chapter. We cannot claim to have included stories of every immigrant group coming to America, nor do we claim that these stories of second-generation Mexican American college students are representative, but they do remind us that the Hispanics whom Huntington sees as a "challenge" are not only a group, but also individuals.

Alma M. Garcia, "María's Story" and "Carmen's Story"

Alma M. Garcia received a B.A. at the University of Texas, El Paso, in 1974 and an M.A. (1978) and Ph.D. (1982) at Harvard. She is a professor of sociology at Santa Clara University, where she directed the women and gender studies program from 1990 to 1996. She is the author of five books, including *Chicana Feminist Thought: The Basic Historical Writings* (1997) and *The Mexican Americans* (2002). In her book, *Narratives of Mexican American Women: Emergent Identities of the Second Generation* (2004), she identifies herself in the preface as a "university professor, daughter of a Mexican immigrant father, and a second-generation Mexican American mother" (xi), whose own life closely parallels those whose stories she tells. Noting that a relatively small percentage of second-generation Mexican American women are likely to attend and complete college, she argues that studies such as hers may help to identify factors that reduce college attendance and to develop policies that will help such students remain in school. The stories that follow reflect the research questions on which she has based her study:

> How is the ethnic identity of second-generation Mexican American women shaped by the experiences of their Mexican immigrant parents?

How does the second generation navigate through the worlds of its immigrant parents, the university setting, and the larger American society?

What meanings do the second generation attach to their ethnicity, and what kinds of ethnic group boundaries do they negotiate?

How does ethnic identity emerge over time for second-generation individuals?

How do gender and social class shape these emergent identities?

In general, how does this second generation recreate and reinvent their ethnic identities? (xi)

Garcia collected the stories used throughout her book from juniors and seniors attending Santa Clara. She describes her interviewing techniques as "semi-structured." As presented in her text, the stories consist of sections quoted verbatim from the taped interview, as well as summaries and her own interpolations.

María's Story

María's parents left their home in Guadalajara to join their relatives, neighbors, and many others who had already made the journey to *El Norte*: the United States. Although her parents did not have any immigration documents, they knew that they would be able to cross La Frontera at Tijuana, Mexico, with the help of their cousins who would be waiting for them, ready to take them to their home in east Los Angeles. Her parents eventually settled into a daily routine, one followed by thousands of immigrants who leave Mexico for a life in the United States in search of the often elusive American Dream. Her father had very little formal education and had worked as part of a construction crew in Mexico, which required him to leave his home to travel to various nearby towns where buildings and roads were being built. Once in the United States, he joined his cousin on a crew that worked for a more established Mexican immigrant who, after about ten years, had started his own gardening business. The two cousins found themselves working side by side, leaving east Los Angeles every morning to tend the yards in the surrounding Los Angeles neighborhoods. María's mother had even less formal education than her husband. She had never worked in the paid labor force in Mexico, and now, in the United States, she continued her traditional role of wife and mother, eventually raising her three American-born daughters.

María says that she remembers her parents telling their story. Even now, at family gatherings, some eighteen years since her parents left Mexico, María tells of how proudly her father recounts their family story, a story that he says is a testimony to what he set out to accomplish the day that he and María's mother left Mexico, crossed the border, and started what they dreamed would be a new life in the United States. After only a year working as a gardener's assistant, María's father and his cousin decided to combine their efforts, save whatever money they could, and go into business for themselves. "My father used to say something like 'I didn't come here [the United States] to work and work and have someone else get most of the money. I wanted more for my children.'" María recounts her father's story of working extra hours, saving as much money as possible, and continuing to live in a crowded, rented house with his cousin's family. Then, a few years later and after he had become an American citizen, his boss told him that he was retiring and wanted to sell the business. He was willing to sell it to him for a small down payment with the balance to be paid over time. This is how María's father became a co-owner of a small gardening business with a long-standing clientele. María says that during her childhood she did not see much of her father; he left early in the morning and took on extra jobs such as painting houses or putting in floors several evenings a week. "I felt like I had only one parent and I felt bad. My mother would tell me that my father had to do this because he wanted more for us. She quickly added that she wanted more for us too." María admits that she sometimes did get tired of hearing the same story over and over again, especially when she was in junior high school:

> But you know, one day we had to do a project for our English class. We were supposed to write a family history. I just wrote down what my father always used to tell us. The day we had to read our stories I felt proud of what my parents had done. I was a little embarrassed at all those times I just didn't want to hear it again.

María soon became interested in her family's history and, given her father's long hours away from home, she began to ask her mother for more information. Her mother's stories paralleled those of her father but eventually took on new dimensions. Her mother spoke of her worries about coming to the United States and raising a family in a place so far from Mexico. Even though she wanted to make a better life for her children, she still worried:

> My mom would tell us that she had heard that "Mexicanos" had problems in the United States. One of her cousins had returned from the United States with a lot of money but had told her that her that life was hard and some people didn't like Mexicans. Her cousin came back home to Mexico. But my mom said that she knew she didn't want to go back. She wanted us to have more things. I guess she meant a better chance to live better. So my mom would say that she put these things, well, behind her and decided to "hacerle la lucha" [take on the struggle] in the United States.

María's mother knew that she and her husband would never go back to Mexico; they were here to stay but they were "Mexicanos." María relates that her family life was indeed a "Mexican" one with all the visible sources of material Mexican culture. Although her parents were able to speak English, they always preferred Spanish. The neighborhood store, El Mercado Mexicano (The Mexican Market), supplied the family kitchen with all the essential ingredients for her mother to maintain "un cocina Mexicana" (a Mexican kitchen). Although María never really liked this Mexican music, her parents, during those rare moments when they were together and able to relax, listened to their favorite Mexican radio station that played "corridos" (Mexican ballads): "They would look sad and I would think that they were really wishing they were back in their home town in Mexico." María remembers that her mother never forgot that she was an immigrant, but she always stressed the importance of her children being American citizens. For María's mother, the family's cultural heritage would always remain Mexican, but her children would move beyond this experience. The life of her second-generation daughter would be different, but her Mexican heritage would shape her ethnic identity. María recalls pensively:

> It took me a long time to figure it out. Now that I am in college and taken some sociology and history classes, I am seeing that my parents wanted us to move beyond them like upward to achieve more.

> I left home to come here [to college], and I keep hearing my family's story in my head. Sometimes it's hard here, so alone, but then it helps to remember how my parents wanted so much for me.

When asked what her parents would want her to remember as long as she lived, María did not hesitate. She said that they would want her to "hacerle la lucha" (take on the struggle) and be proud of her family's story—one of hardship, endurance, and perseverance.

Carmen's Story

Although María's . . . and Carmen's parents [both] left Mexico at about the same time, Carmen's family's immigrant experiences were shaped by their different social class background and, perhaps more importantly, the social class experiences of their relatives who had been living in the United States for almost fifteen years. Carmen's parents lived in the same town as Sonia's parents, but their daily lives were very far removed from the majority of Mexicans who eventually made the trip to the United States. Her parents experienced the same deteriorating economic circumstances that plagued Mexico, but their social class status provided them with some cushion from Mexico's poor economy and, eventually, a distinct context for their immigrant experiences. Carmen's father came from a family of small business owners in their hometown in Michoacán. As owners of a small restaurant and a Mom-and-Pop neighborhood store, Carmen's paternal grandparents had been able to protect themselves from Mexico's economic problems. As entrepreneurs, Carmen's grandparents had secured sufficient capital to purchase a small parcel of land on which they built a modest house, the home in which Carmen's father spent his childhood with his brothers and sisters. Their economic circumstances not only allowed them to weather Mexico's fluctuating economy but also provided them with the financial resources to send their children to a private school. Carmen's father, the eldest child, completed his primary and secondary education and, after his first year in a nearby business school, decided to visit his paternal uncle in the United States.

His uncle had been living in the San Francisco Bay area for over ten years, during which time he started a small, neighborhood Mexican grocery store, established with the savings he brought with him from Mexico. His customers were primarily Mexican immigrants and Mexican Americans living in the surrounding neighborhood. He carried the local Spanish-language newspapers, sold some grocery staples (such as large bags of rice, beans, and flour), and, as a favor to many of his regular customers, allowed them to take incoming calls from Mexico. Carmen's father had intended to visit for only one month, returning to Mexico to finish business school, and then, upon his graduation, marry his longtime hometown girlfriend. This family story took a dramatically different, but not altogether unwelcome, turn. According to Carmen:

> My dad tells it like this. He liked his life in Mexico. I guess he thought he would take over his dad's business and raise a family like that. But he says he liked what he saw here. His uncle's store was really popular and he started telling my dad that he wanted to start another one, but sort of closer to downtown. I guess they just started talking and anyway my dad tells us that's how he decided to come over here after he got married to my mom. He worked and got the other place ready and then was in charge.

Carmen's family joined a community of Mexicans living in the United States whose lives would be affected collectively by immigration experiences of the mid-twentieth century but whose particular, and mostly uncommon, relative social class advantages differentiated them from the majority of Mexican families trying to "hacerle la lucha" in the United States.

Carmen says that her father and uncle became quite successful over the years. She was born two years after her parents settled in San Jose, California, and her brother was born three years later. Her mother, who had graduated from secondary school in Mexico, stayed home and raised the children, but once they started elementary school, she began to work in the family store. She remembers the day that they moved into a small house close to the downtown area, near Japan Town, where she and her family continue to live. Although Carmen's father had attended a private school in Mexico, he enrolled his children in the local public school until a dramatic turn of events unfolded. As their grocery store continued to flourish, Carmen's parents hired regular wageworkers; her mother spent less and less time at the store and, instead, became active in her children's school activities:

> My mom started going to the school meetings, and, when I started playing volleyball, she even helped at some fundraising things, and she brought food from our restaurant. It sold out. I guess I never really thought about it back then. She didn't speak too much English but neither did my friends' moms. They all got along. My brother and I used both English and Spanish, but all day we talked in English and with our friends, too.

Carmen does not remember the exact circumstances herself but recalls her mother's version of the event that would alter Carmen's early educational experience. Her mother told her that some of the parents heard that a certain teacher had been making remarks about "all those illegals" living in San Jose. Some children had also told their parents that some of the Anglo American children had called them names. The parents never heard the teacher make these remarks but relied on the words of other teachers and some students. Although many complained and asked for some kind of explanation, many eventually forgot the issue, but not, as it turns out, Carmen's parents.

> My dad was really upset. He kept saying that he worked just as hard as anybody. He was legal; his kids were born here. I guess he started looking around, and he told me that some of his regular customers told him that our school was getting a bad reputation and that he should look around and maybe put us in a Catholic school. He says that they told him their kids were there and they could tell right away that everything was better there.

Carmen's parents had the financial ability to move their daughters to a private Catholic school, an option limited to only very few Mexican immigrants. In order to meet these new expenses, Carmen's mother took on a job working at a day care center. She also did a little private catering for weddings and baptisms.

> My mom was always figuring out some new ways to make extra money. Once she even went to work at the cannery for about a month in the night shift. But she hated it and quit. My dad was working long hours at the grocery store, but she always tried to be around when we got home from school.

For Carmen's parents, life in the United States represented a 5
dramatic change. Although they had worked hard to make

their grocery store a success, the work responsibilities fell primarily on Carmen's father. Small business ownership brought a certain degree of economic stability. Their decision to open a restaurant in the downtown area provided them with an even deeper economic cushion; they gained a steady clientele of professionals and office workers, most of whom were not Mexican. Still, the high costs of tuition pushed Carmen's parents to work harder at the family businesses. Perhaps more importantly, Carmen's mother quickly diverted her energies as a school volunteer and designed several business enterprises of her own.

> My mom was so hyper all the time. She would be finishing one catering job and then be on the phone making other contacts. Once she wanted to go back to Mexico for a visit and bring back all sorts of things to sell to people, you know like party favors for Quinceañeras. But my dad said she could get in trouble sneaking them over here. Then she started to work on her English. She would try to read the paper and then give up and ask me to help. One summer she took a night class at the community center.

Carmen's parents settled into their world of work and family in the United States with a trip back to Mexico every two years or so, more often if one of their parents became ill. For them, life was hard in the United States, but, as Carmen remembers, the prize was "una vida mejor para nuestras hijas" (a better life for our daughters). Their dreams were the dreams of other immigrant parents who hoped that their children—the second generation—would move closer to the American Dream. María . . . , Carmen, and all the other Mexican American women in this study are daughters of Mexican immigrants living in the United States. As second-generation children, these women have lived in the cultural worlds of their parents and that of the larger American society, a multicultural society whose increased diversity stands as a challenge to these and other children of immigrants. The most recent scholarship on the second generation, however, has challenged the traditional assimilationist model of immigrant adaptation, replacing it with alternative perspectives that can be used to explain various dimensions of both the immigrant and the second generations, including the social construction of their ethnic identities.

Questions about the Passages

1. Specifically, what answers does each story provide to the questions Garcia poses in her preface? In the course of these interviews, is there any direct evidence that Garcia has asked these questions of her interviewees?
2. Compare the two accounts. In each story, how important are the factors of class and income, attitudes towards education, speaking English, and becoming Americans? What other factors or attitudes do you find important in these stories? Which, if any, are predictors of success in college?

Questions about the Argument

1. The stories themselves may not be arguments. Do you think their placement at the start of Garcia's book makes them part of an argument? If so, how might they contribute to or help form an argument?
2. Who do you think is the likely audience for this book? Is Garcia's story-based technique an effective way of appealing to that audience?
3. Once you have read Huntington's article, which follows in this chapter, consider how the material in these stories might either support or undermine his argument.

Samuel P. Huntington, "The Hispanic Challenge"

Samuel P. Huntington (1927–) received a B.A. from Yale, an M.A. from the University of Chicago, and a Ph.D. from Harvard. His early book, *The Soldier and the State* (1957), which argues for the importance of the military in a liberal democracy, disturbed his colleagues and cost him tenure at Harvard. After a four-year stint at Columbia, Huntington was invited back to Harvard and given tenure there. He is currently the Albert J. Weatherhead III University Professor at Harvard. A lifelong Democrat, he has written speeches for Adlai Stevenson and Jimmy Carter, advised Herbert Humphrey on foreign policy, and served at the White House from 1977–78 as Coordinator for Security Planning for the National Security Council. On the academic side, he founded the Olin Institute of Strategic Studies at Harvard, co-founded *Foreign Policy* magazine, and served as president of the American Political Science Association.

Huntington's credentials have not spared him from controversy. His 1996 book, *The Clash of Civilizations*, raised the specter of a collision between eastern and western thought, based on a clash of cultures. His critical view of Islam engendered considerable negative response to his assertions. His most recent book, *Who Are We? The Challenges of America's National Identity* (2004), is well on its way towards raising the hackles of many readers. "The Hispanic Challenge," a chapter from this book first published in *Foreign Policy*, has also provoked immediate criticism. We follow this article with several representative responses. You can decide for yourself whether the critics fairly judge Huntington's argument.

America was created by 17th- and 18th-century settlers who were overwhelmingly white, British, and Protestant. Their values, institutions, and culture provided the foundation for and shaped the development of the United States in the following centuries. They initially defined America in terms of race, ethnicity, culture, and religion. Then, in the 18th century, they also had to define America ideologically to justify independence from their home country, which was also white, British, and Protestant. Thomas Jefferson set forth this "creed," as Nobel Prize-winning economist Gunnar Myrdal called it, in the Declaration of Independence, and ever since, its principles have been reiterated by statesmen and espoused by the public as an essential component of U.S. identity.

By the latter years of the 19th century, however, the ethnic component had been broadened to include Germans, Irish, and Scandinavians, and the United States' religious identity was being redefined more broadly from Protestant to Christian. With World War II and the assimilation of large numbers of southern and eastern European immigrants and their offspring into U.S. society, ethnicity virtually disappeared as a defining component of national identity. So did race, following the achievements of the civil rights movement and the Immigration and Nationality Act of 1965. Americans now see and endorse their country as multiethnic and multiracial. As a result, American identity is now defined in terms of culture and creed.

Most Americans see the creed as the crucial element of their national identity. The creed, however, was the product of the distinct Anglo-Protestant culture of the founding settlers. Key elements of that culture include the English language; Christianity; religious commitment; English concepts of the rule of law, including the responsibility of rulers and the rights of individuals; and dissenting Protestant values of individualism, the work ethic, and the belief that humans have the ability and the duty to try to create a heaven on earth, a "city on a hill." Historically, millions of immigrants were attracted to the United States because of this culture and the economic opportunities and political liberties it made possible.

Contributions from immigrant cultures modified and enriched the Anglo-Protestant culture of the founding settlers. The essentials of that founding culture remained the bedrock of U.S. identity, however, at least until the last decades of the 20th century. Would the United States be the country that it has been and that it largely remains today if it had been settled in the 17th and 18th centuries not by British Protestants but by French, Spanish, or Portuguese Catholics? The answer is clearly no. It would not be the United States; it would be Quebec, Mexico, or Brazil.

In the final decades of the 20th century, however, the United 5
States' Anglo-Protestant culture and the creed that it produced came under assault by the popularity in intellectual and political circles of the doctrines of multiculturalism and diversity; the rise of group identities based on race, ethnicity, and gender over national identity; the impact of transnational cultural diasporas; the expanding number of immigrants with dual nationalities and dual loyalties; and the growing salience for U.S. intellectual, business, and political elites of cosmopolitan and transnational identities. The United States' national identity, like that of other nation-states, is challenged by the forces of globalization as well as the needs that globalization produces among people for smaller and more meaningful "blood and belief" identities.

In this new era, the single most immediate and most serious challenge to America's traditional identity comes from the immense and continuing immigration from Latin America, especially from Mexico, and the fertility rates of these immigrants compared to black and white American natives. Americans like to boast of their past success in assimilating millions of immigrants into their society, culture, and politics. But Americans have tended to generalize about immigrants without distinguishing among them and have focused on the economic costs and benefits of immigration, ignoring its social and cultural consequences. As a result, they have overlooked the unique characteristics and problems posed by contemporary Hispanic immigration. The extent and nature of this immigration differ fundamentally from those of previous immigration, and the assimilation successes of the past are unlikely to be duplicated with the contemporary flood of immigrants from Latin America. This reality poses a fundamental question: Will the United States remain a country with a single national language and a core Anglo-Protestant culture? By ignoring this question, Americans acquiesce to their eventual transformation into two peoples with two cultures (Anglo and Hispanic) and two languages (English and Spanish).

The impact of Mexican immigration on the United States becomes evident when one imagines what would happen if Mexican immigration abruptly stopped. The annual flow of legal immigrants would drop by about 175,000, closer to the level recommended by the 1990s Commission on Immigration Reform chaired by former U.S. Congresswoman Barbara Jordan. Illegal entries would diminish dramatically. The wages of low-income U.S. citizens would improve. Debates over the use of Spanish and whether English should be made the official language of state and national governments would subside. Bilingual education and the controversies it spawns would virtually disappear, as would controversies over welfare and other benefits for immigrants. The debate over whether immigrants pose an economic burden on state and federal governments would be decisively resolved in the negative. The average education and skills of the immigrants continuing to arrive would reach their highest levels in U.S. history. The inflow of immigrants would again become highly diverse, creating increased incentives for all immigrants to learn English and absorb U.S. culture. And most important of all, the possibility of a de facto split between a predominantly Spanish-speaking United States and an English-speaking United States would disappear, and with it, a major potential threat to the country's cultural and political integrity.

A World of Difference

Contemporary Mexican and, more broadly, Latin American immigration is without precedent in U.S. history. The experience and lessons of past immigration have little relevance to understanding its dynamics and consequences. Mexican immigration differs from past immigration and most other contemporary immigration due to a combination of six factors: contiguity, scale, illegality, regional concentration, persistence, and historical presence.

Contiguity Americans' idea of immigration is often symbolized by the Statue of Liberty, Ellis Island, and, more recently perhaps, New York's John F. Kennedy Airport. In other words, immigrants arrive in the United States after crossing several thousand miles of ocean. U.S. attitudes toward immigrants and U.S. immigration policies are shaped by such images. These assumptions and policies, however, have little or no relevance for Mexican immigration. The United States is now confronted by a massive influx of people from a poor, contiguous country with more than one third the population of the United States. They come across a 2,000-mile border historically marked simply by a line in the ground and a shallow river.

This situation is unique for the United States and the world. 10
No other First World country has such an extensive land frontier with a Third World country. The significance of the long Mexican-U.S. border is enhanced by the economic differences between the two countries. "The income gap between the United States and Mexico," Stanford University historian David Kennedy has pointed out, "is the largest between any two contiguous countries in the world." Contiguity enables Mexican immigrants to remain in intimate contact with their families, friends, and home localities in Mexico as no other immigrants have been able to do.

Scale The causes of Mexican, as well as other, immigration are found in the demographic, economic, and political dynamics of the sending country and the economic, political, and social attractions of the United States. Contiguity, however, obviously encourages immigration. Mexican immigration increased steadily after 1965. About 640,000 Mexicans legally migrated to the United States in the 1970s; 1,656,000 in the 1980s; and 2,249,000 in the 1990s. In those three decades, Mexicans accounted for 14 percent, 23 percent, and 25 percent of total legal immigration. These percentages do not equal the

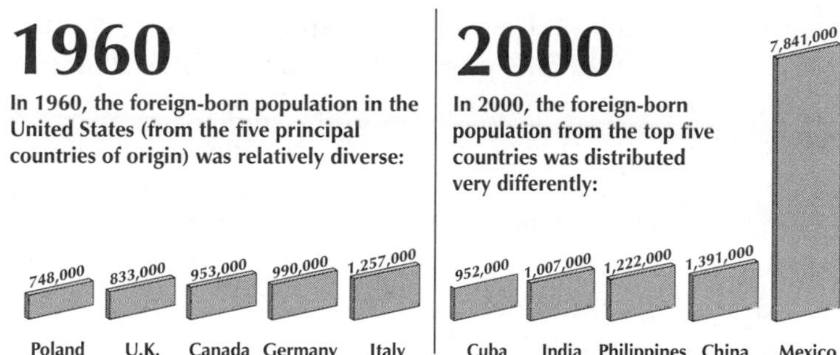

Figure 6-1: *From Diversity to Dominance: Foreign-Born Population Living in the United States*

Sources: Campbell J. Gibson and Emily Lennon's "Historical Census Studies on the Foreign Born Population of the United States 1850-1990" (Population Division Working Paper No. 29. U.S. Census Bureau, February 1999); and "Profile of the Foreign-Born Population in the United States: 2000" (Washington: U.S. Census Bureau, Current Population Reports, Series p.23-206, 2001).

rates of immigrants who came from Ireland between 1820 and 1860, or from Germany in the 1850s and 1860s. Yet they are high compared to the highly dispersed sources of immigrants before World War I, and compared to other contemporary immigrants. To them one must also add the huge numbers of Mexicans who each year enter the United States illegally. Since the 1960s, the numbers of foreign-born people in the United States have expanded immensely, with Asians and Latin Americans replacing Europeans and Canadians, and diversity of source dramatically giving way to the dominance of one source: Mexico. (See Figure 6-1.) Mexican immigrants constituted 27.6 percent of the total foreign-born U.S. population in 2000. The next largest contingents, Chinese and Filipinos, amounted to only 4.9 percent and 4.3 percent of the foreign-born population.

In the 1990s, Mexicans composed more than half of the new Latin American immigrants to the United States and, by 2000, Hispanics totaled about one half of all migrants entering the continental United States. Hispanics composed 12 percent of the total U.S. population in 2000. This group increased by almost 10 percent from 2000 to 2002 and has now become larger than blacks. It is estimated Hispanics may constitute up to 25 percent of the U.S. population by 2050. These changes are driven not just by immigration but also by fertility. In 2002, fertility rates in the United States were estimated at 1.8 for non-Hispanic whites, 2.1 for blacks, and 3.0 for Hispanics. "This is the characteristic shape of developing countries," *The Economist* commented in 2002. "As the bulge of Latinos enters peak child-bearing age in a decade or two, the Latino share of America's population will soar."

In the mid-19th century, English speakers from the British Isles dominated immigration into the United States. The pre-World War I immigration was highly diversified linguistically, including many speakers of Italian, Polish, Russian, Yiddish, English, German, Swedish, and other languages. But now, for the first time in U.S. history, half of those entering the United States speak a single non-English language.

Illegality Illegal entry into the United States is overwhelmingly a post-1965 and Mexican phenomenon. For almost a century after the adoption of the U.S. Constitution, no national laws restricted or prohibited immigration, and only a few states imposed modest limits. During the following 90 years, illegal immigration was minimal and easily controlled. The 1965 immigration law, the increased availability of transportation, and the intensified forces promoting Mexican emigration drastically changed this situation. Apprehensions by the U.S. Border Patrol rose from 1.6 million in the 1960s to 8.3 million in the 1970s, 11.9 million in the 1980s, and 14.7 million in the 1990s. Estimates of the Mexicans who successfully enter illegally each year range from 105,000 (according to a binational Mexican-American commission) to 350,000 during the 1990s (according to the U.S. Immigration and Naturalization Service).

The 1986 Immigration Reform and Control Act contained 15
provisions to legalize the status of existing illegal immigrants and to reduce future illegal immigration through employer sanctions and other means. The former goal was achieved: Some 3.1 million illegal immigrants, about 90 percent of them from Mexico, became legal "green card" residents of the United States. But the latter goal remains elusive. Estimates of the total number of illegal immigrants in the United States rose from 4 million in 1995 to 6 million in 1998, to 7 million in 2000,

and to between 8 and 10 million by 2003. Mexicans accounted for 58 percent of the total illegal population in the United States in 1990; by 2000, an estimated 4.8 million illegal Mexicans made up 69 percent of that population. In 2000, illegal Mexicans in the United States were 25 times as numerous as the next largest contingent, from El Salvador.

Regional Concentration The U.S. Founding Fathers considered the dispersion of immigrants essential to their assimilation. That has been the pattern historically and continues to be the pattern for most contemporary non-Hispanic immigrants. Hispanics, however, have tended to concentrate regionally: Mexicans in Southern California, Cubans in Miami, Dominicans and Puerto Ricans (the last of whom are not technically immigrants) in New York. The more concentrated immigrants become, the slower and less complete is their assimilation.

In the 1990s, the proportions of Hispanics continued to grow in these regions of heaviest concentration. At the same time, Mexicans and other Hispanics were also establishing beachheads elsewhere. While the absolute numbers are often small, the states with the largest percentage increases in Hispanic population between 1990 and 2000 were, in decreasing order: North Carolina (449 percent increase), Arkansas, Georgia, Tennessee, South Carolina, Nevada, and Alabama (222 percent). Hispanics have also established concentrations in individual cities and towns throughout the United States. For example, in 2003, more than 40 percent of the population of Hartford, Connecticut, was Hispanic (primarily Puerto Rican), outnumbering the city's 38 percent black population. "Hartford," the city's first Hispanic mayor proclaimed, "has become a Latin city, so to speak. It's a sign of things to come," with Spanish increasingly used as the language of commerce and government.

The biggest concentrations of Hispanics, however, are in the Southwest, particularly California. In 2000, nearly two thirds of Mexican immigrants lived in the West, and nearly half in California. To be sure, the Los Angeles area has immigrants from many countries, including Korea and Vietnam. The sources of California's foreign-born population, however, differ sharply from those of the rest of the country, with those from a single country, Mexico, exceeding totals for all of the immigrants from Europe and Asia. In Los Angeles,

Hispanics—overwhelmingly Mexican—far outnumber other groups. In 2000, 64 percent of the Hispanics in Los Angeles were of Mexican origin, and 46.5 percent of Los Angeles residents were Hispanic, while 29.7 percent were non-Hispanic whites. By 2010, it is estimated that Hispanics will make up more than half of the Los Angeles population.

Most immigrant groups have higher fertility rates than natives, and hence the impact of immigration is felt heavily in schools. The highly diversified immigration into New York, for example, creates the problem of teachers dealing with classes containing students who may speak 20 different languages at home. In contrast, Hispanic children make up substantial majorities of the students in the schools in many Southwestern cities. "No school system in a major U.S. city," political scientists Katrina Burgess and Abraham Lowenthal said of Los Angeles in their 1993 study of Mexico-California ties, "has ever experienced such a large influx of students from a single foreign country. The schools of Los Angeles are becoming Mexican." By 2002, more than 70 percent of the students in the Los Angeles Unified School District were Hispanic, predominantly Mexican, with the proportion increasing steadily; 10 percent of school-children were non-Hispanic whites. In 2003, for the first time since the 1850s, a majority of newborn children in California were Hispanic.

Persistence Previous waves of immigrants eventually sub- 20
sided, the proportions coming from individual countries fluctuated greatly, and, after 1924, immigration was reduced to a trickle. In contrast, the current wave shows no sign of ebbing and the conditions creating the large Mexican component of that wave are likely to endure, absent a major war or recession. In the long term, Mexican immigration could decline when the economic well-being of Mexico approximates that of the United States. As of 2002, however, U.S. gross domestic product per capita was about four times that of Mexico (in purchasing power parity terms). If that difference were cut in half, the economic incentives for migration might also drop substantially. To reach that ratio in any meaningful future, however, would require extremely rapid economic growth in Mexico, at a rate greatly exceeding that of the United States. Yet, even such dramatic economic development would not necessarily

reduce the impulse to emigrate. During the 19th century, when Europe was rapidly industrializing and per capita incomes were rising, 50 million Europeans emigrated to the Americas, Asia, and Africa.

Historical Presence No other immigrant group in U.S. history has asserted or could assert a historical claim to U.S. territory. Mexicans and Mexican Americans can and do make that claim. Almost all of Texas, New Mexico, Arizona, California, Nevada, and Utah was part of Mexico until Mexico lost them as a result of the Texan War of Independence in 1835–1836 and the Mexican-American War of 1846–1848. Mexico is the only country that the United States has invaded, occupied its capital—placing the Marines in the "halls of Montezuma"—and then annexed half its territory. Mexicans do not forget these events. Quite understandably, they feel that they have special rights in these territories. "Unlike other immigrants," Boston College political scientist Peter Skerry notes, "Mexicans arrive here from a neighboring nation that has suffered military defeat at the hands of the United States; and they settle predominantly in a region that was once part of their homeland. . . . Mexican Americans enjoy a sense of being on their own turf that is not shared by other immigrants."

At times, scholars have suggested that the Southwest could become the United States' Quebec. Both regions include Catholic people and were conquered by Anglo-Protestant peoples, but otherwise they have little in common. Quebec is 3,000 miles from France, and each year several hundred thousand Frenchmen do not attempt to enter Quebec legally or illegally. History shows that serious potential for conflict exists when people in one country begin referring to territory in a neighboring country in proprietary terms and to assert special rights and claims to that territory.

Spanglish As a Second Language

In the past, immigrants originated overseas and often overcame severe obstacles and hardships to reach the United States. They came from many different countries, spoke different languages, and came legally. Their flow fluctuated over time, with significant reductions occurring as a result of the Civil War, World War I, and the restrictive legislation of 1924.

They dispersed into many enclaves in rural areas and major cities throughout the Northeast and Midwest. They had no historical claim to any U.S. territory.

On all these dimensions, Mexican immigration is fundamentally different. These differences combine to make the assimilation of Mexicans into U.S. culture and society much more difficult than it was for previous immigrants. Particularly striking in contrast to previous immigrants is the failure of third- and fourth-generation people of Mexican origin to approximate U.S. norms in education, economic status, and inter-marriage rates. (See Figure 6-2.)

The size, persistence, and concentration of Hispanic immi- 25
gration tend to perpetuate the use of Spanish through successive generations. The evidence on English acquisition and Spanish retention among immigrants is limited and ambiguous. In 2000, however, more than 28 million people in the United States spoke Spanish at home (10.5 percent of all people over age five), and almost 13.8 million of these spoke English worse than "very well," a 66 percent increase since 1990. According to a U.S. Census Bureau report, in 1990 about 95 percent of Mexican-born immigrants spoke Spanish at home; 73.6 percent of these did not speak English very well; and 43 percent of the Mexican foreign-born were "linguistically isolated." An earlier study in Los Angeles found different results for the U.S.-born second generation. Just 11.6 percent spoke only Spanish or more Spanish than English, 25.6 percent spoke both languages equally, 32.7 percent more English than Spanish, and 30.1 percent only English. In the same study, more than 90 percent of the U.S.-born people of Mexican origin spoke English fluently. Nonetheless, in 1999, some 753,505 presumably second-generation students in Southern California schools who spoke Spanish at home were not proficient in English.

English language use and fluency for first- and second-generation Mexicans thus seem to follow the pattern common to past immigrants. Two questions remain, however. First, have changes occurred over time in the acquisition of English and the retention of Spanish by second-generation Mexican immigrants? One might suppose that, with the rapid expansion of the Mexican immigrant community, people of Mexican

Education

The education of people of Mexican origin in the United States lags well behind the U.S. norm. In 2000, 86.6 percent of native-born Americans had graduated from high school. The rates for the foreign-born population in the United States varied from 94.9 percent for Africans, 83.8 percent for Asians, 49.6 percent for Latin Americans overall, and down to 33.8 percent for Mexicans, who ranked lowest.

Education of Mexican Americans by Generation (1989–90)

	First	Second	Third	Fourth	All Americans*
No high school degree (%)	69.9	51.5	33.0	41.0	23.5
High school degree (%)	24.7	39.2	58.5	49.4	30.4
Post high school degree (%)	5.4	9.3	8.5	9.6	45.1

*Except Mexican Americans, 1990.

Source: Rodolfo O. De la Garza, Angelo Falcon, P. Chris García, and John García, "Mexican Immigrants, Mexican Americans, and American Political Culture," in Barry Edmonston and Jeffrey S. Passell (eds.), *Immigration and Ethnicity: The Integration of America's Newest Arrivals* (Washington: Urban Institute Press, 1994); and "Census of Population: Persons of Hispanic Origin in the United States" (Washington: U.S. Census Bureau, 1990).

Intermarriage

In 1977, 31 percent of all U.S. marriages involving Hispanics crossed ethnic lines, compared to only 25.5 percent in 1994 and 28.3 percent in 2000. As the absolute number of Mexican immigrants increases and their high birthrate produces more children, the opportunities for them to marry each other will increase.

Percentage of Asian and Hispanic Women Married Outside of Their Ethnic Group (1994)

	Asian	Hispanic
First Generation (%)	18.6	8.4
Second Generation (%)	29.2	26.4
Third Generation (%)	41.5	33.2

Source: Gregory Rodriguez, "From Newcomers to New Americans: The Successful Integration of Immigrants into American Society" (Washington: National Immigration Forum, 1990), citing "Current Population Survey, June 1994" (Washington: U.S. Census Bureau, 1994).

Economic Status

Mexican immigrants and Mexican Americans lag behind the rest of the nation and other immigrant groups on a variety of economic indicators, including managerial and professional occupations, home ownership, and household income.

Managerial/Professional Positions as a Percentage of Employed Members of Immigrant Groups (2000)

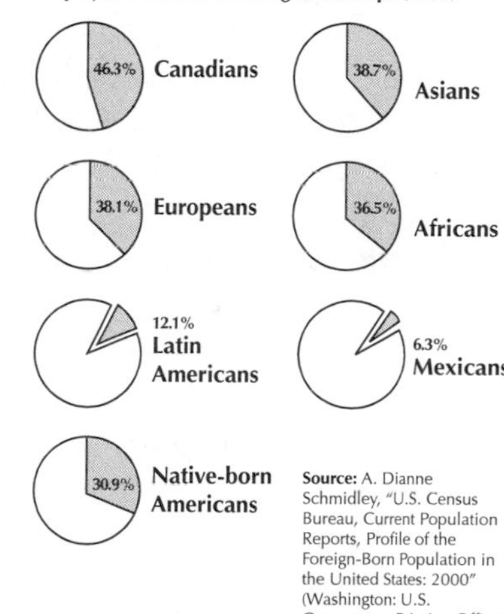

Source: A. Dianne Schmidley, "U.S. Census Bureau, Current Population Reports, Profile of the Foreign-Born Population in the United States: 2000" (Washington: U.S. Government Printing Office,

Home Ownership and Income of Mexican Americans, by Generation (1989–90)

	First	Second	Third	Fourth	All Americans*
Homeowner (%)	30.6	58.6	55.1	40.3	64.1*
Household Income of $50,000 or more (%)	7.1	10.5	11.2	10.7	24.8**

*1990, includes Mexican Americans.
**1990, excludes Mexican Americans.

Source: De la Garza, et al. (1994); "Current Population Survey, March 1990" (Washington: U.S. Census Bureau, 1990); and "Census of Population: Persons of Hispanic Origin in the United States," 1990.

Figure 6-2: *Failure to Assimilate.*

origin would have less incentive to become fluent in and to use English in 2000 than they had in 1970. Second, will the third generation follow the classic pattern with fluency in English and little or no knowledge of Spanish, or will it retain the second generation's fluency in both languages? Second-generation immigrants often look down on and reject their ancestral language and are embarrassed by their parents' inability to communicate in English. Presumably, whether second-generation Mexicans share this attitude will help shape the extent to which the third generation retains any knowledge of Spanish. If the second generation does not reject Spanish outright, the third generation is also likely to be bilingual, and fluency in both languages is likely to become institutionalized in the Mexican-American community.

Spanish retention is also bolstered by the over-whelming majorities (between 66 percent and 85 percent) of Mexican immigrants and Hispanics who emphasize the need for their children to be fluent in Spanish. These attitudes contrast with those of other immigrant groups. The New Jersey-based Educational Testing Service finds "a cultural difference between the Asian and Hispanic parents with respect to having their children maintain their native language." In part, this difference undoubtedly stems from the size of Hispanic communities, which creates incentives for fluency in the ancestral language. Although second- and third-generation Mexican Americans and other Hispanics acquire competence in English, they also appear to deviate from the usual pattern by maintaining their competence in Spanish. Second- or third-generation Mexican Americans who were brought up speaking only English have learned Spanish as adults and are encouraging their children to become fluent in it. Spanish-language competence, University of New Mexico professor F. Chris Garcia has stated, is "the one thing every Hispanic takes pride in, wants to protect and promote."

A persuasive case can be made that, in a shrinking world, all Americans should know at least one important foreign language—Chinese, Japanese, Hindi, Russian, Arabic, Urdu, French, German, or Spanish—so as to understand a foreign culture and communicate with its people. It is quite different to argue that Americans should know a non-English language in order to communicate with their fellow citizens. Yet that is what the Spanish-language advocates have in mind. Strengthened by the growth of Hispanic numbers and influence, Hispanic leaders are actively seeking to transform the United States into a bilingual society. "English is not enough," argues Osvaldo Soto, president of the Spanish American League Against Discrimination. "We don't want a monolingual society." Similarly, Duke University literature professor (and Chilean immigrant) Ariel Dorfman asks, "Will this country speak two languages or merely one?" And his answer, of course, is that it should speak two.

Hispanic organizations play a central role in inducing the U.S. Congress to authorize cultural maintenance programs in bilingual education; as a result, children are slow to join mainstream classes. The continuing huge inflow of migrants makes it increasingly possible for Spanish speakers in New York, Miami, and Los Angeles to live normal lives without knowing English. Sixty-five percent of the children in bilingual education in New York are Spanish speakers and hence have little incentive or need to use English in school.

Dual-language programs, which go one step beyond bilin- 30
gual education, have become increasingly popular. In these programs, students are taught in both English and Spanish on an alternating basis with a view to making English-speakers fluent in Spanish and Spanish-speakers fluent in English, thus making Spanish the equal of English and transforming the United States into a two-language country. Then U.S. Secretary of Education Richard Riley explicitly endorsed these programs in his March 2000 speech, "Excelencia para Todos—Excellence for all." Civil rights organizations, church leaders (particularly Catholic ones), and many politicians (Republican as well as Democrat) support the impetus toward bilingualism.

Perhaps equally important, business groups seeking to corner the Hispanic market support bilingualism as well. Indeed, the orientation of U.S. businesses to Hispanic customers means they increasingly need bilingual employees; therefore, bilingualism is affecting earnings. Bilingual police officers and firefighters in southwestern cities such as Phoenix and Las Vegas are paid more than those who only speak English. In Miami, one study found, families that spoke only Spanish had average incomes of $18,000; English-only families had average incomes of $32,000; and bilingual families averaged more than $50,000.

For the first time in U.S. history, increasing numbers of Americans (particularly black Americans) will not be able to receive the jobs or the pay they would otherwise receive because they can speak to their fellow citizens only in English.

In the debates over language policy, the late California Republican Senator S.I. Hayakawa once highlighted the unique role of Hispanics in opposing English. "Why is it that no Filipinos, no Koreans object to making English the official language? No Japanese have done so. And certainly not the Vietnamese, who are so damn happy to be here. They're learning English as fast as they can and winning spelling bees all across the country. But the Hispanics alone have maintained there is a problem. There [has been] considerable movement to make Spanish the second official language."

If the spread of Spanish as the United States' second language continues, it could, in due course, have significant consequences in politics and government. In many states, those aspiring to political office might have to be fluent in both languages. Bilingual candidates for president and elected federal positions would have an advantage over English-only speakers. If dual-language education becomes prevalent in elementary and secondary schools, teachers will increasingly be expected to be bilingual. Government documents and forms could routinely be published in both languages. The use of both languages could become acceptable in congressional hearings and debates and in the general conduct of government business. Because most of those whose first language is Spanish will also probably have some fluency in English, English speakers lacking fluency in Spanish are likely to be and feel at a disadvantage in the competition for jobs, promotions, and contracts.

In 1917, former U.S. President Theodore Roosevelt said: "We must have but one flag. We must also have but one language. That must be the language of the Declaration of Independence, of Washington's Farewell address, of Lincoln's Gettysburg speech and second inaugural." By contrast, in June 2000, U.S. president Bill Clinton said, "I hope very much that I'm the last president in American history who can't speak Spanish." And in May 2001, President Bush celebrated Mexico's Cinco de Mayo national holiday by inaugurating the practice of broadcasting the weekly presidential radio address to the American people in both English and Spanish. In September 2003, one of the first debates among the Democratic Party's presidential candidates also took place in both English and Spanish. Despite the opposition of large majorities of Americans, Spanish is joining the language of Washington, Jefferson, Lincoln, the Roosevelts, and the Kennedys as the language of the United States. If this trend continues, the cultural division between Hispanics and Anglos could replace the racial division between blacks and whites as the most serious cleavage in U.S. society.

Blood Is Thicker Than Borders

Massive Hispanic immigration affects the United States in two 35
significant ways: Important portions of the country become predominantly Hispanic in language and culture, and the nation as a whole becomes bilingual and bicultural. The most important area where Hispanization is proceeding rapidly is, of course, the Southwest. As historian Kennedy argues, Mexican Americans in the Southwest will soon have "sufficient coherence and critical mass in a defined region so that, if they choose, they can preserve their distinctive culture indefinitely. They could also eventually undertake to do what no previous immigrant group could have dreamed of doing: challenge the existing cultural, political, legal, commercial, and educational systems to change fundamentally not only the language but also the very institutions in which they do business."

Anecdotal evidence of such challenges abounds. In 1994, Mexican Americans vigorously demonstrated against California's Proposition 187—which limited welfare benefits to children of illegal immigrants—by marching through the streets of Los Angeles waving scores of Mexican flags and carrying U.S. flags upside down. In 1998, at a Mexico-United States soccer match in Los Angeles, Mexican Americans booed the U.S. national anthem and assaulted U.S. players. Such dramatic rejections of the United States and assertions of Mexican identity are not limited to an extremist minority in the Mexican-American community. Many Mexican immigrants and their offspring simply do not appear to identify primarily with the United States.

Empirical evidence confirms such appearances. A 1992 study of children of immigrants in Southern California and

South Florida posed the following question: "How do you identify, that is, what do you call yourself?" None of the children born in Mexico answered "American," compared with 1.9 percent to 9.3 percent of those born elsewhere in Latin America or the Caribbean. The largest percentage of Mexican-born children (41.2 percent) identified themselves as "Hispanic," and the second largest (36.2 percent) chose "Mexican." Among Mexican-American children born in the United States, less than 4 percent responded "American," compared to 28.5 percent to 50 percent of those born in the United States with parents from elsewhere in Latin America. Whether born in Mexico or in the United States, Mexican children overwhelmingly did not choose "American" as their primary identification.

Demographically, socially, and culturally, the *reconquista* (reconquest) of the Southwest United States by Mexican immigrants is well underway. A meaningful move to reunite these territories with Mexico seems unlikely, but Prof. Charles Truxillo of the University of New Mexico predicts that by 2080 the southwestern states of the United States and the northern states of Mexico will form *La República del Norte* (The Republic of the North). Various writers have referred to the southwestern United States plus northern Mexico as "MexAmerica" or "Amexica" or "Mexifornia." "We are all Mexicans in this valley," a former county commissioner of El Paso, Texas, declared in 2001.

This trend could consolidate the Mexican-dominant areas of the United States into an autonomous, culturally and linguistically distinct, and economically self-reliant bloc within the United States. "We may be building toward the one thing that will choke the melting pot," warns former National Intelligence Council Vice Chairman Graham Fuller, "an ethnic area and grouping so concentrated that it will not wish, or need, to undergo assimilation into the mainstream of American multiethnic English-speaking life."

A prototype of such a region already exists—in Miami. 40

Bienvenido a Miami

Miami is the most Hispanic large city in the 50 U.S. states. Over the course of 30 years, Spanish speakers—overwhelmingly Cuban—established their dominance in virtually every aspect of the city's life, fundamentally changing its ethnic composition, culture, politics, and language. The Hispanization of Miami is without precedent in the history of U.S. cities.

The economic growth of Miami, led by the early Cuban immigrants, made the city a magnet for migrants from other Latin American and Caribbean countries. By 2000, two thirds of Miami's people were Hispanic, and more than half were Cuban or of Cuban descent. In 2000, 75.2 percent of adult Miamians spoke a language other than English at home, compared to 55.7 percent of the residents of Los Angeles and 47.6 percent of New Yorkers. (Of Miamians speaking a non-English language at home, 87.2 percent spoke Spanish.) In 2000, 59.5 percent of Miami residents were foreign-born, compared to 40.9 percent in Los Angeles, 36.8 percent in San Francisco, and 35.9 percent in New York. In 2000, only 31.1 percent of adult Miami residents said they spoke English very well, compared to 39.0 percent in Los Angeles, 42.5 percent in San Francisco, and 46.5 percent in New York.

The Cuban takeover had major consequences for Miami. The elite and entrepreneurial class fleeing the regime of Cuban dictator Fidel Castro in the 1960s started dramatic economic development in South Florida. Unable to send money home, they invested in Miami. Personal income growth in Miami averaged 11.5 percent a year in the 1970s and 7.7 percent a year in the 1980s. Payrolls in Miami-Dade County tripled between 1970 and 1995. The Cuban economic drive made Miami an international economic dynamo, with expanding international trade and investment. The Cubans promoted international tourism, which, by the 1990s, exceeded domestic tourism and made Miami a leading center of the cruise ship industry. Major U.S. corporations in manufacturing, communications, and consumer products moved their Latin American headquarters to Miami from other U.S. and Latin American cities. A vigorous Spanish artistic and entertainment community emerged. Today, the Cubans can legitimately claim that, in the words of Prof. Damian Fernández of Florida International University, "We built modern Miami," and made its economy larger than those of many Latin American countries.

A key part of this development was the expansion of Miami's economic ties with Latin America. Brazilians, Argentines, Chileans, Colombians, and Venezuelans flooded into Miami, bringing their money with them. By 1993, some $25.6

billion in international trade, mostly involving Latin America, moved through the city. Throughout the hemisphere, Latin Americans concerned with investment, trade, culture, entertainment, holidays, and drug smuggling increasingly turned to Miami.

Such eminence transformed Miami into a Cuban-led, His- 45
panic city. The Cubans did not, in the traditional pattern, create an enclave immigrant neighborhood. Instead, they created an enclave city with its own culture and economy, in which assimilation and Americanization were unnecessary and in some measure undesired. By 2000, Spanish was not just the language spoken in most homes, it was also the principal language of commerce, business, and politics. The media and communications industry became increasingly Hispanic. In 1998, a Spanish-language television station became the number-one station watched by Miamians—the first time a foreign-language station achieved that rating in a major U.S. city. "They're outsiders," one successful Hispanic said of non-Hispanics. "Here we are members of the power structure," another boasted.

"In Miami there is no pressure to be American," one Cuban-born sociologist observed. "People can make a living perfectly well in an enclave that speaks Spanish." By 1999, the heads of Miami's largest bank, largest real estate development company, and largest law firm were all Cuban-born or of Cuban descent. The Cubans also established their dominance in politics. By 1999, the mayor of Miami and the mayor, police chief, and state attorney of Miami-Dade County, plus two thirds of Miami's U.S. Congressional delegation and nearly one half of its state legislators, were of Cuban origin. In the wake of the Elián González affair in 2000, the non-Hispanic city manager and police chief in Miami City were replaced by Cubans.

The Cuban and Hispanic dominance of Miami left Anglos (as well as blacks) as outside minorities that could often be ignored. Unable to communicate with government bureaucrats and discriminated against by store clerks, the Anglos came to realize, as one of them put it, "My God, this is what it's like to be the minority." The Anglos had three choices. They could accept their subordinate and outsider position. They could attempt to adopt the manners, customs, and language of the Hispanics and assimilate into the Hispanic community—"acculturation in reverse," as the scholars Alejandro Portes and Alex Stepick labeled it. Or they could leave Miami, and between 1983 and 1993, about 140,000 did just that, their exodus reflected in a popular bumper sticker: "Will the last American to leave Miami, please bring the flag."

Contempt of Culture

Is Miami the future for Los Angeles and the southwest United States? In the end, the results could be similar: the creation of a large, distinct, Spanish-speaking community with economic and political resources sufficient to sustain its Hispanic identity apart from the national identity of other Americans and also able to influence U.S. politics, government, and society. However, the processes by which this result might come about differ. The Hispanization of Miami has been rapid, explicit, and economically driven. The Hispanization of the Southwest has been slower, unrelenting, and politically driven. The Cuban influx into Florida was intermittent and responded to the policies of the Cuban government. Mexican immigration, on the other hand, is continuous, includes a large illegal component, and shows no signs of tapering. The Hispanic (that is, largely Mexican) population of Southern California far exceeds in number but has yet to reach the proportions of the Hispanic population of Miami—though it is increasing rapidly.

The early Cuban immigrants in South Florida were largely middle and upper class. Subsequent immigrants were more lower class. In the Southwest, overwhelming numbers of Mexican immigrants have been poor, unskilled, and poorly educated, and their children are likely to face similar conditions. The pressures toward Hispanization in the Southwest thus come from below, whereas those in South Florida came from above. In the long run, however, numbers are power, particularly in a multicultural society, a political democracy, and a consumer economy.

Another major difference concerns the relations of Cubans 50
and Mexicans with their countries of origin. The Cuban community has been united in its hostility to the Castro regime and in its efforts to punish and overthrow that regime. The Cuban government has responded in kind. The Mexican community

in the United States has been more ambivalent and nuanced in its attitudes toward the Mexican government. Since the 1980s, however, the Mexican government has sought to expand the numbers, wealth, and political power of the Mexican community in the U.S. Southwest and to integrate that population with Mexico. "The Mexican nation extends beyond the territory enclosed by its borders," Mexican President Ernesto Zedillo said in the 1990s. His successor, Vicente Fox, called Mexican emigrants "heroes" and describes himself as president of 123 million Mexicans, 100 million in Mexico and 23 million in the United States.

As their numbers increase, Mexican Americans feel increasingly comfortable with their own culture and often contemptuous of American culture. They demand recognition of their culture and the historic Mexican identity of the U.S. Southwest. They call attention to and celebrate their Hispanic and Mexican past, as in the 1998 ceremonies and festivities in Madrid, New Mexico, attended by the vice president of Spain, honoring the establishment 400 years earlier of the first European settlement in the Southwest, almost a decade before Jamestown. As the *New York Times* reported in September 1999, Hispanic growth has been able to "help 'Latinize' many Hispanic people who are finding it easier to affirm their heritage . . . . [T]hey find strength in numbers, as younger generations grow up with more ethnic pride and as a Latin influence starts permeating fields such as entertainment, advertising, and politics." One index foretells the future: In 1998, "José" replaced "Michael" as the most popular name for newborn boys in both California and Texas.

Irreconcilable Differences

The persistence of Mexican immigration into the United States reduces the incentives for cultural assimilation. Mexican Americans no longer think of themselves as members of a small minority who must accommodate the dominant group and adopt its culture. As their numbers increase, they become more committed to their own ethnic identity and culture. Sustained numerical expansion promotes cultural consolidation and leads Mexican Americans not to minimize but to glory in the differences between their culture and U.S. culture. As the president of the National Council of La Raza said in 1995: "The biggest problem we have is a cultural clash, a clash between our values and the values in American society." He then went on to spell out the superiority of Hispanic values to American values. In similar fashion, Lionel Sosa, a successful Mexican-American businessman in Texas, in 1998 hailed the emerging Hispanic middle-class professionals who look like Anglos, but whose "values remain quite different from an Anglo's."

To be sure, as Harvard University political scientist Jorge I. Domínguez has pointed out, Mexican Americans are more favorably disposed toward democracy than are Mexicans. Nonetheless, "ferocious differences" exist between U.S. and Mexican cultural values, as Jorge Castañeda (who later served as Mexico's foreign minister) observed in 1995. Castañeda cited differences in social and economic equality, the unpredictability of events, concepts of time epitomized in the *mañana* syndrome, the ability to achieve results quickly, and attitudes toward history, expressed in the "cliché that Mexicans are obsessed with history, Americans with the future." Sosa identifies several Hispanic traits (very different from Anglo-Protestant ones) that "hold us Latinos back": mistrust of people outside the family; lack of initiative, self-reliance, and ambition; little use for education; and acceptance of poverty as a virtue necessary for entrance into heaven. Author Robert Kaplan quotes Alex Villa, a third-generation Mexican American in Tucson, Arizona, as saying that he knows almost no one in the Mexican community of South Tucson who believes in "education and hard work" as the way to material prosperity and is thus willing to "buy into America." Profound cultural differences clearly separate Mexicans and Americans, and the high level of immigration from Mexico sustains and reinforces the prevalence of Mexican values among Mexican Americans.

Continuation of this large immigration (without improved assimilation) could divide the United States into a country of two languages and two cultures. A few stable, prosperous democracies—such as Canada and Belgium—fit this pattern. The differences in culture within these countries, however, do not approximate those between the United States and Mexico, and even in these countries language differences persist. Not many Anglo-Canadians are equally fluent in English and French, and the Canadian government has had to impose penalties to get its top civil servants to achieve dual fluency.

Much the same lack of dual competence is true of Walloons and Flemings in Belgium. The transformation of the United States into a country like these would not necessarily be the end of the world; it would, however, be the end of the America we have known for more than three centuries. Americans should not let that change happen unless they are convinced that this new nation would be a better one.

Such a transformation would not only revolutionize the 55
United States, but it would also have serious consequences for Hispanics, who will be in the United States but not of it. Sosa ends his book, *The Americano Dream*, with encouragement for aspiring Hispanic entrepreneurs. "The Americano dream?" he asks. "It exists, it is realistic, and it is there for all of us to share." Sosa is wrong. There is no Americano dream. There is only the American dream created by an Anglo-Protestant society. Mexican Americans will share in that dream and in that society only if they dream in English.

Questions about the Passage

1. What is Huntington's thesis in paragraph 1? Explain what he means by Anglo-Protestant values in paragraphs 3–5.
2. In paragraph 1, Huntington calls *The Declaration of Independence* "a creed." In paragraph 4, he refers to "the founding culture" and "the bedrock of U.S. identity." What does he mean by each term? Compare this word usage to Antin's in Chapter 4. She refers to *The Declaration* as "fundamental American law" in paragraph 1 and as a "confession of faith" in paragraph 5. Are their assumptions the same? Do they draw the same conclusions from them?
3. Huntington differentiates Hispanic immigration from other waves of immigration, using the following categories: contiguity, scale, illegality, regional concentration, persistence, historical presence, and language retention. In small groups, prepare a brief summary of the point you are assigned. Use these summaries to initiate a class discussion to be sure you have understood what he is saying.

4. After your careful analysis of the piece, reread the last two sentences of paragraph 55. Examine each main clause and decide whether you agree or disagree with each statement. Then explain your position.

Questions about the Argument

1. How do Huntington's credentials qualify him to challenge his readers to a debate about Hispanic immigration? Examine carefully his education, experience, and publications.
2. Find out all you can about the Olin Foundation he founded and about *Foreign Policy.* Draw inferences about both the organization and journal to try to define the kind of audience he is addressing.
3. Identify the assumptions that underlie his argument. Do you agree with his assumptions?
4. Try to formulate his argument as a categorical syllogism.
5. Using the summaries you prepared for each of Huntington's categories, analyze his argument. Examine the evidence, especially statistics, he uses to support each point. Does he use reliable sources for the statistics he presents? Does he draw the correct conclusions from this information? To what degree is he convincing or not?
6. Examine the analogy Huntington makes between Miami (paragraphs 41–47) and other areas with large Hispanic populations like Los Angeles (paragraphs 48–51). Do you think what has happened in Miami is likely to happen in Los Angeles? In Chapter 4, Jacoby also uses an analogy—between Puerto Rican immigrants and Mexican immigrants. Which analogy do you find more persuasive?
7. Does Huntington make use of pathos in his argument? If so, is it a legitimate use of pathos?
8. Where do you think this argument is especially strong? Where particularly weak? Overall, how would you evaluate this argument?

Representations of Mexican Immigrants

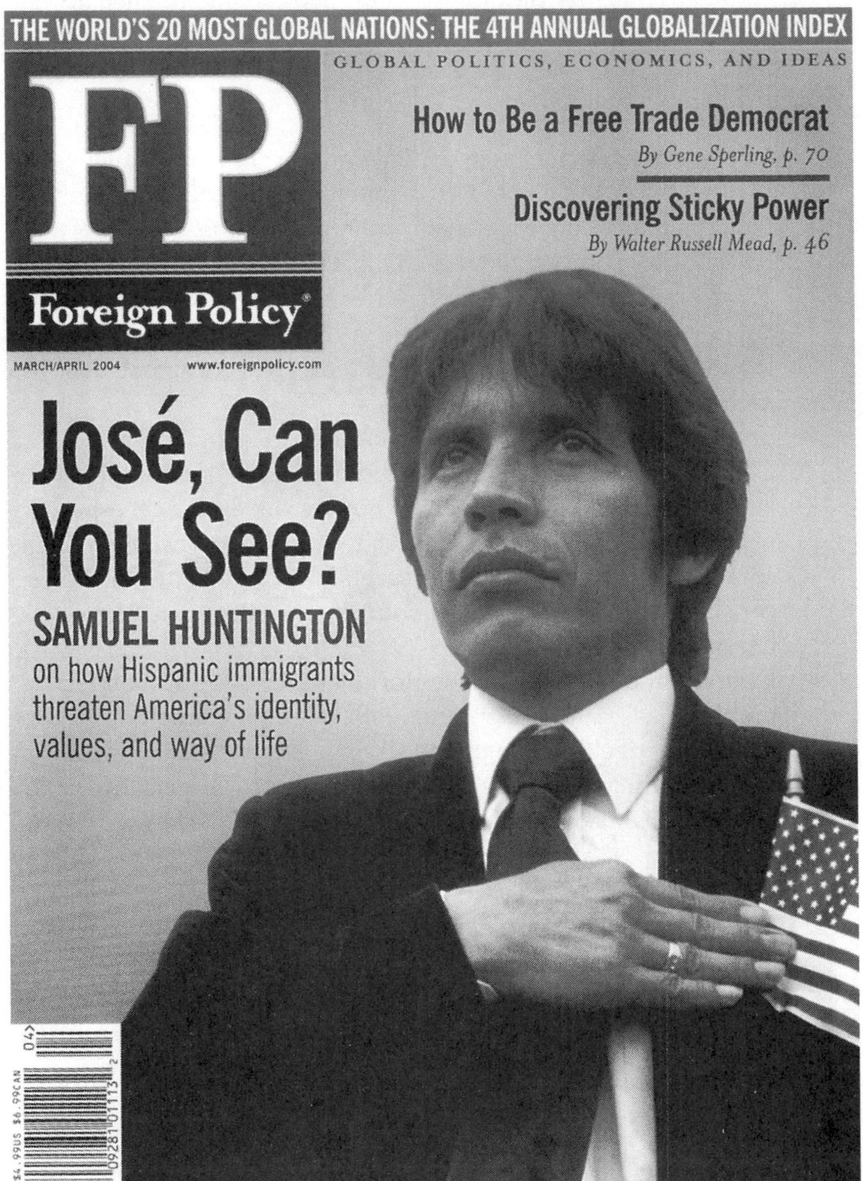

Figure 6-3: *"José, Can You See?," Cover photo of* Foreign Policy, *March/April 2004.*

Figure 6-4: *Lalo Alcaraz, "Americano Gothic," 2001.*

Questions about the Pictures

1. Look at the *Foreign Policy* cover picture (Figure 6-3). Put together the man's gesture and the words "José, Can You See?" What does the phrase or pun allude to? What does the phrase imply about José and, by extension, Hispanics in the United States? How do you think this cover refers to Huntington's article? What attitude towards Hispanics does the cover suggest?
2. What famous painting does the Alcaraz cartoon (Figure 6-4) refer to? Look up (on the Internet or in the library) Grant Wood's "American Gothic." Compare them side by side.
3. How does Alcaraz change the couple on the left from the painting's original couples? Look at their facial expressions, where they are looking, and the way the man holds the pitchfork. Do the same with the couple on the right.
4. Look carefully at the houses behind the couples in the cartoon. Why are the houses identical? Connect the setting to the statement at the top of the cartoon.

Questions about the Arguments

1. Some readers may recognize "José, Can You See?" from an old, widely anthologized joke in which the young José (from Mexico or Puerto Rico) attends his first baseball game at Yankee Stadium. There, he either has to sit near the flagpole (he is given a seat there by the friendly ticket salesman who has no other seats left) or climb the flagpole in order to watch the game. When asked how he liked the game, he is enthusiastic about the friendly Americans who ask (or sing), "José, can you see?" before the game started. What layer of meaning does this allusion add to the message of the cover? Assuming the *Foreign Policy* editors were familiar with the joke, why would they choose this cover? Does the cover fairly represent the content of Huntington's argument? Do you think the cover will attract or alienate possible readers or not affect them at all? What do you think of the decision to use the cover?
2. What argument or arguments is Alcaraz making in "Americano Gothic"? In your groups, brainstorm at least two claims that the cartoon might support. Then make the case for each claim based on evidence from the cartoon.

Responses to Huntington: Louis Menand, Fouad Ajami, and Tamar Jacoby

Louis Menand (1952–), an author, journalist, and academic, has had a long and distinguished career. His Ph.D. is from Columbia, he held the title of Distinguished Professor, Graduate School, English, at CUNY, and is now at Harvard. He is well known as a staff writer for the *New Yorker.* His May 17, 2004, review of Huntington's book, *Who Are We?*, is titled "Patriot Games: The New Nativism of Samuel P. Huntington." We have excerpted the section that deals specifically with "The Hispanic Challenge."

Fouad Ajami (1946–) is Majid Khadduri Professor and Director of the Middle East Studies Program at Johns Hopkins University. His letter in response to Huntington is published in the May/June 2004 issue of *Foreign Policy.*

Tamar Jacoby (1954–) is Senior Fellow at the Manhattan Institute. We have provided a lengthier introduction for her in Chapter 4. Her letter also appears in the May/June 2004 issue of *Foreign Policy.*

You will find a wide range of responses to Huntington in the above-noted issue of *Foreign Policy* as well as Huntington's response to his critics.

Louis Menand

The most inflammatory section of "Who Are We?" is the chapter on Mexican immigration. Huntington reports that in 2000 the foreign-born population of the United States included almost eight million people from Mexico. The next country on the list was China, with 1.4 million. Huntington's concern is that Mexican-Americans (and, in Florida, Cuban-Americans) demonstrate less motivation to learn English and assimilate to the Anglo culture than other immigrant groups have historically, and that, thanks to the influence of bilingualism advocates, unelected judges, cosmopolites, and a compliant Congress, it has become less necessary for them to do so. They can remain, for generations, within their own cultural and linguistic enclave, and they are consequently likely to be less loyal to the United States than other hyphenated Americans are. Huntington believes that the United States "could change . . . into a culturally bifurcated Anglo-Hispanic society with two national languages." He can imagine portions of the American Southwest being ceded back to Mexico.

This part of Huntington's book was published first as an article in *Foreign Policy*, and it has already provoked responses, many in the letters column of that journal. Michael Elliott, in his column in *Time*, pointed out that in the Latino National Political Survey, conducted from 1989 to 1990, eighty-four per cent of Mexican-Americans expressed "extremely" or "very" strong love for the United States (against ninety-two per cent of Anglos). Ninety-one per cent said that they were "extremely proud" or "very proud" of the United States. As far as reluctance to learn English is concerned, Richard Alba and Victor Nee, in "Remaking the American Mainstream: Assimilation and Contemporary Immigration" (Harvard; $39.95), report that in 1990 more than ninety-five per cent of Mexican-Americans between the ages of twenty-five and forty-four who were born in the United States could speak English well. They conclude that although Hispanic-Americans, particularly those who live close to the border, may continue to speak their original language (usually along with English) a generation longer than other groups have tended to do, "by any standard, linguistic assimilation is widespread."

Huntington's account of the nature of Mexican immigration to the United States seems deliberately alarmist. He notes, for example, that since 1975 roughly two-thirds of Mexican immigrants have entered illegally. This is the kind of statistic that is continually cited to suggest a new and dangerous demographic hemorrhaging. But, as Mae Ngai points out, in "Impossible Subjects: Illegal Aliens and the Making of Modern America" (Princeton; $35), a work a hundred times more nuanced than Huntington's, the surge in illegal immigration was the predictable consequence of the reform of the immigration laws in 1965. In the name of liberalizing immigration policy, the new law imposed a uniform quota on all countries, regardless of size. Originally, Western Hemisphere countries were exempted from specific quotas, but the act was amended in 1976, and Mexico was assigned the same annual quota (twenty thousand) as, for example, Belgium. This effectively illegalized a large portion of the Mexican immigrant population. "Legal" and "illegal," as Ngai's book illustrates, are administrative constructions, always subject to change; they do not tell us anything about the desirability of the persons so constructed. (Ngai's analysis also suggests that one reason that Asian-Americans are stereotyped by other Americans as products of a culture that places a high value on education is that the 1965 immigration act gives preference to applicants with professional skills, and, in the nineteen-sixties and seventies, for reasons internal to their own countries, many Asian professionals chose to emigrate. Like professionals from any other culture, they naturally made education a priority for their children.)

Finally, some of Huntington's statistical claims are improperly derived. "Three out of ten Hispanic students drop out of school compared to one in eight blacks and one in fourteen whites," he says, and he cites other studies to argue that Hispanic-Americans are less educationally assimilated than other groups. Educational attainment is not an index of intellectual capacity, though; it is an economic trade-off. The rate of high-school graduation is in part a function of the local economy. For example, according to the Urban Institute and the Manhattan Institute for Policy Research, Florida has one of the worst high-school graduation rates in the United States. This may be because it has a service economy, in which you do not need a diploma to get reasonably steady work. To argue that Hispanic-Americans are disproportionately less likely to finish school, one would have to compare them not with non-Hispanic Americans nationally but with non-Hispanic Americans in the same region. Huntington provides no such comparisons. He is cheered, however, by Hispanic-Americans' high rate of conversion to evangelical Protestantism.

This brings us back to the weird emptiness at the heart of 5
Huntington's analysis, according to which conversion to a fundamentalist faith is counted a good thing just because many other people already share that faith. Huntington never explains, in "Who Are We?," why Protestantism, private enterprise, and the English language are more desirable features of social life or more conducive to self-realization than, say, Judaism, kibbutzim, and Hebrew. He only fears, as an American, their transformation into something different. But how American is that? Huntington's understanding of American culture would be less rigid if he paid more attention to the actual value of his core values. One of the virtues of a liberal democracy is that it is designed to accommodate social and cultural change. Democracy is not a dogma; it is an experiment. That is what Lincoln said in the Gettysburg Address—and there is no more hallowed text in the American Creed than that.

Fouad Ajami

Huntington has paid no court to fashion—or political correctness. He must be reckoned the single most influential and relentless political scientist of the last half century. His article is true to his calling. Its courage is matched only by its clarity. There is an old-fashioned patriotism at the core of Huntington's worldview, and he is not embarrassed to give voice to it.

Our country grows more tribalized by the day, and "hyphenation" has become an unexamined creed of our era. But it wasn't so long ago that the American idea was much simpler: The door was open (I walked through it four decades ago), but the assumption was that older loyalties would be set aside. It was, after all, the "newness" of the New World that had created its magnetic appeal. In saying that there is no "Americano dream," Huntington restates the case for that simpler and older American dream.

Culture matters, Huntington would say—indeed he already has in the title of one of his countless books. A decade ago, Huntington was prescient when he wrote of the coming clash of civilizations. I, along with many others, dissented and wrote a critique of his idea. I had fallen back on the universalism of modern civilization. But history acquiesced with his brooding, darker view as the 1990s drew to a close and as the death pilots of September 11, 2001, blew our way. I have since conceded Huntington's wisdom and the feebleness of my own hopes.

Now Sam plays it again, this time with the American idea itself in the balance. This time I cast my lot with him.

Tamar Jacoby

There is so much to rebut in Professor Huntington's essay that it is hard to know where to start. Consider just one of his arguments—that today's Latino immigrants to the United States are not learning English as quickly or as readily as earlier newcomers. Virtually every study of Latino language acquisition refutes this claim. As in every immigrant generation, foreign-born adults and new arrivals often have trouble with English, leading to the alarming-sounding statistics Huntington cites. Yet U.S. census data show that nearly all children of Latino immigrants speak English proficiently; even in what the census labels "Spanish-speaking homes," between 70 and 80 percent of the children speak English "well" or "very well." And by the third generation, nearly two thirds of Hispanics speak only English. As for Huntington's claim that significant numbers of Latinos "oppose" English and seek an officially bilingual culture, nothing could be further from the truth. The ethnic-activist professors he cites speak only for themselves. Hispanic parents understand perfectly that their children's future will be in English.

Huntington is also wrong about U.S. identity and what it means for immigrants to assimilate. Apart from the English language, U.S. identity has never been about culture. We ask newcomers to buy into our political values by understanding and embracing the Constitution and its ideals. We require that they identify with the United States by swearing loyalty to the nation and committing to its defense when necessary. But we have never demanded that newcomers adopt any particular cultural habits, Anglo Protestant or otherwise. As long as they adopt our ideas about freedom, tolerance, and equality before the law, we have left them to do as they pleased in the private sphere. We have always been confident that U.S. political values—the very act of living in this republic—would eventually transform their attitudes toward matters as deeply personal as the role of the individual, ambition, opportunity, self-reliance, responsibility, how merit and initiative should be rewarded, and the proper place of ethnicity in the larger commonweal. And transform them our free and tolerant way of life always has.

The notion that our political values are inherently Anglo or Protestant is also incorrect. Many of the Enlightenment ideas upon which the U.S. Constitution is based originated in the British Isles, but that does not make them inherently British—any more than Christianity, which originated on the shores of the Mediterranean, is inherently Middle Eastern or Italian. Americans long ago appropriated Enlightenment ideals and used them to shape distinctively American institutions, which have been subtly influenced and improved by input from a long succession of immigrant groups.

Samuel Huntington is entitled to his fears and his pessimism. But it is troubling to see such a distinguished scholar adopt a mistaken, counterfactual view of the tried and tested traditions that have made the United States and its social cohesion the envy of the world.

Questions about the Passages

A. Menand

1. In paragraph 1, does Menand state fairly the claims that Huntington is making?
2. What authorities does Menand cite to rebut Huntington's claim that Hispanics are reluctant to learn English?
3. According to Menand, "Huntington's account of the nature of Mexican immigration seems deliberately alarmist." What does Menand mean and why does he make the statement?
4. According to Menand, which of Huntington's statistics are "improperly derived"? Go back to Huntington's article to be sure that you understand what Menand is arguing.

B. Ajami

1. Why does Ajami say that "Huntington has paid no court to fashion—or political correctness"?
3. Why did Ajami originally dissent from Huntington's view of civilizations? What changed his mind?
3. "This time" why does Adjami cast his lot with Huntington?

C. Jacoby

1. Jacoby rebuts three main points Huntington makes: that Latino immigrants are not learning English as quickly as other immigrant groups; that we require they adopt Anglo-Protestant cultural habits; and that "our political values are inherently Anglo or Protestant." Be sure you understand each of the counter-points she makes and then summarize each carefully.

Questions about the Arguments

A. Menand

1. Is Menand qualified by training and experience to review Huntington's book? Why or why not? Be sure to research his curriculum vitae, including his publications.
2. Menand cites several authorities in his rebuttal. Are they used effectively to support his contentions? Is Menand correct that Huntington's statistics are improperly derived?
3. Examine the *New Yorker*. What can you determine about its audience from the subject of its articles, the level of writing, and its advertising? Can you locate any specific strategies that indicate Menand's awareness of that audience?
4. Has Menand's critique affected your estimation of Huntington's argument?

B. Ajami

1. Do Ajami's training and experience qualify him to critique both *The Clash of Civilizations* and "The Hispanic Challenge"?
2. Look at the contents of *Foreign Policy.* Does the readership of this journal differ significantly from that of the *New Yorker*? What can you infer about that readership from the authors of the letters published in the May/June 2004 edition?
3. Does Ajami supply a strong defense of Huntington? Why or why not?

C. Jacoby

1. Is Jacoby's rebuttal of Huntington's argument in line with her article on immigration printed in Chapter 4? Does she criticize him for the same reasons she criticizes the restrictionists?
2. Does she provide sufficient evidence to undermine Huntington's claims? If yes, which do you think is her strongest point? If not, where does she need additional support?

Writing Assignments

Conversations

1. Invite Jefferson, Antin, and Huntington to meet you for coffee. You have noticed that both Antin and Huntington make use of *The Declaration of Independence*. Ask them to explain how this document is important to their debate. Does Jefferson find their uses of his work valid and/or persuasive?
2. Set up a debate on immigration. Decide on the proposition you wish to debate, placing restrictionists on one side and those advocating a more open policy on the other. Of the following thinkers, whom would you place on each side: Jacoby, Antin, Beecher, Jefferson, Huntington? What reasons would each give for the assigned position? How would each counter arguments from the other side?
3. In class, conduct your own debate on one of the following propositions. Resolved: The immigrant stories we have read support the argument for continuing the current immigration policy. Or Resolved: The restrictionists are right. Too much immigration is damaging to our country. Or Resolved: The open door policy is the only just immigration policy.

Writing Sequence One: Huntington Right or Wrong?

1. In a two-page paper, explore the assumptions Huntington sets up in paragraphs 1–4, drawing on what you've read elsewhere in the book and on class discussions to help you discover whether you accept these assumptions fully or partially or reject them.
2. Read all the responses to Huntington in the May/June 2004 issue of *Foreign Policy* and group them according to whether they support or attack Huntington. Decide whether you can categorize the

responses on each side. In a two-page paper, summarize these arguments.

3. Write your own four- to five-page critique or defense of Huntington. Be sure to weigh carefully his ethos, assumptions, claim, and reasons in support of his claim, evidence, and use of pathos. As support, use at least some of the responses you analyzed in question 2. You may also include the stories that begin this chapter. Take care to cite properly from both primary and secondary sources.

Writing Sequence Two: Discover Your Own Position on Immigration

1. In a brief paper, explore your views on immigration. Where do you find yourself on the continuum between the total restrictionist position and the wide-open borders position? How have the readings influenced you to think as you do? What experiences (your own, your family's, or your friends'), if any, have contributed to your view?
2. Summarize briefly but carefully at least two readings that support your position and at least two that undermine it. Be sure to include both narratives and argumentative works.
3. Now construct a four- to five-page argument in which you enunciate precisely the position (claim) you take on the question of immigration and why you take that position (reasons), and provide the specific evidence that will at least convince your readers that you have a claim and support meriting their attention. Be sure to address and refute the concerns your readers are likely to raise. As always, cite all sources carefully.

APPENDIX

Research Topics and Selected Immigration Bibliography

Suggestions for Research Topics

1. It is often asserted that immigrants frequently become a drag on society (through use of welfare and other social services). Investigate this assertion thoroughly and write an argumentative essay based on the conclusion you have drawn. Start with Census Bureau data; you might also examine materials put forward by both pro- and anti-immigration associations.
2. Patrick Buchanan, in his recent book, *The Death of the West: How Dying Populations and Immigrant Invasions Imperil our Country and Civilization* (2002), draws an analogy between the barbarian invasions of Rome and the immigrant "invasions" of Western countries, including the United States. After reading Buchanan, research his claim and develop your own position on it. Be sure to look at reviews of Buchanan's book to help you identify important issues.
3. Lyman Beecher, Patrick Buchanan, and Samuel P. Huntington have all been called "nativists." Define what the term *nativism* has meant in American history through research. Which, if any, of these writers would you label as a nativist? Defend your answer.
4. Why did immigrants from your own ethnic group (or another that interests you) come to America? Develop an argument that

delineates the specific causes, taking care to note any disagreements among historians and supporting your own view. You might begin by reading a good encyclopedia entry about the immigrant group. Check the bibliography listed there as well as the bibliographies in the Selected Bibliography in this appendix. Another good source is immigrant narratives, some of which are listed in the Selected Bibliography. See also the very complete listing in Thomas Dublin's *Immigrant Voices: New Lives in America, 1773–1986*, which indicates the immigrant's country of origin.

5. Collect biographical accounts (including narratives, letters, interviews, and so on) of one particular immigrant group. Good sources are listed in the Selected Bibliography, but be sure to consult your library's catalog as well. What evidence do you find that the immigrants have tried to assimilate, have succeeded or failed to assimilate, or do not wish to assimilate? What factors seem to account for this result? Definition is important here: what does the term *assimilation* mean for the purposes of your argument?
6. Investigate one of the major acts that restricted immigration to the United States, such as the Chinese Exclusion Act of 1882 or the Immigration Act of 1924. What were the historical circumstances around the act's passage? Which immigrant groups were especially targeted? What effect did the law have on immigration? After exploring these issues, argue that the immigration law was beneficial or harmful to the country, using the historical data you have gathered to support your position.
7. The huge numbers of immigrants from southern and eastern Europe who arrived in the late nineteenth and early twentieth centuries posed major problems for many American communities, especially large cities like New York and Chicago. One important response was the "settlement house," a place in the immigrant neighborhood where middle- and upper-class volunteers provided educational, social, and vocational services for immigrants. What made the settlement movement distinctive was that the workers also lived in the settlement house itself, rather than coming into the district from their own wealthy communities. One of the most famous of these settlements was Hull-House in Chicago, founded by Jane Addams. Another, founded by nurse Lillian Wald, was the House on Henry Street in New York City. Select one of these settlement houses or another one (there were multiple settlements in many cities), and research it. Assess the contribution that the settlement house made to immi-

grants' lives. Did the settlement house acknowledge the importance of the immigrant's home culture? Did it help the immigrants deal with the specific problems they faced in coming to a new country, such as finding employment, housing, medical care, and education? Some critics have charged that settlement houses were essentially means of social control. Choose one of these issues and argue for your well-researched position on it.

8. Investigate the philosophies of the founders and participants in the settlement houses. What do their ideas tell us about the attitudes towards immigration and towards the immigrants themselves? What visions of American society did the settlement founders and workers have?
9. Several first-person accounts by immigrants who were settlement house clients are listed in our Selected Bibliography (Polacheck, Ets, and Cohen). You may be able to find additional accounts. Examine the settlement house from the immigrant's viewpoint. How did the immigrants view these early social workers? For these specific writers, how central were their settlement house experiences in their lives? Were the settlement house workers truly helping immigrants? In what ways?
10. Immigrants have formed self-help groups to aid newcomers. Determine whether there are any such immigrant self-help organizations in your own community. Obtain their mission statements and a list of services they provide. You might check whether they have a website or visit their offices. Interview a staff member about the goals of the organization and the particular problems facing its immigrants. If possible, interview one or more immigrants who use the organization's services. Assess the role the organization plays in the immigrants' lives. How important is the organization? Is it effective?
11. Trace the development of a refugee policy after World War II. Why did the United States define a new category of immigrant? How important has refugee status been for immigration since the 1940s? Do we need this category of immigrant? Defend your position.
12. Choose one of the theories of immigration presented in Chapter 5: assimilation, segmented assimilation, or transnationalism. Consult the bibliography of the author(s) you have chosen and read some of the sources. Find out as much as you can about this theory. What are its strengths and weaknesses for explaining immigrant experience and acculturation? Write your own assessment of the theory, taking a position on its utility.

Selected Bibliography

These are good places to start your research. The footnotes and bibliographies in these sources will lead you to other pertinent material.

Bibliographies on Immigration

Brye, David L. European Immigration and Ethnicity in the United States and Canada: A Historical Bibliography. Santa Barbara: ABC-Clio, 1983.

Buenker, John D., and Nicholas C. Burckel. Immigration and Ethnicity: A Guide to Information Sources. Detroit: Gale, 1977.

Gabaccia, Donna R. Immigrant Women in the United States: A Selectively Annotated Multidisciplinary Bibliography. New York: Greenwood P, 1989.

Janeway, W. Ralph. Bibliography of Immigration in the United States, 1900–1930. Columbus, OH: H. L. Hedrick, 1934.

Mageli, Paul D. The Immigrant Experience : An Annotated Bibliography. Pasadena: Salem P, 1991.

Meadows, Paul. Recent Immigration to the United States: The Literature of the Social Sciences. Research Institute on Immigration and Ethnic Studies Bibliographic Studies 1. Washington: Smithsonian Institution P, 1976.

General Sources on Immigration

Antin, Mary. They Who Knock at Our Gates: A Complete Gospel of Immigration. Boston: Houghton Mifflin, 1914.

Brown, Mary Elizabeth. Shapers of the Great Debate on Immigration: A Biographical Dictionary. Westport, CT: Greenwood P, 1999.

Capaldi, Nicholas. Immigration: Debating the Issues. Amherst, NY: Prometheus Books, 1997.

Chang, Iris. The Chinese in America: A Narrative History. New York: Viking, 2003.

Chavez, Leo R. Covering Immigration: Popular Images and the Politics of the Nation. Berkeley: U of California P, 2001.

Daniels, Roger. Coming to America: A History of Immigration and Ethnicity in American Life. 2nd ed. New York: Perennial, 2002.

—. Guarding the Golden Door: American Immigration Policy and Immigrants Since 1882. New York: Hill and Wang, 2004.

Gjerde, Jon. Major Problems in American Immigration and Ethnic History: Documents and Essays. Boston: Houghton Mifflin, 1998.

Handlin, Oscar. The Uprooted. 2nd enlarged ed. Boston: Little, Brown, 1973.

Isbister, John. The Immigration Debate: Remaking America. West Hartford, CT: Kumarian P, 1996.

Jacobson, David. The Immigration Reader: America in a Multidisciplinary Perspective. Malden, MA: Blackwell, 1998.

Jones, Maldwyn Allen. American Immigration. 2nd ed. Chicago: U of Chicago P, 1992.

Millman, Joel. "Going Nativist." Columbia Journalism Review 37.5 (1999): 60–64.

Pozzetta, George E. Contemporary Immigration and American Society. American Immigration & Ethnicity 20. New York: Garland, 1991.

—. The Immigrant Religious Experience. American Immigration & Ethnicity 19. New York: Garland, 1991.

—. Nativism, Discrimination, and Images of Immigrants. American Immigration & Ethnicity 15. New York: Garland, 1991.

Riis, Jacob A. How the Other Half Lives: Studies Among the Tenements of New York. New York: Dover, 1971.

Schneider, Dorothee. "'I Know All About Emma Lazarus': Nationalism and Its Contradictions in Congressional Rhetoric of Immigration Restriction." Cultural Anthropology 13.1 (1998): 82–99.

Segal, Uma Anand. A Framework for Immigration: Asians in the United States. New York: Columbia U P, 2002.

Simon, Rita James, and Susan H. Alexander. The Ambivalent Welcome: Print Media, Public Opinion, and Immigration. Westport, CT: Praeger, 1993.

The Rise of New Immigrant Gateways. 2004. Center on Urban and Metropolitan Policy, The Brookings Institution. <http://www.brookings.edu/urban/pubs/20040301%5Fgateways.pdf>.

Wyman, Mark. Round-Trip to America: The Immigrants Return to Europe, 1880–1930. Ithaca: Cornell U P, 1993.

Yans-McLaughlin, Virginia, et al. Immigration Reconsidered: History, Sociology, and Politics. New York: Oxford U P, 1990.

Theories of Immigration

Alba, Richard D., and Victor Nee. Remaking the American Mainstream: Assimilation and Contemporary Immigration. Cambridge: Harvard U P, 2003.

Basch, Linda G., Nina Glick Schiller, and Cristina Szanton Blanc. Nations Unbound: Transnational Projects, Postcolonial Predicaments, and

Deterritorialized Nation-States. Langhorne, PA: Gordon and Breach, 1994.

Dewind, Josh, and Philip Kasinitz. "Everything Old is New Again? Processes and Theories of Immigrant Incorporation." The International Migration Review 31.4 (1997): 1096–1111.

Gerber, David A. "Forming A Transnational Narrative: New Perspectives on European Migrations to the United States." The History Teacher 35.1 (2001): 61–77.

Gordon, Milton Myron. Assimilation in American Life: The Role of Race, Religion, and National Origins. New York: Oxford U P, 1964.

Holli, Melvin G. "E Pluribus Unum: The Assimilation Paradigm Revisited." Midwest Quarterly 44.1 (2002): 10–26.

Portes, Alejandro, and Rubén G. Rumbaut. Immigrant America: A Portrait. 2nd ed. Berkeley: U of California P, 1996.

——. Legacies: The Story of the Immigrant Second Generation. Berkeley: U of California P; New York: Russell Sage, 2001.

Pozzetta, George E. Assimilation, Acculturation, and Social Mobility. American Immigration & Ethnicity 13. New York: Garland, 1991.

Rumbaut, Rubén G., and Alejandro Portes. Ethnicities: Children of Immigrants in America. Berkeley: U of California P; New York: Russell Sage, 2001.

Schiller, Nina Glick, Linda G. Basch, and Cristina Szanton Blanc. Towards a Transnational Perspective on Migration: Race, Class, Ethnicity, and Nationalism Reconsidered. Annals of the New York Academy of Sciences 645. New York: New York Academy of Sciences, 1992.

Schiller, Nina Glick, and Georges Eugene Fouron. Georges Woke Up Laughing: Long-Distance Nationalism and the Search for Home. Durham: Duke U P, 2001.

Schuck, Peter H., and Rainer Münz. Paths to Inclusion: The Integration of Migrants in the United States and Germany. New York: Berghahn Books/American Academy of Arts and Sciences, 1998.

Zhou, Min. "Segmented Assimilation: Issues, Controversies, and Recent Research on the New Second Generation." The International Migration Review 31.4 (1997): 975–1008.

Immigrant Narratives

Abinader, Elmaz. Children of the Roojme: A Family's Journey from Lebanon. Madison: U of Wisconsin P, 1997.

Agueros, Jack, and Thomas C. Wheeler. The Immigrant Experience: The Anguish of Becoming American. New York: Dial, 1971.

Albert, Félix. Immigrant Odyssey: A French-Canadian Habitant in New England, A Bilingual Edition of Histoire d'un Enfant Pauvre. Orono: U of Maine P, 1990.

Anderson, Mary, and Mary Nelson Winslow. Woman at Work: The Autobiography of Mary Anderson as Told to Mary N. Winslow. Minneapolis: U of Minnesota P, 1951.

Antin, Mary. From Plotzk to Boston. Boston: W. B. Clarke, 1899.

—. The Promised Land. Princeton: Princeton U P, 1969.

Barton, H. Arnold. Letters from the Promised Land: Swedes in America, 1840–1914. Minneapolis: U of Minnesota P for the Swedish Pioneer Historical Society, 1975.

Bost, Théodore, Sophie Bost, and Ralph Henry Bowen. A Frontier Family in Minnesota: Letters of Théodore and Sophie Bost, 1851–1920. Minneapolis: U of Minnesota P, 1981.

Bulosan, Carlos. America Is in the Heart: A Personal History. New York: Harcourt Brace, 1946.

Cahan, Abraham. The Education of Abraham Cahan. Philadelphia: Jewish Publication Society of America, 1969.

Chan, Sucheng. Hmong Means Free: Life in Laos and America. Philadelphia: Temple U P, 1994.

Christowe, Stoyan. My American Pilgrimage. Boston: Little, Brown, 1947.

Cohen, Rose. Out of the Shadow. New York: George H. Doran, 1918.

Colon, Jesus. A Puerto Rican in New York, and Other Sketches. New York: Mainstream Publishers, 1961.

Conway, Alan. The Welsh in America: Letters from the Immigrants. Minneapolis: U of Minnesota P, 1961.

Dublin, Thomas. Immigrant Voices: New Lives in America, 1773–1986. Urbana: U of Illinois P, 1993.

Duus, Olaus Fredrik, and Theodore Christian Blegen. Frontier Parsonage: The Letters of Olaus Fredrik Duus, Norwegian Pastor in Wisconsin, 1855–1858. Northfield, MN: Norwegian-American Historical Association, 1947.

Espiritu, Yen Le. Filipino American Lives. Philadelphia: Temple U P, 1995.

Ets, Marie Hall. Rosa, the Life of an Italian Immigrant. Minneapolis: U of Minnesota P, 1970.

Frank, Louis Frederick, comp. German-American Pioneers in Wisconsin and Michigan: The Frank-Kerler Letters, 1849–1864. Ed. Harry

H. Anderson. Trans. Margaret Wolff. Milwaukee: Milwaukee County Historical Society, 1971.

Freeman, James M. Hearts of Sorrow: Vietnamese-American Lives. Stanford: Stanford U P, 1989.

Gamio, Manuel. The Life Story of the Mexican Immigrant: Autobiographic Documents. New York: Dover P, 1971.

García, Alma M. Narratives of Mexican American Women: Emergent Identities of the Second Generation. Walnut Creek, CA: Altamira P, 2004.

Gonzales, Ramón, and John J. Poggie. Between Two Cultures: The Life of an American-Mexican, as Told to John J. Poggie, Jr. Tucson: U of Arizona P, 1973.

Handlin, Oscar. Children of the Uprooted. 2nd Ed. Enlarged. Boston: Little, Brown, 1951.

Herscher, Uri D. The East European Jewish Experience in America: A Century of Memories, 1882–1982. Cincinnati: American Jewish Archives, 1983.

Hoflund, Charles J., and H. Arnold Barton. Getting Ahead: A Swedish Immigrant's Reminiscences, 1834–1887. Carbondale: Southern Illinois U P, 1989.

Holt, Hamilton. The Life Stories of Undistinguished Americans as Told by Themselves. New York: J. Pott, 1906.

Kalergis, Mary Motley. Home of the Brave: Contemporary American Immigrants. New York: Dutton, 1989.

Kamphoefner, Walter D., Wolfgang Johannes Helbich, and Ulrike Sommer. News from the Land of Freedom: German Immigrants Write Home. Ithaca: Cornell U P, 1991.

Katzman, David M., and William M. Tuttle, eds. Plain Folk: The Life Stories of Undistinguished Americans. Urbana: U of Illinois P, 1982.

Kessner, Thomas, and Betty Boyd Caroli. Today's Immigrants, Their Stories: A New Look at the Newest Americans. New York: Oxford U P, 1981.

Kim, Elaine H., and Eui-Young Yu. East to America: Korean American Life Stories. New York: New P, 1996.

LaGumina, Salvatore John. The Immigrants Speak: Italian Americans Tell their Story. New York: Center for Migration Studies, 1979.

Lee, Joann Faung Jean. Asian American Experiences in the United States: Oral Histories of First to Fourth Generation Americans *from China, the Philippines, Japan, India, the Pacific Islands, Vietnam, and Cambodia*. Jefferson, NC: McFarland, 1991.

McCunn, Ruthanne Lum. *Chinese American Portraits: Personal Histories 1828–1988*. San Francisco: Chronicle, 1988.

McKay, Claude. *A Long Way from Home.* New York: Harcourt Brace, 1970.

Mendoza, Louis Gerard, and Subramanian Shankar. *Crossing into America: The New Literature of Immigration*. New York: New P, 2003.

Metzker, Isaac. *A Bintel Brief: Sixty Years of Letters from the Lower East Side to the Jewish Daily Forward*. New York: Ballantine, 1977.

Morrison, Joan, and Zabusky, Charlotte Fox. *American Mosaic: The Immigrant Experience in the Words of Those Who Lived It*. New York: Dutton, 1980.

Mullen, Pat. *Man of Aran*. Cambridge: MIT P, 1970.

Namias, June. *First Generation: In the Words of Twentieth-Century American Immigrants*. Urbana: U of Illinois P, 1992.

Ngor, Haing, and Roger Warner. *A Cambodian Odyssey*. New York: Warner Books, 1989.

Peck, Abraham J., and Uri D. Herscher. *Queen City Refuge: An Oral History of Cincinnati's Jewish Refugees from Nazi Germany*. West Orange, NJ: Behrman House, 1989.

Polacheck, Hilda Satt. *I Came a Stranger: The Story of a Hull-House Girl*. Ed. Dena J. Polacheck Epstein. Urbana: U of Illinois P, 1989.

Rockaway, Robert A. *Words of the Uprooted: Jewish Immigrants in Early Twentieth-Century America*. Ithaca, NY: Cornell U P, 1998.

Rubin, Steven Joel. *Writing Our Lives: Autobiographies of American Jews, 1890–1990*. Philadelphia: Jewish Publication Society, 1991.

Santoli, Al. *New Americans: An Oral History: Immigrants and Refugees in the U.S. Today*. New York: Viking, 1988.

Schweizer, Johannes, et al. *The Old Land and the New: The Journals of Two Swiss Families in America in the 1820's*. Minneapolis: U of Minnesota P, 1965.

Surmelian, Leon Z. *I Ask You, Ladies and Gentlemen*. New York: Dutton, 1945.

Thomas, Piri. *Down These Mean Streets*. New York: Knopf, 1967.

Zempel, Solveig. *In Their Own Words: Letters from Norwegian Immigrants*. Minneapolis: U of Minnesota P with the Norwegian-American Historical Association, 1991.

Settlement Houses

Addams, Jane. Twenty Years at Hull-House with Autobiographical Notes. Boston: Bedford/St. Martin's, 1999.

Addams, Jane, and Charlene Haddock Seigfried. Democracy and Social Ethics. Urbana: U of Illinois P, 2002.

Brown, Victoria. The Education of Jane Addams. Philadelphia: U of Pennsylvania P, 2004.

Bryan, Mary Lynn McCree, et al. 100 Years at Hull-House. Bloomington: Indiana U P, 1990.

Cohen, Rose. Out of the Shadow. New York: George H. Doran Co., 1918.

Johnson, Mary Ann, ed. The Many Faces of Hull-House: The Photographs of Wallace Kirkland. Urbana: U of Illinois P, 1989.

Lissak, Rivka Shpak. Pluralism & Progressives: Hull House and the New Immigrants, 1890–1919. Chicago: U of Chicago P, 1989.

Philpott, Thomas Lee. The Slum and the Ghetto: Immigrants, Blacks, and Reformers in Chicago, 1880–1930. Belmont, CA: Wadsworth, 1991.

Polacheck, Hilda Satt. I Came a Stranger: The Story of a Hull-House Girl. Ed. Dena J. Polacheck Epstein. Urbana: U of Illinois P, 1989.

Simkhovitch, Mary K. Neighborhood: My Story of Greenwich House. New York: Norton, 1938.

Wald, Lillian D. The House on Henry Street. New York: Henry Holt, 1915.

Hispanic Immigration and Response to Samuel P. Huntington

Also see Hispanic immigrant narratives above.

"A Question of Identity." Economist, 6 March 2004: 32.

Brooks, David. "The Americano Dream." New York Times 24 Feb. 2004, late ed.: A25.

Carlson, Peter. "Hey, Professor, Assimilate This." Washington Post 9 March 2004, Style: C01.

Castañeda, Jorge. "Immigration Reform Would Help Warm Mexicans to U.S. 'Melting Pot.'" Christian Science Monitor 9 April 2004: 9.

Connor, Walker. Mexican-Americans in Comparative Perspective. Washington, D.C: Urban Institute P, 1985.

Glaister, Dan. "On the Border of Disaster?" Guardian 15 March 2004, Guardian Features: 4.

Glenn, David. "Scholars Cook Up a New Melting Pot." Chronicle of Higher Education 13 February 2004: A10, A12.

Grow, Brian, et al. "Hispanic Nation." Business Week 15 March 2004: 58+.

Gutiérrez, David. Between Two Worlds: Mexican Immigrants in the United States. Wilmington, DE: Scholarly Resources, 1996.

Mormino, Gary Ross, and George E. Pozzetta. The Immigrant World of Ybor City: Italians and Their Latin Neighbors in Tampa, 1885–1985. Urbana: U of Illinois P, 1987.

APPENDIX

B

Using Sources in an Argumentative Research Essay

I. Research Resources

Writing an argumentative research essay demands that you learn to do many things—read arguments critically, synthesize other writers' work, and organize and support your own argument. But before you can do any of these things, you must locate relevant, reliable, and thoughtful sources for your essay. The types of critical skills you exercise in reading the texts in this book are also necessary for doing good research. Finding sources may be easy, but finding good sources is often hard because we must be able to distinguish the good from the bad, the thoughtful from the superficial, the reliable from the fly-by-night, and the open-minded from the biased.

Research often begins when you have chosen your research topic but not yet narrowed it or developed a working thesis or claim (see Chapter 3). What you discover about your research topic will help you to narrow your focus and then to take your own position. Students just beginning research in the modern college library have great resources to draw upon. But where should you begin?

There are four types of resources for the research you will likely do for a college argumentative research essay:

1. Field research, such as observations, interviews, surveys, and questionnaires
2. Your library (and connected libraries) catalog

3. InfoTrac College Edition, other databases, and other electronic sources such as CD-ROMs
4. The Internet

Field Research

The information and ideas necessary to understand some current topics can be obtained through research "in the field," direct observation and collection of material in the world. You might, for example, conduct an oral history interview with a veteran to learn how people experienced a particular war. You might e-mail civil disobedience activists and ask them their opinions of current world events; they will often respond to thoughtful questions from serious students. It is important to prepare well for field research, so be sure that you have carefully constructed your questions or interview procedure before you begin.

Library Catalogs

Every library maintains a catalog of its holdings of books, periodicals, and electronic publications, normally cataloged according to the Library of Congress or Dewey Decimal System. College and university libraries, as well as many public libraries, are often part of larger library networks that enable you to search the holdings of thousands of other libraries. You should become very familiar with the method to search your own library's catalog and with using the reference materials available in the library. Learn to use the search functions in your online library catalog. Consult the reference librarians; they are extremely knowledgeable and will assist you to do better searches in the library. Remember that most scholarship in the world is still found in the books and journals you can locate through the library catalog.

InfoTrac College Edition, Databases, and Other Electronic Sources

Libraries subscribe to databases that contain bibliographic information—indexes to publications, citations, and abstracts—and to databases that include full-text services that allow the user to read and download complete sources. Investigate what your library has available and how to access it. Many databases are now available to library patrons from off-campus via the library's website.

The Internet

The Internet can be a wonderful source for information and ideas for the careful researcher. Government bodies, universities, publishers, individual scholars, and scholarly and professional organizations have published millions of valuable pages on the World Wide Web. Many newspapers and magazines now publish online versions of their current issues, although earlier material may not be accessible or free. Other material available is much more dubious, ranging from personal obsessions to deceptive websites that are selling a product or an ideology. It is vital to depend upon the guidance of your librarian or instructor as well as on your own critical analysis in evaluating websites. See your library website or your librarian for recommended sites when you begin your research.

You will also wish to search directly for your topic on the Internet. You can use keywords and subjects to locate material using search engines such as Google and Yahoo! Evaluate the sites you find this way using the steps below. Remember to record all publication information and the date you accessed the site because you will need these to use and cite the source in your essay.

Example of Doing Research

Suppose you were interested in exploring whether the Vietnam War could be considered a just war. How would you go about finding adequate and reliable sources?

Look at the four types of research resources above. You would probably not begin with *field research* because you would need to educate yourself before you interviewed or questioned anyone. You should begin with your library catalog.

Library Catalog

Our library catalog at Loyola University Chicago found two books when we entered the keywords *Vietnam* and *just war* in the keyword catalog search:

Boyd Andrew J. *The Theory of Just War and Its Application to the American War in Vietnam.* Chicago: Loyola UP, 1991.

McNeal, Patricia F. *Harder than War: Catholic Peacemaking in Twentieth-Century America.* New Brunswick: Rutgers UP, 1992.

Internet Site Evaluation Checklist

1. Is the site peer reviewed?
2. Does it give information about how to cite it? Such information is a good indication that the authors see themselves as part of the scholarly conversation.
3. Is there a named author? Who is it? What are his or her credentials? You may have to do research on the author.
4. Check the home page or welcome page. Is there a sponsoring organization? Have you heard of it? Is it reliable? What do the authors say about themselves? Do you have any way to check on them? Are they a recognized authority such as a university or well-known organization? Do not use websites where no author or no sponsoring organization is named.
5. Is there any kind of editorial policy or statement of purpose given? Read it carefully so you can judge the intention of the authors.
6. If the sites include text from other sources, can you be sure it is reliably reproduced? If material is scanned in, there is no way to tell if it was correctly and completely added. Look for PDF texts because you can see the original pages and locate the original in the library. You must be able, at the least, to verify the material, so there must be accurate citation of original publication data and/or hyperlinks to original material locations.
7. When was the site last updated? If some years ago, it may no longer be accurate or have been a fly-by-night project to begin with.
8. If it is a commercial site, what sorts of ads appear? Look carefully to see if the site is in fact only an advertisement disguised as information. Ads can also lead you to make critical judgments about the intended audience of the website, helping you to evaluate its contents.
9. Finally, there is no substitute for reading critically. You are the judge of the ethos of the website. Are you confident that the site is reliable, authoritative, and honest?

We can print all the publication information and library call number or save it to a file on our computer. We can even e-mail the information to ourselves or to someone else.

Once the books are located in the library, we can see if they lead in an interesting direction. Almost as important, we can use their bibliographies to find the names of other books and articles and can search the catalog for them.

InfoTrac College Edition and Other Databases

A search of InfoTrac College Edition for the keywords *Vietnam* and *just war* together finds three sources. One that looks especially promising is reprinted below as it appears:

KERREY'S CULPABILITY: Vietnam & the just-war tradition. (participation of former Senator Bob Kerrey in Vietnam War and moral culpability implied by just-war theory) Gordon Marino.

Commonweal June 1, 2001 v128 i11 p9 Mag.Coll.: 107M0094

Using InfoTrac College Edition assures us that the source has been selected as appropriate for college research. If we need to know more, we can pursue information about both Senator Bob Kerrey and the author, Gordon Marino, in other databases available in the library. Sen. Kerrey is easy to find through many standard biographical reference sources. However, Marino is harder. He is not, for example, in *Who's Who* or *Contemporary Authors*. We can try to see if there is a note about the author in the publication itself, where we learn he is an associate professor of philosophy and director of the Hong/Kirkegaard Library at Saint Olaf College. If further research about him were necessary, we would look for other of his publications and for information about him on Saint Olaf's website.

We can also click on the Link button next to his article to find many other sources related to Vietnam. These need to be followed up. *Just war* by itself and *Vietnam* by itself as keywords will locate more sources as well.

The Internet

Using *Vietnam "just war"* to search Google finds 12,700 Web documents. One is a page on a website for the 15th Field Artillery Regiment http://www.landscaper.net/peace.htm. There is quite a bit of material on this website, but how much can you use? For example, this page includes a definition of just war that is not credited to an author or source. This is not a particularly reliable source for just war theory. The writers of the website are not authorities and do not claim to be authorities on just war. What could you use? The regimental history by the regimental historian, who is named, would be authoritative. You can check to see the statement of purpose and the history of the website. You can contact the Webmaster and ask questions. You can follow the links and evaluate them as well. Excerpts from other sources and quotations should not be used unless you can verify them.

Some research topics make evaluation especially difficult. For example, if you were researching World War II, you might use the words *German, WW II, British,* and *Jews* to search in Google. You would then come across the website http://www.heretical.com/mkilliam/wwii.html, which seems to have a large number of quotations from primary sources and newspapers. Initially, you might think the site was one you could use in your research.

However, the author's name is given, but not information about the author. And, as you begin to read, if you know anything about the subject, you will see the author is a Hitler supporter and twists facts terribly. If you then turn to the main page and click on some links, you will see it is a neo-Nazi site selling anti-Semitic books; there is even a swastika on one page. But if you knew nothing about the subject, you might believe this to be objective or at least truthful. Thus the Internet may not be a good place to begin research on a topic you know very little about.

II. Integrating Sources into Your Writing

In general, you will demonstrate your knowledge and credibility as a writer by controlling your use of source material. Remember that you are in charge, not the sources. Certainly utilize the ideas and facts another writer offers, but employ those to support your argument. Do not allow the sources to overshadow your claims.

Avoiding Plagiarism

Plagiarism is a form of fraud or theft in which a writer takes others' words or ideas and presents them as his or her own. Some plagiarism is the result of ignorance or carelessness. More seriously, some is deliberate, such as buying papers to hand in as your own or copying sources and passing them off as your own writing. All kinds of plagiarism violate the basic rules of the conversations we participate in. Inadvertent plagiarism prevents researchers from following up on sources and learning from them directly because sources are not named. Of course, deliberate plagiarism is equivalent to lying to people—never a good basis for a conversation. In addition, plagiarism often leads to severe penalties in both the academic and publishing worlds.

To avoid plagiarism, you must cite your source wherever you paraphrase, summarize, or quote. Both the sources of information—facts, dates, and events—and of ideas must be cited. You must give complete bibliographic data about all sources you use. You must use either the exact words of the source as a quotation or paraphrase or summarize the source's information or ideas in your own words.

Introducing Source Material

There are three ways to use material you have found in your research in your own argument: summary, paraphrase, and quotation. Each has its place. Whether you summarize, paraphrase, or quote, you need to introduce the material in some way. The easiest way is to begin with an attribution:

- According to Richard Falk, . . .
- As John Yoder points out, . . .

Be sure to give the full name of an author you are mentioning for the first time; thereafter you may use the last name only. It can add to your own authority as a writer to identify the authority of your source:

- The Islamic legal scholar Majid Khadduri notes . . .
- University of Chicago Divinity School professor Jean Bethke Elshtain believes that . . .

Give a context or other opening to make sense of a quotation, and be sure that your quotation is part of a grammatical sentence.

Summary

When you wish to state briefly information or an idea from a source, use summary. Use your own words to sum up the main facts or notions; leave out the details. Summary is especially appropriate for information.

Paraphrase

When you want to use information or ideas at greater length from a source, paraphrase it. To paraphrase means to put the passage into your own words, changing the structure as well as the words.

Quotation

Judicious quotation adds authority and credibility to your argumentative research writing. Choose passages that are important to your argument, that are well stated, or that you wish to examine in detail. Avoid using too many quotations. No reader wants to read a patchwork quilt of quotations stitched together by a writer with no words of his or her own. Introduce quotations carefully: Do not just plop them in. Quotations longer than four lines should be set off by indenting them ten spaces. If you remove anything from a quoted passage, you must indicate you have done so with ellipses. If you add anything to a quotation, perhaps to clarify a word, place square brackets around the addition.

III. Documenting Sources: MLA and APA Styles

All sources of information and ideas must be cited; you must state what the source is and which part of it you used. The exception is items that are common knowledge, such as, for instance, that the United States fought in World War II or that Christianity is the dominant religion of the West. Both the Modern Language Association (MLA) and the American Psychological Association (APA) have extensive guidelines for preparing papers and publications that include distinct styles of source citation. The styles both require that you keep careful records of your research so that you can accurately cite your sources. Instructors in the humanities generally require students to follow MLA guidelines. In the social sciences, instructors usually require APA format. Use the format your instructor assigns.

Both the MLA and APA formats work by giving a short reference to the source at the end of the passage quoted, paraphrased, or summarized. The reference is keyed to a complete bibliographic entry at the end of the paper, the Works Cited page for MLA, the References or Bibliography for APA.

For more extensive discussions of documentation forms, see the *MLA Handbook for Writers of Research Papers,* 6th edition, and the *APA Publication Manual,* 5th edition. In addition, both the MLA and the APA have advice about documenting sources, particularly electronic ones, on their respective websites, www.mla.org and www.apastyle.org.

Parenthetical Citation

The MLA format requires that you give the author's name and the page number in parentheses following the quotation, summary, or paraphrase. For APA, the author's name, the date or year of publication, and the page numbers are given. In either style, you do not need to repeat the author's name if you give it in the text.

MLA Style

1. Direct Quotation

One major concern is "that America's pre-emptive war will lead directly to the use of the weapons whose mere possession the war is supposed to prevent" (Schell 15).

2. Author Named with Direct Quotation

As Kelsay points out, "with respect to the example of Muhammad, then, it was possible to speak of use of lethal force which was right, in the sense of divinely sanctioned—even, divinely commanded" (45).

3. Summary or Paraphrase

After the September 11, 2001, terrorist attacks, there were condemnations from almost all governments around the world, although in the Middle East there was public rejoicing in the streets at Americans' suffering (Longworth 19).

4. Two or Three Authors

The main difference between the assassination of John F. Kennedy and that of Abraham Lincoln was that Kennedy was "a remembered physical presence" while Lincoln was "an image of the plastic arts" (Kempton and Ridgeway 63).

5. Two Books by the Same Author

To distinguish between two books by the same author that appear in your Works Cited, either include the title in the introduction to the passage or use a short version of the title in the parenthetical citation.

Khadduri explains: "The world surrounding the Islamic state, composed of all other nations and territories that had not been brought under its rule, was collectively known as the 'territory of war'" (Islamic Law of Nations 12).

6. **Corporate Author**
Some publications are published under the name of an organization or other group. You can use the name of the organization just as you would an author. It is preferable to give the name in the introduction to the cited passage.

```
    The Chicago Public Schools Office of School
and Community Relations notes that Local School
Councils may set dress-code policy (vi).
```

7. **Article in an Anthology**
If you use an article in a book such as this casebook or any anthology, use the name of the author of the article, not the author or editor of the book.

8. **No Author**
Use the title in the parenthetical citation if there is no author. You should use a shortened title if possible, starting with the word by which it is alphabetized in the Works Cited.

```
    "We are menaced less by fleets and armies than
by catastrophic technologies in the hands of the
embittered few" (National Security Strategy 1).
```

9. **Indirect Source**
When you wish to use a passage quoted in another source and cannot locate the original, you may cite the source by naming the author of the quoted passage and placing the source you found it in the parenthetical citation.

```
    Burton Leiser describes terrorism as "seem-
ingly senseless" (qtd. in Khatchadourian 35).
```

10. **Scriptures**
References to the names and parts of sacred writings, such as the Bible, the Qur'an, and the Upanishads, are not underlined. Biblical citations give the book, chapter, and verse, and the standard abbreviations are preferred.

```
    "They have healed the wound of my people
lightly, saying, 'Peace, peace,' when there is no
peace" (Jer.6:14).
```

11. Electronic Sources

When citing sources from databases and the Internet, follow the rules for in-text parenthetical citation as much as possible. If there are no page numbers given, you must cite the entire work. If the source numbers its paragraphs, then include those as (par. 2) or (pars. 8–9). It is a good idea to name the source in the text.

Alexander warns that it is easier to list Just War principles than to apply them to a specific instance.

The Works Cited list gives Alexander's article retrieved through a full-text database from The Providence Journal-Bulletin.

According to Prados, "There were no significant changes in the CIA's intelligence sources on Iraq, and in fact there was no real change in what the agency was reporting" (29).

This article, from The Bulletin of the Atomic Scientists, was retrieved as a PDF from InfoTrac College Edition. Therefore, a page number can be given. If you retrieve it directly from the Bulletin's website, you will not be able to cite a page number.

The White House Web site's History & Tours section attributes Jefferson's election to the vice presidency under John Adams to "a flaw in the Constitution."

12. A Television or Radio Program, a Sound Recording, a Film or Video Recording, a Lecture, an Interview, or a Cartoon

These are all cited in the text as entire works. Thus the preferred method is to include the title or the name of the person (such as the director, performer, interviewee, or speaker) in the text. The title or name should be the element that begins the entry in your Works Cited.

The Ramirez cartoon expresses a strong prowar position. (The entry in the Works Cited list gives the specific cartoon under the cartoonist's name, Mike Ramirez.)

Kathy Kelly inspired the students with her lecture on working for peace. (The lecture is listed under Kelly.)

Mrs. Wayani was married twice and has four

children. (The interview with Mrs. Wayani appears under her name in the Works Cited list.)

Phillis Wheatley went to England with her master's son, Nathaniel Wheatley, as Africans in America explains. (The video recording is listed in the Works Cited list by its title.)

APA Style

1. Author with Direct Quotation

One major concern is "that America's pre-emptive war will lead directly to the use of the weapons whose mere possession the war is supposed to prevent" (Schell, 2003, p.15).

2. Author Named with Direct Quotation

As Kelsay (1993) points out, "with respect to the example of Muhammad, then, it was possible to speak of use of lethal force which was right, in the sense of divinely sanctioned—even, divinely commanded" (p.45).

3. Summary or Paraphrase

After the September 11, 2001, terrorist attacks, there were condemnations from almost all governments around the world, although in the Middle East there was public rejoicing in the streets at Americans' suffering (Longworth, 2001, p.19).

4. Two or Three Authors

APA uses an ampersand (&) between names in the parenthetical citation but not in the text itself.

The main difference between the assassination of John F. Kennedy and that of Abraham Lincoln was that Kennedy was "a remembered physical presence" while Lincoln was "an image of the plastic arts" (Kempton & Ridgeway, 1968, p.63).

5. Two Books by the Same Author

In the APA style, the different dates distinguish the different books. Khadduri's other book was published in 1955.

Khadduri (1966) explains: "The world surrounding the Islamic state, composed of all other nations and territories that had not been brought under its rule, was collectively known as the 'territory of war'" (p.12).

6. **Corporate Author**

The Chicago Public Schools Office of School and Community Relations (2000) notes that local school councils may set dress code policy (p.vi).

7. **Article in an Anthology**

As with MLA format, use the author of the article in the collection, not the author or editor of the book.

8. **No Author**

"We are menaced less by fleets and armies than by catastrophic technologies in the hands of the embittered few" (National Security Strategy, 2003, 1).

9. **Indirect Source**

Burton Leiser (1979) describes terrorism as "seemingly senseless" (as cited in Khatchadourian, 2003, p.35).

10. **Scriptures**

Identical to MLA format, references to the names and parts of sacred writings, such as the Bible, the Qur'an, and the Upanishads, are not underlined. Biblical citations give the book, chapter, and verse, and the standard abbreviations are preferred.

11. **Electronic Sources**

Give the author's name, the date of publication, and page or paragraph numbers, if they are available, just as you would with a print source. If no author is given, use a shortened version of the title. If no date is given, use n.d. to indicate no date.

Alexander (2003) warns that it is easier to list Just War principles than to apply them to a specific instance.

The References list gives Alexander's article retrieved through a full-text database from *The Providence Journal-Bulletin.*

According to Prados (2003), "There were no significant changes in the CIA's intelligence sources on Iraq, and in fact there was no real change in what the agency was reporting" (p.29).

This article, from *The Bulletin the Atomic Scientists,* was retrieved as a PDF from InfoTrac College Edition. Therefore, a page number can be given. If you retrieve it directly from the *Bulletin*'s website, you will not be able to cite a page number.

The White House Web site's History & Tours section attributes Jefferson's election to the vice presidency under John Adams to "a flaw in the Constitution."

12. A Television or Radio Program, a Sound Recording, a Film or Video Recording, a Lecture, an Interview, or a Cartoon
As in the MLA format, these sources are all cited in the text as entire works. Thus, the preferred method is to include the title or the name of the person (such as the director, performer, interviewee, or speaker) in the text. Unlike in MLA format, APA format considers an interview or unpublished lecture unrecoverable data and therefore does not include it in the References list, but it may be cited in the text as a personal communication.

Mrs. Wayani was married twice and has four children (personal communication, October 17, 2003).

Phillis Wheatley went to England with her master's son, Nathaniel Wheatley, as *Africans in America* explains.

The video recording is listed in the References list by its title.

The Works Cited and References Lists

All parenthetical citations refer to a work listed on the Works Cited page (MLA) or References list (APA). The reader must be able to find every source named in the body of your essay in the bibliographic listing, which appears at the end of the essay. Therefore the list is alphabetized by the authors' last names or, if no author is given, by the title of the source (excluding *a, an,* and *the* at the beginning of the title).

If you have kept a computer file of all your sources, you can easily arrange them alphabetically. Similarly, if you have kept bibliography notecards, you can alphabetize these. If you have already prepared an annotated bibliography, remove the annotations and attach it to the paper.

MLA Style

The Works Cited page is double-spaced. The entries are typed in the "drop-and-hang" style: the first line of the entry is flush against the left margin, and each subsequent line of the entry is indented five spaces. A student paper using MLA style is printed at the end of this Appendix.

MLA Form for Books

Author. Title of Book. City: Publisher's Name in Shortened Form, date of publication.

Note that all the important words in the title are capitalized. MLA prefers that titles be underlined rather than italicized, but your instructor might prefer italics for titles. Publishers' names should be abbreviated; use UP for *University Press.*

1. **Book by One Author**

   Kelsay, John. Islam and War: A Study in Comparative Ethics. Louisville: Westminster, 1993.

2. **Book by Two or More Authors**

   If a book has two or three authors, list them in the order they appear on the title page. Reverse only the name of the first author listed and separate the names by commas. If there are more than three authors, use the abbreviation et al. (Latin for *and others*) after the first author, or you may choose to list all the authors.

   Hammer, Michael, and James Champy. Reengineering the Corporation: A Manifesto for Business Revolution. New York: HarperBusiness, 1993.

   Perls, Frederick, Ralph E. Hefferline, and Paul Goodman. Gestalt Therapy: Excitement and Growth in the Human Personality. New York: Dell, 1951.

3. Book with an Editor or Translator

Jack, Homer A., ed. The Gandhi Reader: A Sourcebook of His Life and Writings. New York: Grove, 1956.

Zohn, Harry, and Karl F. Ross, trans. What If—? Satirical Writings of Kurt Tucholsky. New York: Funk, 1967.

4. Corporate Author

List the book by the corporate author, such as an association or commission, even if there is an editor listed as well.

Central Conference of American Rabbis. A Passover Haggadah: The New Union Haggadah. Ed. Herbert Bronstein. New York: Central Conference of American Rabbis, 1974.

5. Article or Other Piece in an Anthology

Use the author of the article as the author. Put the title of the article in quotation marks. Give the editor's name after the title of the anthology, which is underlined. Follow the period after the date of the publication with the inclusive pages where the article is found.

Chang, Edward T. "America's First Multiethnic 'Riots.'" The State of Asian America: Activism and Resistance in the 1990s. Ed. Karin Aguilar-San Juan. Boston: South End, 1994. 101-17.

Kempton, Murray, and James Ridgeway. "Romans." The Sense of the Sixties. Ed. Edward Quinn and Paul J. Dolan. New York: Free, 1968. 63-67.

6. Article in a Reference Book

Cite an article in an encyclopedia or dictionary the way you would one in an anthology (see above) except do not list the editor of the reference work. If the author of the article is given, use the name; otherwise, cite by the title of the article. Common reference books that are published often in new editions do not need full publication data. You need only give the edition (if you can) and the date of publication. You may omit volume and page numbers if the entries are arranged alphabetically.

"Justice." The American Heritage College Dictionary. 3rd ed. 1997.

Kelly, P. M. "Gaia Hypothesis." The Harper Dictionary of Modern Thought. Ed. Alan Bullock and Stephen Trombley. Rev. ed. New York: Harper, 1988.

MLA Form for Articles

Author. "Title of the Article." Journal volume number (year): page numbers.

Author. "Title of the Article." Newspaper date of publication, edition: page numbers.

Author. "Title of the Article." Magazine date of publication: page numbers.

1. Article in a Scholarly Journal

Do not use the issue number unless the journal does not number pages continuously throughout the volume.

Windholz, Anne M. "An Emigrant and a Gentleman: Imperial Masculinity, British Magazines, and the Colony That Got Away." Victorian Studies 42 (1999-2000): 631-58.

Flanzbaum, Hilene. "Unprecedented Liberties: Re-Reading Phillis Wheatley." MELUS: The Journal of the Society for the Study of the Multi-Ethnic Literature of the United States 18.3 (1993): 71-81.

2. Article in a Newspaper

Schmetzer, Uli, "Spanish, Italian Backers of Iraq War Survive Vote." Chicago Tribune 27 May 2003, late ed., sec 1: 6.

3. Article in a Magazine

Schell, Jonathan. "The Case against the War." The Nation 3 March 2003: 11-23.

Meyerson, Harold. "The Most Dangerous President Ever." American Prospect May 2003: 25-28.

MLA Form for Electronic Sources

For electronic sources, you need to collect more information than you do for print sources because there is no uniform publication format as yet for Internet, World Wide Web, and other electronic publications. Be sure to record as much publication data as you can find about electronic sources, including especially the date you accessed the source. Electronic sources can disappear in a way print ones do not, so record your information right away. It is also a good idea to download and save or print a copy of the source.

Publication data you should collect and use to cite electronic sources:

1. Author's name (if given)
2. Title of the document
3. Information about print publication (if published previously or simultaneously in print)
4. Information about electronic publication (title of publication or Internet site)
5. Access information (date of access and URL of the document—but see exceptions below)

The basic Works Cited form is:

Author's name. "Title of the Document." Information about print publication. Information about electronic publication. Access information.

1. Article in a Periodical on the Web

Prados, John. "A Necessary War? Not According to U.N. Monitors—or to U.S. Intelligence, Which Has Watched the Situation Even More Carefully." Bulletin of the Atomic Scientists 59.3 (2003): 8 pp. 27 May 2003 <http://www.thebulletin.org/issues/2003/mj03/mu03prados.html>.

Sometimes the URL becomes so long and complicated that it is difficult to transcribe. In such cases, give the URL of the site's search page instead.

Gonzalez, David. "A Town of Tents and Civil Disobedience." New York Times on the Web. 1 Aug. 2001. The New York Times Company. 9 Feb. 2002 <http://www.nytimes.com>.

2. **Article through a Library Subscription Service**

   Often the URLs from these services are unique to the institution, are extremely long, or require access through your institution. In this case, access information should include the name of the database (underlined), the name of the service, the name of the library, and the date of access.

Robnett, Belinda. "African-American Women in the Civil Rights Movement, 1954-1965: Gender, Leadership, and Micromobilization." American Journal of Sociology 101 (1996): 1661-1693 JSTOR. Loyola U Chicago Lib. 2 March 2003 <http://www.jstor.org>.

3. **Article from an Organization's Website**

"Not In Our Name: A Statement of Conscience against War and Repression." Not In Our Name. 2002. Not In Our Name. 9 Jan. 2003 <http://www.nion.us/NION.HTM>.

4. **Entire Internet Sites, Such as Online Scholarly Projects or Professional Sites**

Digital Schomburg African American Women Writers of the 19th Century. 1999. The New York Public Library. 10 June 2002 <http://149.123.1.8/schomburg/writers_aa19/toc.html>.

MLA Form for Nonprint Sources

1. **A Film or Video Recording**

Africans in America. Prod. Orlando Bagwell. WGBH Educational Foundation. Videocasette. PBS Video, 1998.

2. **A Television or Radio Program**

"White House Pressed to Stir Revolt in Iran." Narr. Steve Inskeep. All Things Considered. Natl Public Radio. WBEZ, Chicago. 31 May 2003.

3. An Interview

Wayani, Shashi. Personal Interview. 17 October 2002.

4. A Lecture or Speech

Kelly, Kathy. Keynote Address. English Dept. Shared-Text Project. Loyola University, Chicago. 18 Sept. 2002.

5. A Cartoon or Comic Strip

Follow the cartoonist's name with the title if there is one. Use the label of either *Cartoon* or *Comic Strip* and then give the regular publication information.

Donnelly, Liza. Cartoon. <u>New Yorker</u> 21 and 28 April 2003: 66.

APA Style

The References page is double-spaced. The entries are typed in the "drop-and-hang" style: the first line of the entry is flush against the left margin; each subsequent line of the entry is indented five spaces.

APA format differs from MLA in a number of important ways: Use only the initial or initials of an author's first and middle names with his or her last name: *Adams, J. Q.* Follow the name of the author with the date of publication in parentheses.

Capitalize only the first word of titles of books and articles and the first word after a colon. Do capitalize the main words of journals and newspapers. Do not put quotation marks around the titles of articles.

Italicize the titles of books and names of journals, newspapers, and magazines. Do not shorten publishers' names, although you may omit unimportant words such as *Publishers, Inc.,* or *Co.*

APA Form for Books

Author. (date of publication). *Title.* City of publication: Publisher.

1. Book by One Author

Kelsay, J. (1993). *Islam and war: A study in comparative ethics.* Louisville: Westminster/John Knox Press.

2. **Book by Two or More Authors**
APA only uses et al. if there are more than six authors. Use an ampersand to connect the last two authors.

Hammer, M., & Champy, J. (1993). *Reengineering the corporation: A manifesto for business revolution.* New York: HarperBusiness/Harper Collins.

Perls, F., Hefferline, R. E., & Goodman, P. (1951). *Gestalt therapy: Excitement and growth in the human personality.* New York: Dell.

3. **Book with an Editor or Translator**
Jack, H. A. (Ed.). (1956). *The Gandhi reader: A sourcebook of his life and writings.* New York: Grove Press.

Zohn, H., & Ross, K. F. (Trans.). (1967). *What if—? Satirical writings of Kurt Tucholsky.* New York: Funk & Wagnalls.

4. **Corporate Author**
Central Conference of American Rabbis. (1974). *A Passover haggadah: The new union hagaddah.* H. Bronstein (Ed.). New York: Author.

5. **Article or Other Piece in an Anthology**
Use the author or title of the article as the beginning of the entry. Put the inclusive page numbers after the title of the book in parentheses.

Chang, E. T. (1994). America's first multiethnic "riots." In K. Aguilar-San Juan (Ed.), *The state of Asian America: Activism and resistance in the 1990s* (pp.101–117). Boston: South End Press.

Kempton, M., & Ridgeway, J. (1968). Romans. In E. Quinn & P. J. Dolan (Eds.), *The sense of the sixties* (pp.63–67), New York: Free Press.

6. **Article in a Reference Book**
Justice. (1997). *The American heritage college dictionary* (3rd ed., p.738). Boston: Houghton Mifflin.

Kelly, P. M. (1988). Gaia hypothesis. In A. Bullock & S. Trombley (Eds.), *The Harper dictionary of modern thought* (p.341). New York: Harper & Row.

APA Form for Articles

Author. (date of publication). Title of article. *Title of publication, volume number,* page numbers.

1. **Article in a Scholarly Journal**

Windholz, A. M. (1999-2000). An emigrant and a gentleman: Imperial masculinity, British magazines, and the colony that got away. *Victorian Studies, 42,* 631-58.

Flanzbaum, H. (1993). Unprecedented liberties: Rereading Phillis Wheatley. *MELUS: The Journal of the Society for the Study of Multi-Ethnic Literature of the United States, 18*(3), 71-81.

2. **Article in a Newspaper**

Schmetzer, U. (2003, May 27). Spanish, Italian backers of Iraq war survive vote. *Chicago Tribune,* Sec. 1, p.6.

3. **Article in a Magazine**

Schell, J. (2003, March 3). The case against the war. *The Nation,* 11-23.

Meyerson, H. (2003, May) The most dangerous president ever. *American Prospect,* 25-28.

APA Form for Electronic Sources

Author. (Date of publication). Title of article. *Journal title, volume number,* issue number, page numbers [if given]. Retrieved date of access, from where: source URL.

1. **Article in a Periodical on the Web**

Give the retrieval date and URL only if you believe the electronic version differs from the print version.

Prados, J. (2003). A necessary war? Not according to U.N. monitors—or to U.S. intelligence, which has watched the situation even more carefully. *Bulletin of the Atomic Scientists, 59*(3). Retrieved May 27, 2003, from http://www.thebulletin.org/issues/2003/mj03/mj03prados.html.

2. **Article through a Library Subscription Service**
   Give the date of retrieval and the name of the database service. Follow it with the article number if the database provides one.

Robnett, B. (1996) African-American women in the civil rights movement, 1954-1965: Gender, leadership, and micromobilization. *American Journal of Sociology, 101,* 1661-1693. Retrieved March 2, 2003, from JSTOR database.

3. **Article from an Organization's Website**

Not in Our Name (2002). *Not in our name: A statement of conscience against war and repression.* Retrieved January 9, 2003, from http://www.nion.us/NION.HTM.

4. **Entire Internet Sites, Such as Online Scholarly Projects or Professional Sites**

The New York Public Library. (1999) *Digital Schomburg African American women writers of the 19th century.* Retrieved June 10, 2002, from http://149.123.1.8/schomburg/writers_aa19/toc.html.

APA Form for Nonprint Sources

1. **A Film or Video Recording**

Bagwell, O. (Producer). (1998). *Africans in America.* [Videotape]. Boston: WGBH Educational Foundation/PBS Video.

2. A Television or Radio Program

Inskeep, S. (Reporter). (2003, May 31). White House pressed to stir revolt in Iran. *All things considered* [Radio Program]. Chicago: WBEZ.

3. An Interview

Because interviews cannot be retrieved as a source, APA does not list them in the References list.

4. A Lecture or Speech

Unless the lecture was recorded, it is also considered a source that cannot be retrieved and is not listed in the References list.

5. A Cartoon or Comic Strip

Donnelly, L. (2003, April 21 & 28). [Cartoon]. *New Yorker*, 66.

IV. Sample Student Paper in MLA Style

Format

Print or type your paper in an easily readable font type and size, such as Times New Roman 12 point. Justify the lines of the paper at the left margin only. Print only on one side, and use white, good-quality, 8½ × 11-inch paper. Be sure to keep a backup copy on disk. Use one-inch margins on the sides and the top and bottom of the paper (except for page numbers). Double-space your paper, including quotations and the Works Cited list. Leave only one space after the period unless your instructor prefers two.

Put your name and the title of the paper on the first page as follows:

Name
Instructor's Name
Course Number
Date

Double-space and then center the title of your paper on the next line. Do not underline the title, put it in quotation marks, or type it in all capital letters. Capitalize the main words and underline only the words (such as a book title) you would underline in the text of the paper. Use the header function of your word-processing program to place your name and consecutive page numbers in the upper right corner of your pages

You can see what a properly formatted research paper looks like in Caitlin Cunninghams's paper that follows.

Caitlin Cunningham

Dr. Walsh

English 106, Section 066

16 November 2003

The Underground Railroad as a Case of Civil Disobedience

Alan Gewirth presents a generally accepted definition of civil disobedience in his essay "Civil Disobedience, Law and Morality: An Examination of Justice Fortas' Doctrine;" "Civil disobedience," he indicates, "consists in violating some law on the ground that it or some other law or social policy is morally wrong, and the manner of this violation is public, nonviolent, and accepting of the legally prescribed penalty for disobedience" (107). The Underground Railroad is not a classic case of civil disobedience, then, in that its participants violated the Fugitive Slave Law of 1850 secretly so as to avoid capture and punishment. Does the railroad's underground aspect allow for categorization within even a more flexible definition of civil disobedience? Almost certainly, as slaves, legally lacking other nonviolent alternatives, escaped inhuman treatment and living conditions furtively only to ensure their survival. Despite the harsh penalties facing anti-slavery activists, many courageous whites and free African-Americans helped care for, disguise, and move along these fugitive slaves; upon reaching free territory, they could then devote themselves to proving slavery unjust, rallying support, and bequeathing to their descendants the liberty to follow in their footsteps. In its participants' lack of open action and willingness to suffer legal consequences, the Underground Railroad is a unique case of civil disobedience, but a case of civil disobedience nonetheless.

The Underground Railroad, not really a railroad at all, was an illegally operated network leading fugitive slaves to emancipation in the free states or Canada prior to the abolition of slavery in the United States. As acknowledged in Colonel William M. Cockrum's <u>The History of the Underground Railroad</u> and Ryan Dougherty's "A Quest for Freedom," the organization's action violated the Fugitive Slave Law of 1850, which declared captured runaways unworthy of a trial by jury and imposed a $1,000 fine (Cockrum 11-12), property seizure, or a prison sentence upon any individual caught aiding their escape (Dougherty 52). Suggesting this system either had to run clandestinely or not at all,

William Breyfogle asserts in Make Free: The Story of the Underground Railroad the devoted secretiveness exhibited by those involved (22). "In spite of the best efforts of Southern agents, professional slave-catchers and former owners, the secrets were well kept [...] It was a conspiracy, and it is the essence of conspiracies that they remain secret" (Breyfogle 35, 174). John Brown, in his autobiographical work Slave Life in Georgia: A Narrative of the Life, Sufferings, and Escape of John Brown, a Fugitive Slave, Now in England, illustrates slave owners' bewilderment at their rapid loss of property and inability to trace runaway slaves' travels beyond Ohio. Masters became suspicious that escaped slaves had developed a means for leading fellow slaves to freedom via a subterranean network, and abolitionists coined the term "the Underground Railroad to Freedom" (217). Lacking any additional information about the well-kept secrets of the Underground, ignorant masters could not raise solutions to the problem. Even Jake Davis, a runaway unknowingly traveling by and receiving assistance from the Underground Railroad, knew nothing of the system due to a lack of volunteers' verbal or active clues (Breyfogle 32-34). Breyfogle points out that Underground participants kept

Cunningham 4

secrets so well, in fact, that even today little is known about the system; in an attempt to avoid exposure, conductors concealed their identities and workers kept few records, many of which were later destroyed to ensure slave owners' unawareness (34, 173).

The classic view of civil disobedience does not allow for this secretiveness and unwillingness to accept consequences. Abe Fortas, in his article "Concerning Dissent and Civil Disobedience," builds on Robert Bolt's statement, "To break the law of the land is always serious, but it is not always wrong" (qtd. in Fortas 91). He contends, however, that civil disobedients must be punished for illegal actions, no matter how pure their intentions. Fortas backs his argument, though, by suggesting that individuals challenging the justness of a particular law utilize their constitutional rights in protest (103). This option was not available to nineteenth century African-Americans. As a result, they fit what Herbert J. Storing labels 'subjects,' as opposed to citizens, in "The Case Against Civil Disobedience." Just as Fortas, Martin Luther King, Jr., a civil disobedient himself, insisted that any protestors violating laws do so overtly and suffer their penalties (Storing 96). Storing questions the reasoning of King by asking, "Indeed, why *should* the breaker of an unjust law do so 'openly, lovingly and with a willingness to accept the penalty?'" He concludes that while violating a law must be done this way in a "fundamentally just regime," a subject denied political involvement need not act accordingly (104, 117). Slaves, considered mere property, and even free African-Americans did not possess legal rights such as access to the ballot box or freedoms of speech and the press. Instead, they turned to the next best option, secretive, nonetheless nonviolent, escape; upon emancipation, African-Americans could then take steps towards obtaining constitutional rights and protesting injustices in a legal manner.

Clearly essential to the Underground Railroad's survival, its concealment allowed fugitive slaves to attain emancipation and thus the opportunity to reveal the injustice of slavery through personal stories and achievements. John Brown, for instance, efficiently utilized his newly achieved freedom after escaping with the assistance of the one-way railroad he so praised; selling copies of his personal narrative to earn income, Brown longed to help end slavery by dedicating himself to lowering the market value of goods produced within the

Cunningham 6

institution (206-209). After all, as Breyfogle stresses, "The whole purpose of the Underground Railroad was to put itself out of business" (140). The renowned fugitive slave Frederick Douglass, as explained in J. Blaine Hudson's Fugitive Slaves and the Underground Railroad in the Kentucky Borderland, emphasized that escape from oppression was but a small step towards African-Americans' recognition as equals (3). Martin Luther King, Jr., as quoted in "Martin Luther King, Jr.: Ethics, Nonviolence, and Moral Character" by Ron Large, suggests that upon freeing oneself from physical slavery and ultimately eliminating a need for the Underground Railroad, an African-American could also gradually escape mental slavery (12). Overcoming oppression through daring acts of escape, runaway slaves provided reasons for fellow African-Americans to have hope for the advancement of their race. "It is perfectly fitting," thus concludes Hudson, "that the biological and ideological children, grandchildren and great-grandchildren of fugitive slaves and those who assisted them would become the leaders of black America" (164). Having acted courageously to arrive at emancipation, fugitive slaves opened doors of opportunity for their offspring. These children, who were born into freedom became capable of receiving an education and assuming important positions in their community. These descendants built upon their predecessors' attempts at proving African-Americans worthy of equal treatment. Volunteer workers and runaways both risked their lives but, because of the harsh punishments they faced, had to act in secret to ensure that they might live to achieve freedom and opportunity for future generations. Thus, the Underground, secretive as it was, was a product not of cowardice, but of courage.

"As much as I deplore violence," once declared Martin Luther King, Jr., "there is one evil that is worse than violence, and that's cowardice" (Large 44). The subterranean network remained a mystery to those not personally involved, and some might have considered its secret operation a product of weakness, using King's statement to strengthen their argument. However, working for or traveling by means of the Underground, despite its concealment, required tremendous courage. Conductors of the Underground Railroad, volunteers sacrificing their time and wealth with no expectation of reimbursement, led equally brave fugitive slaves to freedom (Breyfogle 35). Regarding these workers, John Brown writes, "The slave-owners would doubtless pay a heavy sum to the man who would point out to them exactly where the underground line commences, and thus enable them to complete its survey for their own purposes. But abolition knows its duty better" (214). Owners made slave catching profitable in offering considerable rewards to any person who returned his missing property; slaves, after all, had monetary value as property and in labor, and, in the case of female slaves, the potential children, additional property at no cost. Masters typically published a description of and any additional information concerning missing slaves in antebellum newspapers to promote slave catching (Hudson 31). Men and women of various ethnic, economic, and religious backgrounds united together to aid runaways in their clearly perilous escape from oppression; battling inclement weather conditions and the threat of disease, starving fugitive slaves traveled north primarily at night (Dougherty 52), attempting to avoid capture by such greedy slave catchers (Cockrum 60). Oftentimes fugitives, as was the case for John Brown, followed the North Star unaccompanied as a safety precaution. Groups of escapees were far more likely to draw unwanted public attention to themselves than individual runaways. Receiving directions from one inconspicuous station to the next only by informed sources' word of mouth, Brown faced these dangers alone (157-158).

A fugitive's journey was so dangerous, in fact, that runaways often had to develop cunning schemes to escape oppression via the Underground Railroad. Harriet Tubman, an escaped slave herself, helped free nearly 300 African-Americans (Dougherty 52). Despite rewards of up to $40,000 offered for her capture, Tubman's optimism and cleverness prevented her own capture and that of any fugitive under her guidance. Once faced with the threat of a white man seeing her runaway group, Tubman and her companions lay hidden in a swamp for an entire day (Breyfogle 175, 179). Ellen Craft, a light-skinned African-American, traveled into free territory posing as a white master seeking medical attention with her alleged slave, actually her dark-skinned husband William (Dougherty 52). In another case, white Underground volunteers stood in for a carriage full of runaway slaves spotted by slave-hunters. While the slave-catchers pulled ahead to notify law officials, the African-Americans hid in a nearby chimney as the volunteers packed into the carriage. The white workers then presented themselves before the magistrate, leaving the

Cunningham 10

slave-catchers no choice but to admit a mistake and concede that the travelers were obviously free citizens. Such quick thinking allowed for the fugitive slaves, though publicly observed, to reach Canada and escape oppression (Brown 225-227). King suggests that in facing and conquering fear of death, courageous disobedients, such as those of the Underground, can gain the upper hand over oppressors and expose injustices (36).

Nineteenth century African-Americans, even the five to ten percent not enslaved, were provoked to make such daring escapes having suffered great injustices based entirely on skin color (Hudson 3). Cockrum, explaining the brave assistance his family offered to fugitive slaves, reasons, "They [African-Americans] are possessed of fidelity, gratitude, good humor and kindness, and have souls the same as you and I, and deserve to enjoy the great freedom of this country the same as you and I" (74). John Brown's personal story illustrates that Cockrum's beliefs were not so common among slave owners. Though sometimes slaves fled out of an utter longing for liberty and opportunity, frequently a "trigger event" such as physical or sexual abuse sent them running (Hudson 55-56). Brown, claiming that some of his experiences were too inhuman to speak of publicly, describes the unreasonable workloads and living conditions of slaves; a master, he contends, would have found slaves' duties, housing, and meals unfit for even his cattle (190-191). Still more degrading than the one or two blankets and sets of clothes owners provided their slaves with each year was the fact that slaveholders could legally oppress African-Americans (Brown 198).

Just as the law refused to recognize slaves as human beings, so masters rejected the idea of their deserving civilized treatment (Brown 202). Henry Ward Beecher argued in <u>Readings in Indiana History</u>:

> This American people have laws within which men may violate every sentiment of humanity, smother every breath of Christianity, outrage the feeling of a whole community, crush an innocent and helpless family, reduce a citizen of universal respect and proved integrity, to the level of a brute, carry him to the shambles, sell him forever away from his church, his children, his wife. All this may be done without violating the laws of the land--nay, by the laws and under the direction of a magistrate. (qtd. in Cockrum 220-221)

Gewirth notes that laws which inflict suffering upon some groups but are not followed by

Cunningham 12

others are unjust; he also labels as unreasonable any acts of cruelty imposed upon innocent people of a particular ethnicity (110, 114). It follows that the Fugitive Slave Law of 1850 was unjust, as were laws preventing African-Americans from testifying against whites in court and so allowing slave killers to go free (Cockrum 60). Many times owners mistreated their slaves despite realizing that their actions were unjust; Brown notes the trend of dying owners, unable to rest peacefully with their cruel actions in mind, begging their slaves' forgiveness. He also suggests that masters might have better recognized this injustice and detached themselves from the institution of slavery if not for its profitable nature (200-205).

Despite the harsh treatment slaves endured, they typically sought to conquer their oppressors through nonviolent means. Participants in the Underground Railroad acted in agreement with a statement once made by King, an advocate of nonviolent protest: "Something must happen to touch the hearts and souls of men that they will come together, not because the law says it, but because it is natural and right" (10). The unwillingness of the network's volunteers and runaways to act openly and accept punishment allowed for African-Americans to achieve freedom and prove themselves intelligent contributors to a community, the certain "something" uniting different races. Isaac Hopper, a member of the devoutly peaceful Quakers, helped establish and run the Underground Railroad (Breyfogle 167-168). As Breyfogle implies, discouraged slaves might have acted aggressively if not for the nonviolent option Hopper assisted in creating. The reappearance of forceful revolutions like those led by repressed African-Americans in Santo Domingo in 1791 would have been a backwards step in demonstrating equality (35-36).

Ending as unceremoniously as it began, the Underground Railroad quickly faded into nonexistence in 1865, when the United States government put a lawful end to slavery (Breyfogle 275, Dougherty 52). The network's operation may be appropriately classified as a valid act of civil disobedience despite the secretive nature of its workers and escapees. As asserts Robert Stanton, former National Park Service Director and contributor to the organization's Underground Railroad guide, "For all Americans in search of a shared past, it proves that brutal systems and laws can be overturned from within.

Cunningham 14

It speaks the power of freedom and justice" (as quoted in Dougherty 52). Participants in the railroad acted inconspicuously not out of cowardice or feelings of superiority towards the law, but out of desire to ensure that they could survive in order to attain and utilize freedom in making known the injustices of slavery. "And in its lawlessness, its altruism and its ultimate success," adds Breyfogle, "it was essentially native and proper to the soil of this continent and the history of this people" (276). Unable to implement legal means of nonviolently protesting the Fugitive Slave Law of 1850, African-Americans established and made use of the Underground Railroad, though in secret; runaways accordingly turned to an alternative far more effective, responsible, and well thought-out than violent measures. In ultimately attaining emancipation, African-Americans demonstrated their equality and went on to make notable contributions to the development of the United States.

Works Cited

Breyfogle, William. Make Free: The Story of the Underground Railroad. Philadelphia: Lippincott, 1958.

Cunningham 15

Brown, John. *Slave Life in Georgia: A Narrative of the Life, Sufferings, and Escape of John Brown, a Fugitive Slave, Now in England*. Ed. Louis Alexis Chamerovzow. 1855. Electronic Edition. Documenting the American South. Chapel Hill: U of North Carolina, 2001. <http://docsouth.unc.edu/neh/jbrown/jbrown.html>

Cockrum, Col. William M. *The History of the Underground Railroad*. 1915. New York: Negro Universities P, 1969.

Dougherty, Ryan. "A Quest for Freedom." *National Parks* 77.1/2 (Jan/Feb 2003): 52.

Fortas, Abe. "Concerning Dissent and Civil Disobedience." *Civil Disobedience*. Ed. Paul Harris. Lanham, MD: U P of America, 1989. 91-105.

Gewirth, Alan. "Civil Disobedience, Law and Morality: An Examination of Justice Fortas' Doctrine." *Civil Disobedience*. Ed. Paul Harris. Lanham, MD: U P of America, 1989. 107-119.

Hudson, J. Blaine. *Fugitive Slaves and the Underground Railroad in the Kentucky Borderland*. Jefferson, NC, 2002.

Large, Ron. "Martin Luther King, Jr.: Ethics, Nonviolence, and Moral Character." *Journal of Religious Thought* 48.1 (Summer/Fall 1991): 51-63.

Storing, Herbert J. "The Case Against Civil Disobedience." *On Civil Disobedience: American Essays, Old and New*. Ed. Robert A. Goldwin. Chicago: Rand McNally, 1968. 95-120.

Index

Note: Italicized page locators refer to tables/figures.

Credits

This page constitutes an extension of the copyright page. We have made every effort to trace the ownership of all copyrighted material and to secure permission from copyright holders. In the event of any question arising as to the use of any material, we will be pleased to make the necessary corrections in future printings. Thanks are due to the following authors, publishers, and agents for permission to use the material indicated.

Chapter 4.

58: The Declaration of Independence, 1776, Thomas Jefferson; **63:** From A Plea for the West (1835) by Lyman Beecher; **69:** William and Sophie Seyffardt, "Letters Home to Germany, 1851–1863" from Louis F. Frank, comp., German-American Pioneers in Wisconsin and Michigan: The Frank-Kerler Letters, 1849–1864, trans. Margaret Wolff, ed. Harry H. Anderson. Milwaukee: Milwaukee County Historical Society, 1971, pp. 101, 104, 106, 116, 131, 145, 173–175, 224, 232, 289, 290, 304, 320, 336, 337, 343, 350, 409, 450, 451, 518, 519, 524, 544, 545; **86:** "The Life Story of an Irish Cook" reprinted from Hamilton Holt, ed., The Life Stories of Undistinguished Americans. New York: James Pott, 1906, pp. 143–149; **90:** Marie Hall Ets, "An Italian Immigrant in a Missouri Mining Camp" from Marie Hall Ets, Rosa: The Life of An Italian Immigrant. Minneapolis: University of Minnesota Press, 1970, pp. 172–177; **96:** Hilda Satt Polacheck, "Chicago Sweatshop" from I Came a Stranger: The Story of a Hull-House Girl, pp. 56–60. Copyright © 1989 by the Board of Trustees of the University of Illinois. Used with permission of the University of Illinois Press; **103:** "Have We Any Right to Regulate Immigration?" by Mary Antin. Reprinted from Mary Antin, They Who Knock at Our Gates: A Complete Gospel of Immigration. Boston: Houghton Mifflin, 1914, pp. 1–16; **110:** Library of Congress, Prints and Photographs Division: Reproduction No. LC-USZ62-22399; **111:** Courtesy HarpWeek, LLC; **112:** Mike Keefe, The Denver Post, 7 September 2001; **113:** Clay Bennett / © 2002 The Christian Science Monitor (www.csmonitor.com). All rights reserved; **114:** Tamar Jacoby, "Too Many Immigrants?" Commentary, April 2002, pp. 34–44.

Chapter 5.

136: Bharati Mukherjee, "Two Ways to Belong in America," New York Times, 22 September 1996, Op-Ed Section, p. E13; **141:** Bong Hwan Kim, "As American as Possible," in Elaine H. Kim and Eui-Young Yu, eds., East to America: Korean American Life Stories, New York: New Press, 1996, pp. 343–352; **152:** From "Tradition," from New Americans: An Oral History by Al Santoli, pp. 87–90, 97–102. Copyright © 1988 by Al Santoli. Used by permission of Viking Penguin, a division of Penguin Group (USA) Inc.; **161:** From THE PUBLIC INTEREST, No. 119 (Spring 1995), pp. 3–18. Copyright © 1995 by National Affairs, Inc. Reprinted with permission of the author; **177:** Alejandro Portes and Rubén Rumbaut, "Not Everyone Is Chosen," from Alejandro Portes and Rubén G. Rumbaut, Legacies: The Story of the Immigrant Second Generation, pp. 44–54. Berkeley: University of California Press. Copyright © 2001 The Regents of the University of California. Used by permission of the publisher; **193:** Annals of the New York Academy of Sciences, Volume 645, Towards a Transnational Perspective on Migration: Race, Class, Ethnicity, and Nationalism Reconsidered, pp 1–24 © 1992, "Transnationalism" by Nina Glick Schiller, Linda Basch, and Cristina Blanc-Szanton. Copyright 1992 New York Academy of Sciences, U. S. A.

Chapter 6.

203: "Maria's Story" from Narratives of Mexican American Women: Emergent Identities of the Second Generation, pp. 1–4. Walnut Creek, CA: Altamira Press/Rowman & Littlefield, 2004; **206:** "Carmen's Story" from Narratives of Mexican American Women: Emergent Identities of the Second Generation, pp. 8–11. Walnut Creek, CA: Altamira Press/Rowman & Littlefield, 2004; **211:** Samuel P. Huntington, "The Hispanic Challenge" Foreign Policy, March/April 2004, pp. 31–39, 42–45; **234:** FOREIGN POLICY by HUNTINGTON. Copyright 2004 by FOREIGN POLICY. Reproduced with permission of FOREIGN POLICY in the format Textbook via Copyright Clearance Center. www.foreignpolicy.com; **235:** LALO ALCARAZ © 2001 Dist. by UNIVERSAL

PRESS SYNDICATE. Reprinted with permission. All rights reserved; **237:** "Patriot Games: The New Nativism of Samuel P. Huntington," from Louis Menand, New Yorker, 17 May 2004, pp. 96–98; **239:** FOREIGN POLICY by FAOUD AJAMI. Copyright 2004 by FOREIGN POLICY. Reproduced with permission of FOREIGN POLICY in the format Textbook via Copyright Clearance Center. www.foreignpolicy.com; **240:** FOREIGN POLICY by TAMAR JACOBY. Copyright 2004 by FOREIGN POLICY. Reproduced with permission of FOREIGN POLICY in the format Textbook via Copyright Clearance Center. www.foreignpolicy.com.

Appendix.
280: Courtesy of Caitlin Cunningham.